OUR LADY OF THE ROCK

OUR LADY OF THE ROCK

VISION AND PILGRIMAGE
IN THE MOJAVE DESERT

LISA M. BITEL

PHOTOGRAPHS BY MATT GAINER

Cornell University Press   *Ithaca and London*

First published 2015 by Cornell University Press
First printing, Cornell Paperbacks, 2015

Printed in the United States of America

Library of Congress Cataloging-in-Publication Data

Bitel, Lisa M., 1958– author
    Our Lady of the Rock : vision and pilgrimage in the Mojave Desert / Lisa M. Bitel ; photographs by Matt Gainer.
        pages cm
    Includes bibliographical references and index.
    ISBN 978-0-8014-4854-6 (cloth : alk. paper)
    ISBN 978-0-8014-5662-6 (pbk. : alk. paper)
    1. Mary, Blessed Virgin, Saint—Apparitions and miracles—Mojave Desert. I. Gainer, Matt, illustrator. II. Title.
    BT652.U6B58   2015
    232.91'70979495—dc23   2014029088

Cornell University Press strives to use environmentally responsible suppliers and materials to the fullest extent possible in the publishing of its books. Such materials include vegetable-based, low-VOC inks and acid-free papers that are recycled, totally chlorine-free, or partly composed of nonwood fibers. For further information, visit our website at www.cornellpress.cornell.edu.

Cloth printing   10 9 8 7 6 5 4 3 2 1
Paperback printing   10 9 8 7 6 5 4 3 2 1

For Peter, who saw God in a fjord.

Lisa Bitel

*For Mom and Trang for helping me see clearly,
and for Mela and Chloe, that you may too.*

Matt Gainer

Contents

Impressions: Our Lady of the Rock, 2006–2011, *a photo essay by Matt Gainer, follows page 48.*

October 13, 2006

Preface
Looking the Wrong Way

In 2006 I was browsing the Internet for the latest news of apparitions and miracles when I stumbled across the story of Maria Paula Acuña. A 1997 article printed in the *Los Angeles Times* reported that she claimed to see the Virgin Mary at a place called Our Lady of the Rock, just outside California City in the Mojave Desert north of Los Angeles.[1] On the thirteenth of every month, hundreds of men, women, and children followed Acuña into the desert to watch. Only Maria Paula could see and speak with the Virgin, the article explained, but onlookers searched the skies for signs from heaven, gazing directly into the sun and snapping photographs of the sky.

Apparitions come as no surprise to a medievalist. In the pages of ancient manuscripts and in the carvings of crumbling churches, I have encountered far more bizarre apparitions than the Blessed Virgin. Premodern Christians (and followers of other faith traditions) regularly spotted saints, angels, demons by the dozen, flying ships, rains of blood, fireballs, ghosts, and shape-shifters, among other marvelous sights. Maria Paula Acuña and her followers seemed to offer me a rare chance to witness religious visions in process rather than in the pages of a document, and to pose questions that I might take back to the past. What might this moving picture of ancient practices, I wondered, reveal to me? It tempted me like time travel. I decided to go see for myself.

I had mixed feelings when I first witnessed Maria Paula Acuña fall to her knees and address thin air. After all, as an anthropologist friend had told me recently, "We're researchers—we test the credibility of stuff." Apparitions of the Virgin Mary seem less plausible these days than other kinds of invisible phenomena, such as black holes in space or devices of nanotechnology. I tried to look through Maria Paula's eyes, but of course that is impossible—only Maria Paula knows what she sees. I considered causes for her behavior and wondered about her background and motives. I pondered her relation to the witnesses who accompany her to Our Lady of the Rock in the Mojave Desert. Still, while I might be able to rule out some causes for her sightings, I lack evidence—aside from my unwillingness to believe in the intervention of the Blessed Virgin—to prove that Maria Paula does *not* see what she says she sees. Like other witnesses to religious visions, I must make a decision about the seer's integrity based on my own observations and interpretations.

"Do you really think she sees the Virgin?" people ask me. It is often hard to tell whether they are asking, "What does Maria Paula see?" or "Does she see anything?"[2] Academics want to know whether Maria Paula believes she sees supernatural phenomena or whether she only pretends. Sociologists and anthropologists study prophets and shamans in terms of ethnic identity and power; scholars of religion focus on visions and revelations in the context of charismatic movements, doctrinal debates, and grassroots reforms. Psychologists, physicians, and brain scientists wonder about physiological and neurological causes of her trances and ecstasies. But in fact none of us can know what Maria Paula sees. We have not learned how to look through Maria Paula's eyes. As Courtney Bender has explained in her study of modern mystics, it is precisely this invisibility or "untranslatability" of Maria Paula's visionary experience that renders it meaningful and even authoritative—not just to her followers but also to scientists, academics, and Doctors of the Church who might notice and try to assess it.[3]

As it turned out, the discerners of Maria Paula's visions have more interesting stories to tell than the self-identified visionary. Pilgrims to Our Lady of the Rock are not the glassy-eyed cultists and hysterics of documentary films about latter-day prophets. They are ordinary men and women who live in a practical world of jobs, families, rents, and car trouble. Not all of them are convinced of Maria Paula's intercessory capability. At each vision event, they watch for proof of God's concern and the Virgin Mary's attention to Maria Paula, to themselves, and to the larger world of Christian believers. They learn how to spot clues that most people cannot detect, like the cloud in the shape of an angel or the unexpected scent of roses, which help them evaluate Maria Paula's efficacy.

Nor have they abandoned institutional religion. Most go to churches of one kind or another and consider themselves Catholics, members of another Christian denomination, or both. They are not refugees from earlier centuries laboring to revive outdated folk devotions, defy the Vatican, or smuggle native goddesses into California parishes. La Señora de la Roca is no rallying point for demonstrations of ethnic identities or immigration status either. On the contrary, pilgrims travel purposefully into the desert in order to experience firsthand one of the oldest and most fundamental promises of Christianity: the revelations of God, made possible by the resurrection of Jesus and facilitated by heavenly messengers, particularly Mary, the Virgin Mother of Christ the Savior.

Some of what they do in the Mojave resembles the venerable practices of other Jesus followers. More recent regional customs, politics, shifts in visual culture, and technological advances also influence pilgrims' practices in the Mojave. To label their collective activities "folk" or "popular," as some Catholic leaders and many scholars still do, is unhelpful in explaining their motivations. Such simplistic categorization, as one scholar points out, ignores the "often practical, crassly material, and decidedly modern aspects of so much popular religion" and the fact that plenty of people who share the daily struggles of pilgrims do not seek relief in worship.[4]

In the pages that follow, I offer a less reductive explanation for why so many people choose to watch Maria Paula and how they have made religion at Our Lady of the Rock. Although I cannot discern the spiritual authenticity of Maria Paula's visions or describe exactly what each individual pilgrim witnesses, I can tell you how they look (in both senses of the verb). I also suggest why they go to the desert to see what they can—and cannot—see.

I worked with my friend and colleague, the photographer Matt Gainer, to make this book about modern ways of religious looking. For six years we trailed pilgrims to Our Lady of the Rock, jointly and on individual missions. While I took notes, Matt took pictures. His photographs capture both the narrative structure of the monthly vision event and the simultaneous activities of the crowd on any given thirteenth day of the month—one woman's moment of intense interiority in the midst of noisy chaos, the diffident posture of a critical pilgrim, the visual irony of witnesses displaying photos of the invisible Virgin to the visionary who presents them to the camera. The images reveal patterns in the recurring liturgy of visions yet also chronicle changes at the site over the years. The photos offer a prosopography of witnesses too. A chapter of twenty-nine color photographs tells Matt's version of a typical thirteenth of the month at Our Lady of the Rock. Forty black-and-white photographs also appear throughout the book as clarifications and comments on the textual narrative. The rest of his thousands of shots and recorded interviews have provided evidence for my analysis of the vision event. Unpublished pictures skulk like ghosts behind my pages of words. The names of all informants except Maria Paula Acuña and Sister Thelma, who are public figures, and Juan Rubio, who gave explicit permission, have been changed to preserve their anonymity.

The Virgin Mary's previous apparitions and miracles have been well documented at Lourdes, Fátima, Marpingen, Knock, Garabandal, Medjugorje, Betania, Zeitoun, the Basilica of Our Lady of Guadalupe, and a multitude of less famous places. I cite many admirable studies of these religious phenomena in the notes of this book, along with the works of historians and theologians who have explicated diverse traditions of prophecy, vision, and dreaming among Christians. Many authors have probed the long history of extraordinary sights of, and human contacts with, the supernatural. Modern devotees of Mary—priests and other pious Catholics but also novelists and journalists—have written movingly and also critically about personal relationships with their Blessed Mother.[5] A whole library of possible explanations already exists as to why apparitions of the Virgin Mary proliferated suddenly in the nineteenth century and have continued multiplying ever since. One entire aisle in that imaginary library is devoted to the Second Vatican Council (1962–65), the famous gathering of Catholic leaders that loosened the clergy's strict control of devotional practices but that, at the same time, raised standards for the discernment of spirits. Another aisle of that imaginary library concentrates on visual religion after the Big Bang of electronic technologies and communication networks and the resultant spread of globalized religious and visual cultures.

What, then, can a medievalist, in cahoots with a photographer of social protest movements, relying on a virtual library of visionary religion, add to our collective understanding of modern visions and apparitions—besides a naive eagerness to spot the Virgin Mary in the clouds? Three credentials qualify me to write this book. First, I watched and listened carefully to Maria Paula and her witnesses for more than six years as they built their religion in the desert. Second, my coconspirator, Matt, can see things with his camera that I cannot. As his witness and interpreter, I report and explicate here what we both saw at Our Lady of the Rock because only words and images together can account for visionary religion.

Third and most important, I am an expert on what some historians call the *longue durée*—the long haul—of Christian visionary and visual traditions. Religion is an ever-mutating but inherently backward-looking phenomenon; in order to comprehend the meaning of contemporary mariophanies, one must grasp the enduring drama of Christian revelation and the history of the Savior's mother over the long haul of twenty centuries, as set down in sacred scriptures, rehearsed in rituals through the ages, argued in doctrines and theologies, probed endlessly in literature, represented in art and architecture, and repeatedly reenacted by believers around the world. If you know how to look at the unseen past, it becomes much easier to spot the invisible in our own post-Enlightenment present. Maria Paula and her associates are not the only modern believers scanning for signs of the divine. Other vision seekers are doing similar things in the plazas of small villages and parks of major cities, on street corners, and under freeways. They find the Virgin in shrines, fields, parking lots, factories, living rooms, and kitchens. In garages and backyards. On windows. In food products and tree trunks.

Thus chapter 1 of this book explains what happens at Our Lady of the Rock each month and how two thousand years of Christian revelatory tradition prepared the way for Maria Paula to meet Mary in the desert. Chapter 2 investigates the ancient tradition of desert pilgrimage that led Maria Paula and her pilgrims to transform a corner of the Mojave into a holy place of pilgrimage, as earlier deserts in other parts of the world once summoned other prophets and seers. Chapter 3 examines historical models for religious visionaries, especially those who see the Virgin. Chapter 4 focuses on the pilgrims: who they are, where they come from, why they go to the vision event, and how they practice the Christian discernment of spirits and visions. This chapter also analyzes changes in the rituals, iconographies, and environment of Our Lady of the Rock over several years. Chapter 5 follows three pilgrim informants out of the desert as they return home with relics and proofs of visions, where, out of Maria Paula's sight, they too confessed to be practicing visionaries. Chapter 6 examines the discernment of contemporary visionary religion carried out by reporters, photographers, videographers, and creators of Internet media. In conclusion, I reconsider Christian ways of looking.

Throughout the book, I try to locate Maria Paula and modern pilgrims in appropriate local historical and cultural contexts: demographic changes on the borderlands of Mexico and the United States, recent religious trends and Catholic politics, reports of apparitions and miracles from around the world, the latest developments in American communications and visual technologies, and the seemingly endless debate among academics, faith leaders, scientists, and citizen observers about sight, perception, reason, and belief. Nowhere in the book do I render an opinion on the reality of apparitions, nor do I intend my analysis to debunk the vision event, demean the visionary, or dismiss the witnesses to her desert visions. To paraphrase a fellow vision hunter, I pray that nothing in these pages will challenge anyone's devotion to la Virgen de la Roca.[6]

Many invisible helpers deserve my gratitude. A grant from the American Council of Learned Societies funded one year of research on this project. The Center for Interdisciplinary Research at the University of Southern California sponsored a collaborative research project with Norberto Grzywacz on the neurological basis of religious vision. Andrew Fogleman, Margaret Wertheim, Colum Hourihane, David Morgan, Jon Miller, and Deirdre de la Cruz all posed challenging questions for my research. Sandra Ruiz transcribed and translated some video and audio recordings. Sherry Velasco corrected my Spanish; all unattributed translations are my own. Students at USC and the University of California at Santa Barbara contributed field notes and bibliography for this book. Oren Margolis deserves special thanks for a preliminary site visit and also for cataloging references to contemporary visionaries. Jake Bloch's field notes and splendid video interviews provided crucial evidence. The Center for Religion and Civic Culture at the University of Southern California, funded by the Pew Foundation, generously supported research for the book, including the sponsorship of three international conferences on religious visions and visionaries and a photography show. I thank the many distinguished scholars who took part in those conferences and whose work has improved this book.

I am particularly grateful for the input of Roberto Lint Sagarena, who tutored me in modern Latino/a Catholicisms and accompanied me to the desert. Luis Corteguera, who also went to the desert with me, has been my debating partner on religious and historical topics for fifteen years; his insights are hidden in this book. In addition to our editor, Michael McGandy, and the anonymous and enormously helpful reviewers for Cornell University Press, Lester Little also read the manuscript with his usual care and astuteness. Bill Christian, too, critiqued the manuscript; he has been my mentor and guide on vision-hunting expeditions and my patron in the academic community of visioneers. I hope this book reveals how much I have learned from him.

It goes without saying that this book could not exist without the collaboration of writer and photographer. Matt Gainer and I debated every detail of the vision event as we drove back and forth to the desert, awaited the Virgin's arrival under the sizzling sun, and lunched on bad burritos in California City diners. Our arguments about the visionary and her witnesses have provoked the best ideas printed on these pages. The cost of publishing Matt's images in this book were generously subvented by the deans of USC Dornsife College of Letters, Arts, and Sciences and the dean of the USC Libraries, the School of Religion at USC, and the USC-Huntington Institute for California and the West.

Even my children helped me interpret Christian visions taking place in the California desert. Nick clambered around Lopez Canyon in search of Maria Paula's original vision site. Sophie confronted me with a crucial question: How does one recognize an apparition of the Virgin? Or, as she put it more colloquially, "How do they know it's not just some random–ass dead guy?" That question led to my hypothesis about choosing to look the right way. Finally, as always, I thank Peter. He may believe none of it, but he knows how important it is to me, and he read every word.

October 13, 2006

Our Lady of the Rock

Déjà Vu

1

Pilgrims have been driving to Our Lady of the Rock since 1995. Every month, on the morning of the thirteenth, Angelenos and other southerners load up cars, trucks, and vans and head north, cutting through the San Gabriel Mountains on Highway 14 to descend into the desert. At the town of Mojave, travelers turn eastward through miles of scrub toward California City, where they pick up the Randsburg Mojave Road, which turns into the old Twenty Mule Team Road. They pass the state reserve for desert tortoises, the parking lot of Borax Bill Park, and miles of unpeopled terrain until eventually they spot—if they look sharp—a hand-lettered sign tacked to a telephone pole. The sign points left to Our Lady of the Rock. Watchful drivers head deeper into the desert on the ambitiously named Lincoln Boulevard (really just a dirt track), where they join a line of vehicles from near and far. They have come down from Fresno and Oakland; in from Vegas; up from San Diego, Texas, Mexico, Guatemala, and Peru; from as far west and east as the Philippines or India; and occasionally even from Europe. They all arrive at this junction by motor vehicle. Short of walking for days or riding a horse, there is no other way to reach the place where Maria Paula Acuña sees the Blessed Virgin Mary.

Between 1995, when Maria Paula Acuña moved to California City, and 2009, when the Marian Movement of Southern California completed a long-planned "grotto" at Our Lady of the Rock, the schedule for vision days was largely the same. Señora Acuña and pilgrims conducted a liturgy that they had developed together, in response to the Virgin's appearances, over the years. The rituals were similar to those played out in shrines and churches around Catholic Christendom: group prayer with rosaries, the processional, the main service—at Our Lady of the Rock, this included Maria Paula's vision—the sermon, and the benediction before departure. Pilgrims knew what to do when commanded to recite the Sorrowful Mysteries or sing an Ave Maria. They borrowed iconography from other holy places. Newcomers could easily join in. Everywhere a pilgrim's gaze rested, there was something familiar to see and hear. Even the desert was a homely vista for anyone who lived in northern Mexico or the American Southwest.

The script and rhythm of each vision day may have seemed the same, but the players always improvised. Maria Paula's behavior and moods shifted from month to month depending on her health and the Virgin's messages. Pilgrims constantly chose what to do from minute to minute of the daylong event, as Maria Paula prayed or exhorted her audience. They might listen as she whispered to the Virgin or mumble their own pleas to the Blessed Mother or carry on with some other business. Their principal occupation was scrutiny of the sky. They constantly raised their eyes, as well as cameras and cell phones, in the direction of (what they supposed to be) the Virgin's presence. The crowd's composition varied as new pilgrims arrived or previous witnesses stayed away. If the vision event fell on the weekend, the audience swelled with younger adults and entire families. Weather affected the crowd's size, too, and forced alterations in the monthly routine. News about regional events or the Catholic Church inspired variations upon the day's activities. Sometimes Maria Paula arrived late or waited hours before actually having her vision, and the entire ritual schedule accelerated. As the grotto neared completion in late 2009, however, the crowd's focus split between the Virgin's shrine, which sheltered her statue, and the skies overhead. The vision event began to change in more radical and permanent ways.

Maria Paula is the only person who claims to see the Lady of the Rock in the Mojave on the thirteenth of every month, although most witnesses have learned to detect signs of the Virgin's invisible presence. She alone converses with the apparition. I refer to this experience variously as a vision, revelation, epiphany, theophany, or mariophany. Both "epiphany" and "theophany" refer to the visual manifestation of God or a deity to humans, although epiphany can also mean "revelation" more generally; "mariophany" refers to a similar visual manifestation of the Virgin. In Catholic terms, an apparition may be either corporeal—that is, visibly present to the human eyes—or present only in a symbolic or spiritual way, with or without participation of the human senses (called imaginative or intellectual vision in Catholic doctrinal terms.) Still, whatever Maria Paula Acuña experiences as visual and aural manifestations of the Virgin Mary, Mother of Jesus Christ, other Catholics have perceived before.[1] Her description of the Lady evokes Marian apparitions from ten, thirty, or hundreds of years ago. Her vocabulary for the apparitions, her gestures, her responses to the invisible, and even her choice of venues reflect ancient traditions of epiphany and prophecy. Señora Acuña would never have entered the desert to meet the Virgin if, two thousand years ago, the Jesus of scriptures had not taught his followers to see the signs of their own forthcoming salvation. Christian visions, prophecies, and revelations have always been at once singular and familiar, private and shared, never-before-witnessed and old news.

Maria Paula says that her first encounter with the Mother of God came as a surprise. Nonetheless, she was prepared for the Virgin long before they met on a hilltop in Lopez

Canyon. Like every attentive believer, the visionary—I grant her that provisional title throughout this book without arguing her right to it—collected exemplary role models and pertinent legends over the course of her lifetime.[2] She absorbed the visionary catechism from the material environments that daily surrounded her at home, at work, at social gatherings, in church, or in public media. She learned about the extraordinary visual experiences of others by watching television or films, readings newspapers and gossiping. Perhaps her mother or grandmother spoke to her of saints and seers. Maria Paula represents herself as ignorant and naive, but she knows how to dress and behave as a holy woman and she skillfully exploits symbolic images. Without much formal education, she has harvested her lessons from the visible world around her.

As many scholars have noted, today's global citizens have learned how to select meaningful information from among the many competing sources of visual culture and memory that confront them daily.[3] As a small girl and young woman, Maria Paula must have seen images of the local version of the Virgin in her church in Sonora, and various other madonnas in home shrines, both in the United States and in Mexico. She has participated in Marian devotions and fiestas. She clearly grasps the patriotic importance of the ubiquitous Virgin of Guadalupe. In 1989, when she caught the scent of roses and blinked at the radiant mist that preceded the Mother of God's appearance before her eyes, Maria Paula suspected who was coming. She reacted, as she has confessed, exactly as historic visionaries did, long ago, to hints of the Virgin's presence. After all, those venerable seers confronted the very same Mary, mother of Jesus, who also spoke to Maria Paula. No one witnessed Maria Paula's initial vision of Mary, but none of the pilgrims has publicly challenged her account of that first encounter either. Her imitation of other visionaries, although it may seem like mere mimicry to critics of Marian apparitions, is both homage to historical visionaries and proof that Maria Paula's experience was legitimately Catholic.

Her witnesses, too, have spent their lives absorbing the cues to authentic religious experience. Professed Catholics know the look and feel of a holy place, whether inside a church or out in the wilderness. They can distinguish between sacred and profane moments. Devotees of the Virgin Mary cherish her icons and the legends of those who have been blessed to see her apparitions, and they rely on both icons and historical models when evaluating new claims to visionary experience. They have gathered this wisdom from literally all over the place: from half-remembered sermons at Mass, holiday celebrations, classroom lectures, church decor, home shrines, and holy cards. They have harvested religious concepts and visual memories from television programs and movies, books, Bibles, billboards, news reports, casual conversation, the Internet, and innumerable other oral, documentary, and visual sources.[4]

Each witness's mental archives of Christian concepts, vision history, and religious images shape his or her expectations of visions, visionaries, and the Virgin. Pilgrims seek out Our Lady of the Rock for many different reasons. They share their understanding of the Virgin, their assessment of Maria Paula, and the meaning of the vision event when they gather in the desert. Pilgrims may not agree about the details of famous apparitions or Maria Paula's abilities, but they know some reliable signs of a bona fide visionary in direct contact with a genuine apparition of the one and only Mother of God—a mariophany—and they anticipate spiritual rewards for witnessing such a phenomenon.

The vision event in the Mojave repeats a predictable pattern every month. What follows below is a synthetic description of a typical thirteenth of any month between 1995, when Maria Paula moved to California City and began to meet the Virgin in the desert, and the winter of 2009–2010, when Our Lady of the Rock gained a permanent monument in the Mojave. The event is predictable—it happens at the same place, with the same ritual elements and same kind of crowd, and it looks much the same every month—but it is not uniform. Subsequent chapters will complicate this postcard picture of a single day at Our Lady of the Rock, teasing out the historical background of this and other apparitions, unique details of particular vision events in the Mojave, the personality of Maria Paula and her pilgrim witnesses, and multiple interpretations that participants and external observers have offered for whatever happens at Our Lady of the Rock. The ritual routine on each thirteenth connects one month's event to the next.

The visionary and her supporters understand that Marian iconography and devotions at Our Lady of the Rock strategically rehearse previous appearances of the Virgin elsewhere. Maria Paula's personal history and behavior recall visionaries from earlier times. The desert setting lends biblical authenticity to the vision event, and at the same time its seeming emptiness frees pilgrims from both the burdens of daily life and the scrutiny of church authorities and nonbelievers, as subsequent chapters of this book explain.

On the Thirteenth of the Month, 1995–2009

Pilgrims always arrived at Our Lady of the Rock early in the day to await the advent of Maria Paula Acuña and the Virgin Mary. Some came on the evening of the twelfth to camp and keep vigils in the desert, especially on summer weekends or Catholic feast days. By ten o'clock on the morning of the thirteenth, anywhere from several dozen to several hundred vehicles had parked in orderly rows and spilled their riders into the landscape. In earlier years, thousands of onlookers would attend, often in busloads, but after 2000, audiences apparently grew smaller. No one could explain why, although some witnesses suggested growing disenchantment with Maria Paula, especially when she had some money trouble around 2006. Nonetheless, several hundred witnesses continued to gather each month, and the crowd swelled on important feast days in May and December.

Savvy pilgrims always planted their lawn chairs, tents, and umbrellas near the inner sanctuary to stake out spots with good views. They spread blankets for the family and positioned portable barbecues and coolers filled with drinks and snacks. Later in the day, fatigued onlookers would ask permission to stand in someone else's shade or borrow an empty chair. Tamale vendors and purveyors of religious items erected long tables of goods for sale. Freelance merchants remained outside the sanctuary, where they hawked plastic umbrellas to protect against the sun, as well as tacos, tiny icons of Mary or Jesus, and pamphlets—meditations on suffering, brief hagiographies of Padre Pio and martyrs of the Mexican civil war, basic catechisms, and self-help guides based on the life of Jesus. Rosaries in various plastics and charm bracelets featuring a variety of Virgins and saints were always popular. Near the low picket fence, which surrounded the inner sanctuary of about sixty feet across, a table manned by the Marian Movement of Southern California dispersed Xeroxed brochures and collected donations. They also displayed and sold photographs from previous vision events and historic apparitions. Flowers were everywhere—in wrapped bouquets, in buckets of water, and clutched in pilgrims' hands—although none were native to the desert.

Inside the enclosure stood a modest temporary stage, about twenty feet across and six feet deep; in earlier years, before the stage, witnesses surrounded a simple low platform instead. Fiesta streamers crossed from the roof of the stage to tall poles set around the perimeter fence. Barn-style doors hung open on either side of the stage, suggesting how it could be closed up when day was done. A small tree and some creosote bush grew nearby. Behind the stage, outside the fence, stood a giant steel cross. On the other side of the

October 13, 2006

sanctuary was a tumble of white boulders, quartz or marble, surrounded by chain link fencing, which gradually grew into a building site.

As the crowd gathered in the morning, a few men would bustle around the stage and sanctuary. Like the ladies at the Marian Movement's table, they wore specially printed T-shirts. The front featured an image of the Lady of the Rock—or, rather, the statue of the Lady of the Rock carried in the monthly procession, which Maria Paula said resembled the apparition exactly. On the back was the text of the Ave Maria (in Spanish). Movement members distributed buckets of flowers around the sanctuary and tested audio equipment, shifted icons and candles, and positioned a large crucifix, a statue, or an image of La Virgen de Guadalupe on the back wall of the stage. One tall old Anglo named Ron always led the crowd in recitation of the rosary, droning into a microphone, sometimes echoed by a Spanish speaker. Occasionally Ron interrupted himself to issue instructions to the crowd or to convey bulletins about Maria Paula Acuña's impending arrival. In summer, the audience hid under vividly colored umbrellas to avoid the already brutal sun, which often heats the desert to 115 degrees Fahrenheit in August. In winter, they wrapped themselves in blankets against blasts of wind. By ten thirty or eleven, the able-bodied would drift along Lincoln Boulevard back toward the Randsburg highway, lining the road in anticipation of the visionary's appearance. She was always among the last to arrive at Our Lady of the Rock. These days she rides in a white SUV, but for years she came in some other modest vehicle, always accompanied by a small flock of white-garbed attendants. Maria Paula calls them *monjas, monjitas,* or *hermanas*—nuns or sisters—although none of them belong to an official order. If the visionary's diabetes or another ailment weakened her, she was driven all the way to the picket fence. On good days, though, her ride parked at the highway junction so that she could lead a procession of witnesses back to the sanctuary. Maria Paula would hop out of whatever car had brought her, dressed in spotless white from veil to sneakers, sporting huge round sunglasses and always smiling. From the moment the car door opened, she would direct the monjas and the rest of her retinue, including the man who managed a portable microphone and speakers, and the litter bearers of the Blessed Virgin's statue, all of whom hurried to perform her bidding.

When everyone gained his or her proper place, all of them would begin pacing slowly through the scrub toward the sanctuary. Pilgrims trailed along. If someone surged excitedly ahead, one of Maria Paula's handlers would halt him so that the visionary and the Virgin's statue, lifted high on her bearers' shoulders, led the way again. Together, visionary and witnesses prayed and sang Aves as they advanced. Often a guitarist or a horn player accompanied them. On some feast days, traditional *matachine* dancers shuffled back and forth in rhythm, tiny bells jingling from leather shin cuffs tied over their white pants. Children always ran along beside the line, and mamas pushed sleepy babies in their strollers over the bumpy ground. Some witnesses paused for individual devotions along the way. Women bowed their heads and murmured over their decades of rosary beads. It was not unusual to see a sturdy man squat on his heels, cover his eyes with one hand, and weep.

December 13, 2006

At some point during the procession, its most elusive and crucial participant would silently join the congregation. When Maria Paula turned her face skyward, raised a sudden hand, or dropped to her knees, everyone knew that the Virgin had come. They shushed each other, although no one except Maria Paula could hear or see (or would confess to seeing and hearing) the Mother of God. The visionary would gaze at what seemed like empty air above the pilgrims' heads and address the Lady in a high, breathless voice. Sometimes she channeled the Virgin Mary, speaking the Virgin's words. At other times, the visionary repeated what the Virgin said or spoke in dialogue with the Blessed Mother, although the audience heard only one side of those conversations. Onlookers listened, watched, and prayed. The visionary would occasionally stage-whisper parenthetical cues: "She is here!" or "You can be taking the pictures now!" Pilgrims aimed cameras at the airspace above Maria Paula. They tried to capture on Polaroid or regular film, or in digital pixels, some evidence of the holy presence. When Maria Paula rose to begin walking again, pilgrims would continue to snap photos as they ambled on. Eventually the procession reached the sanctuary, which the visionary and monjas would circle several times before settling down to pray. They knelt on the ground as sturdy men hoisted the statue atop a table onstage. The visionary's handlers disposed themselves around the sanctuary.

April 13, 2008

Although elements of this monthly ritual were choreographed—the visionary's arrival, the procession, the kneeling, and the photographing—the crowd moved constantly in all directions. No single pair of eyes could catch everything happening simultaneously. Even while the visionary prayed or spoke with the Virgin, onlookers murmured at the edge of the crowd. They took more pictures. Many of the watchers had participated in the ceremony before, but just as many were curious newcomers learning the routine. First-timers often knew the hymns and prayers from church. They were familiar with religious processions at Mass and on feast days. They had handled rosaries before. They had heard that miracles happen in this place, or they knew someone who had been healed of illness here. They may have known about the Polaroid photographs of solar phenomena that pilgrims took at vision events elsewhere. The Internet is littered with such images, if you know where to look.[5]

Within the sanctuary, Maria Paula would kneel before the stage with her monjas and finish her conversation with the Lady or the Rock. Occasionally, members of the T-shirt-clad Marian Movement joined the women at prayer. Sometimes a special guest shared the sacred space at Maria Paula's invitation—a priest from Peru or Colombia or a perilously ailing pilgrim. They all faced the stage, backs to the crowd, praying toward the statue of the Virgin. Only Maria Paula looked up at the apparition. To their right, near the single tree, visitors had carefully arranged devotional items for blessing: small statues, framed prints of famous icons, rosaries, flasks of water, rocks. Larger jugs of water and buckets of flowers sat nearby. Later, the visionary would bless these objects and pilgrims would take them home. She would sprinkle some of the water on selected suppliants. Her helpers sold the roses for five dollars each to benefit the Marian Movement and to support the sisters. They often raffled off one of the blessed statues, although occasionally the prize was something crafted by Maria Paula and the monjas, such as a rosary or wreath.

Each month, pilgrims ringed the sanctuary, shielding themselves from the sun with raised hands and vivid umbrellas and awaiting the moment when Maria Paula would rise to repeat what the Virgin had told her that day. As the entourage prayed, some members of the crowd also knelt silently. But not everyone was reverent. Kids were always running or digging in the dirt. Observers wandered to the refreshment stand for drinks or queued up for a turn at the portable toilet. Families would retire to their vans for naps, returning later for the sermon. Some pilgrims followed their own devotional schedules, repeating the rosary, raising arms and faces to heaven, bowing their heads, and moaning softly. Many witnesses took the opportunity to greet old friends or catch up with family members who had come along for the ride; almost all cars arrived full of passengers. Religious and social obligations blurred when a family of pilgrims took a lunch break and discussed their photos, inviting a curious stranger to learn the code of the Polaroids, then glancing up to check Maria Paula's progress around the congregation.

The crowd could guess when the Virgin departed by listening for Maria Paula's mournful "Adiós, Madre!" Prayers finished, the visionary would take up a wireless microphone and lecture the congregation. Her topic varied each month, as did many details of the event, but themes recurred in Maria Paula's transmissions. Through her, the Lady of the Rock regularly admonished her children to pray, repeat the rosary, and repent. She warned against sexual sins and promiscuity. She decried abortion and divorce. She urged preservation of the nuclear family. She begged for peace. Sometimes Maria Paula reported Mary's sorrow and Jesus' annoyance at wayward Catholics. She referred to events both recent and historical to illustrate her points. On one December 13, day after the feast of Our Lady of Guadalupe, the visionary used her sermon to emphasize the need for conversion to Catholicism. She recalled the Christianization of Mexico's indigenous population long ago, begged the crowd to follow native example, and shouted "Viva Mexico! Viva Nuestra Señora de Guadalupe!" In a sermon preached after the 2008 earthquake in China, Maria Paula repeated the Virgin's request for prayers on behalf of the victims. Sometimes the visionary's sermons seemed like faithful reports of Mary's wishes, while at other times Maria Paula delivered first-person commentary in Spanish and bits of English. As she spoke, she would stroll and turn, gesturing dramatically. She broke suddenly into smiles or tears, her voice falling to a sigh or rising to wail.

After the sermon, Maria Paula would circle the sanctuary, speaking briefly with individual witnesses. They crowded close to the picket fence, reaching out to touch her hand or her veil as she wended her way around the circle, always followed closely by one or two of the monjas. As Maria Paula chatted with pilgrims, Sister Thelma would take notes. Thelma, a former nurse who comes from the Philippines, is the best educated of the sisters and is also fluently bilingual. Meanwhile, Juan, a tough-looking, burly young man in mirrored sunglasses, usually trailed them at a little distance, keeping a suspicious eye on the crowd. Maria Paula's companions always tried to keep her moving so that she could greet everyone, but the visionary would pause to lay a hand on this one's forehead or to bless another. She cuddled babies and embraced sickly pilgrims.

People tried to tell her complicated stories of injuries, troubles, and miracles. They wanted to share their own experiences so that Maria Paula could help interpret what they dreamed, thought they saw, or otherwise sensed. Some pilgrims offered Maria Paula photographs of the sky or snapped her portrait. If a pilgrim's request seemed heartfelt, then bespectacled Thelma, notebook in hand, would jot down details for the visionary's later reference. Maria Paula greeted some onlookers with special affection because she knew they came to witness her vision every month. Some had been her friends before she moved to California City. Others she had visited at home or in the hospital or had met at Mass at Our Lady of Lourdes church. Eventually, after an hour or two of these exchanges, the visionary would take up the microphone once more to bless the crowd and send them back to their lives. Her helpers would extricate her from the sanctuary, although she sometimes lingered to speak with the especially needy who had arranged an interview in advance—a group of pilgrims with Down syndrome, for instance, or in wheelchairs. Finally, she would retire with the monjas and her family members, including several of her six children, to a trailer behind the tamale stand. There she would rest before climbing back into the SUV and driving off.

Before, during, and after the vision event pilgrims stared at the sun and sky and took pictures. Except at dramatic moments of Maria Paula's speech, the photography never ceased. Witnesses constantly shot and shared images. In earlier years of the vision event, they would cluster over shiny squares of sticky Polaroid paper, awaiting the revelation of developed pictures. By 2008, when Polaroid announced it would quit manufacturing film, most people had already switched to digital cameras. Whichever technology they employed, though, they still haggled over the meanings of their images, openly but congenially disagreeing about what they could see. Is that the Gate of Heaven? Look, there's an angel in the corner, a rosary at the top. What do you see there? No, over here. Sometimes they would rotate an image and begin the explication process anew. Repeat visitors brought along photographs taken in previous months. Some veteran pilgrims carted whole albums to the desert, just in case they needed to check a shot or compare a particularly meaningful record of the skies. First-time witnesses peered over the shoulders of regulars to get lessons in taking and interpreting photos. Some photographers graciously offered use of their cameras or bestowed snapshots as keepsakes on curious strangers.

Meanwhile, members of the Marian Movement sold reprints of classic shots at their table, along with photos taken by Maria Paula herself and a few photographs of historic apparitions at other places. The visionary would happily examine the Polaroids and digital screens of her witnesses. Later, in the spring of 2010, Maria Paula suddenly tried to halt the taking and selling of photographs because, she announced, the church did not approve. However, the photos returned a few months later, and nothing more was said about the Catholic leadership's opinion of the coded pictures.

Pilgrims typically began packing up and drifting off to their cars even before Maria Paula had finished moving among them. By late afternoon, only a few stragglers usually remained to fold up tents and umbrellas and load their coolers into their cars. The T-shirt brigade finished picking up trash. They collected forgotten flowers, emptied the buckets, and closed the stage. By sundown, the desert always seemed empty of religion.

One and Many Virgins

Most pilgrims to Our Lady of the Rock are familiar with the basic parameters of Christian religious vision, although they might not use the same terminology as preachers and theologians. They are well aware, too, that the majority of Americans reject the possibility of seeing the Virgin Mary with their own eyes, although that majority believe firmly in the participation of angels and demons in human events, as well as frequent miracles. Even people who profess to believe in angels do not always welcome the Virgin Mary.[6] Nonetheless, many Catholics believe—or at least entertain the possibility—that the Virgin is somehow immanent in images of her and at places associated with her.

Visitors to the shrine outside California City are familiar with other famous manifestations of the Virgin. Everyone knows about Nuestra Señora de Guadalupe, whose image is ubiquitous in the southwestern United States, although their understanding of, and relations with, the patron saint of Mexico varies.[7] Many have also heard about famous European apparitions or the regional Virgins popular across Latin America, including the Ladies of Luján, Copacabana, Chiquinquirá, Caacupé, Quinche, and Coromoto, among many others.[8] Regular churchgoers as well as pilgrims who attended religious school or catechism classes recognize less popular elements of Catholic visionary iconography. They may know all the Sorrowful and Joyful Mysteries that adorn rosaries or grasp the meaning of the snake depicted under the Virgin's foot on a devotional card or understand how various icons of Mary differ in appearance.[9] Pamphlets about historic apparitions and pictures of other Virgins and visionaries, especially from Fátima (Portugal) and Medjugorje (Bosnia-Herzegovina), often appear for sale on concessions tables at Our Lady of the Rock. Some pilgrims fondly recollect local devotions at hometown shrines dedicated to a previous apparition of La Virgen. Others have participated in the exciting chaos of religious festivals or pilgrimages dedicated to the Virgin in major cities of the United States, Latin America, Europe, or Asia. Somewhere in the world there is always someone celebrating a feast day in honor of Mary.

The Lady of the Rock who appears to Maria Paula is the same Mary who gave birth to the Christian Savior and the Mary who has repeatedly returned to earth in visions, apparitions, and other manifestations across Christendom. Yet the pale Lady in shining white garments is also unique to her shrine in the Mojave. She is historically, doctrinally, and visibly distinguishable from any other manifestation of Mary. One regular witness, called here Adelia, says that she saw the Lady of the Rock in her own backyard. Adelia knew her at first sight, even though that Virgin did not resemble Maria Paula's white

October 13, 2006

Lady. Yet other pilgrims, when questioned about the variable colors of the Virgin's hair, skin, and costume in her many apparitions, explain that they're all the same Virgin.

Catholic doctrine preaches this paradox of a Virgin who is one and many. The latest Catholic catechism of 1992 explains that Mary was the historical Galilean woman who gave birth to Jesus sometime in (what we now call) the first century CE. In the fifth century, Christian bishops proclaimed Mary the only *theotokos*—"God bearer"—of human history.[10] According to centuries of theological discussion summed up in the recent catechism, Mary was divinely predestined and prepared for the task. According to the doctrine of the Immaculate Conception—debated for centuries but declared as dogma by Pope Pius IX only in 1854—she was the only sinless human ever to walk the earth. (Jesus does not count because he was both God and man, according to Christians across the denominational spectrum.) Mary was conceived without sex by her mother, Saint Anne, and thus without the carnal pollution inherent in other human bodies and souls. As Pius IX explained, "The most Blessed Virgin Mary was, from the first moment of her conception, by a singular grace and privilege of almighty God and by virtue of the merits of Jesus Christ, Savior of the human race, preserved immune from all stain of original sin."[11] Only this flawless virgin was fit to bear the son of God. Designated by her divine child as the universal mother to humankind, she is bound to the Savior in intimate ways unfathomable to ordinary mortals. She remains the ideal Catholic, "symbol and the most perfect realization of the church" on earth.[12]

Over the last century and a half, church leaders and Catholic laity have continued to struggle with definitions of Mary's purpose, powers, and meaning for modern Christians. Catholic pontiffs and clerical assemblies repeatedly reaffirmed Mary's presence and special influence as the Mother of God, beginning with Pope Pius XII's bull, *Munificentissimus Deus* in 1950. At the Second Vatican Council, which began in 1965, churchmen again debated the Virgin's role as intercessor between believers and their God. Was she a mediatrix with special powers to secure the protection of those who prayed to her, they wondered, or even a co-redemptrix with Jesus, who died and rose again for humankind? Popes, bishops, and cardinals argued for recognition of the Holy Mother's increasing importance in both private devotions and universal liturgies, as did Marian organizations.[13] Ultimately, though, the keepers of doctrine and liturgy decided that Mary's mediation supported "the dignity and power of Christ the one mediator," and that her major purpose in Christian eschatology was to work with the saints and God to "gather" men, women, and children to the one God of the Trinity in anticipation of Judgment Day.[14]

Twenty years after Vatican II, Pope John Paul II (1987) encouraged Marian enthusiasts with his own special devotion to the Blessed Mother. He dedicated his papacy to Mary and decreed a special anniversary year of the rosary, the devotional instrument most associated with the Virgin, during which he devised a series of new mysteries to be contemplated while repeating the rosary's prayers. John Paul II was also fervently attached to the Lady of Fátima, who had purportedly bestowed three secrets upon the Portuguese children who saw her apparition in 1917. Many Catholics of the late twentieth century believed that the first secret had been a vision of hell, warning believers of what awaited them should they not heed the Virgin's warning about their bad behavior; earlier in the century, the vision was widely interpreted as a call to confront communism as well as a prophecy of World War I. The second secret had been a warning of World War II if Russia's people refused to return to Christianity. The third secret vision seemed to foretell the assassination of a pontiff and resulting breakdown of society, which would culminate in the reign of the Antichrist, if and when believers neglected to promote proper devotion to the Immaculate Hearts of Mary and Jesus. John Paul II understood this third secret to refer to the foiled attempt on his life made by a Bulgarian in 1981.

However, Marian devotees around the world stubbornly continued to suspect that Vatican insiders had conspired to hide the full or original text of the last secret of Fátima. Rumors have long suggested that the Virgin divulged far more horrifying predictions to the three children, including desperate feuds within the church, the Antichrist's capture of the Vatican, Satan's appearance on earth, and the imminent Apocalypse.[15] When the last secret was made public in 2000, then Cardinal Ratzinger agreed that it might have referred to the attack on John Paul yet also cautioned that "those who expected exciting apocalyptic revelations about the end of the world or the future course of history are bound to be disappointed. Fatima does not satisfy our curiosity in this way." He added that Mary had changed history when she agreed to give birth to Jesus: "The *fiat* of Mary, the word of her heart, has changed the history of the world, because it brought the Saviour into the world—because, thanks to her *Yes*, God could become man in our world and remains so for all time."[16]

Ratzinger was a young theologian at Vatican II, which did not diminish Marian devotions but, on the contrary, seemed to encourage a proliferation of new Marian devotions and apparitions aimed at preventing Armageddon. Conservative Catholic lay groups, such as the Legion of Mary (founded in Dublin, 1921), along with the various armies, confraternities, and sodalities of Mary have since spread across the continents in missionary and charismatic movements.[17] Liberation theologians, particularly from Franciscan and Marian orders, as well as feminist and Latino/a theologians, have also helped promote the Virgin's popularity among disenfranchised and oppressed groups of Catholics. At the same time, both feminists and anthropologists continue to argue over the benefits brought by *marianismo*—the church-sanctioned, ideological counterpart to machismo—to Latina devotees of the Virgin.[18] The material cult of the Virgin—made obvious at traditional shrines, in pilgrimages, on feast days, and in private devotions such as praying the rosary—both reinforces and is bolstered by new theological developments regarding Mary's importance to Catholics.[19] Meanwhile, apparitions continue to drop from heaven at an increasing rate.

In 2005, after Benedict XVI became pope, bishops and cardinals met at Fátima to discuss the Virgin Mary's role as "Unique Cooperator in the Redemption," a term also used by John Paul II. The conferees petitioned Benedict to consider declaring certain of their discussion points as church dogma, including the Virgin's roles as co-redemptrix (that is, as helper but not source of human salvation), mediatrix, and advocate for Catholics with her son, Jesus. Despite a second petition sent three years later by cardinals from India, Puerto Rico, the Philippines, and Mexico, Pope Benedict declined to declare a new dogma.[20] He confirmed the Virgin's doctrinal significance during a visit to Mary's shrine at Lourdes in 2008 but also tried to dampen devotional fervor by emphasizing that Mary works beside and at the direction of Jesus in the job of human salvation. Nonetheless, in the fiftieth anniversary year of Vatican II, Catholic clergy seemed to be regretting the suppression of Marian devotions that had begun in the 1960s. Pope Benedict's public statements about the Virgin became less restrictive, although he did not revise his stance on Mary's theological relation to the triune God of Christians. On the Feast of the Queenship of Mary, August 22, 2012, Benedict preached to pilgrims at Castel Gandolfo: "Dear friends, devotion to Our Lady is an important part of spiritual life. In our prayer, we should not fail to turn to her, confident that Mary will intercede for us with her Son."[21] This is in keeping with the catechism, which sums up twenty centuries of Mariology in a sentence: "What the Catholic faith believes about Mary is based on what it believes about Christ, and what it teaches about Mary illumines in turn its faith in Christ."[22] Interpreted in light of cumulative Catholic doctrine and theology, then, the Lady of the Rock—the Virgin who appears once each month to Señora Acuña—is the symbolic mother of believers and the paradigmatic Jesus follower, who gives a sympathetic hearing to all prayers and requests, which she then refers to her son for consideration and possible intervention. The Virgin's job is to keep a loving eye on God's children. Her doctrinal, devotional, and apparitional histories prepare each generation of pilgrims to anticipate her immanence—if not visibly, then in the eyes of someone else whom she has chosen for revelations.

Mary's biblical history and her literary personae in Christian literature and legends help pilgrims understand why and how the Mother of God, who lived so long ago, might come to comfort them once more in the desert. The New Testament, written between about 65 and 110, contains the oldest evidence for Mary's existence in its Gospels, Acts, and letters but few details about her life. As early modern Protestants liked to point out, two of the four canonical Gospels hardly mention her at all. In the Gospel of Mark, Mary hovered in the background of Jesus' ministry. The mystical Gospel of John granted her a single nameless notice. Jesus' disciple Paul—who wrote his epistles in the mid-first century before the Gospels took final shape—did not mention Mary in his letters to budding Christian communities, although he referred to the unidentified mother of Jesus (Gal 4:4–5). Matthew and Luke called her by the common Hebrew name of Miriam or Mariam (Hebrew מִרְיָם; Greek Μαρίαμ).[23] Many other Mariam-Miriams-Marias-Marys also passed through these early stories of Jesus.[24]

Matthew and Luke both began Mary's story with the miraculous conception of her child. According to Luke, an angel arrived at Mary's childhood home to ask that she conceive and give birth to God's only begotten son. Mary wondered about the logistics. "How will this be since I am a virgin?" she asked. Nonetheless, she modestly consented.[25]

Luke prefigured Mary's remarkable pregnancy with a story about her kinswoman Elizabeth, who after many years of barrenness bore a boy that she named John. As an adult, John predicted Jesus' coming and baptized him in the Jordan River. All these scenes became favorite subjects for Christian artists in later centuries, as did images of Mary and the newborn Jesus at the Nativity.

The evangelists kept quiet, though, about most of the thirty or so years of life that Mary and Jesus shared with Joseph, Mary's husband. It is not clear, for instance, whether Mary accompanied Jesus as he traveled and preached. According to John's version, she provoked her son's first public miracle by asking him to intervene when the wine ran out at a wedding feast in Cana.[26] Yet the canonical Gospelists also described how Jesus sometimes chided or ignored his mother. She may or may not have witnessed his death. Although later artists commonly depicted her at the scene of Jesus' crucifixion, weeping at his feet or cradling his lifeless body, only John's Gospel (the latest of the four) located her there.[27] According to the Acts of the Apostles, probably written by the Gospelist called Luke at the end of the first century, several Marys were among the followers of the resurrected Christ when the Holy Spirit brought the gift of prophecy to the apostles. However, no one depicted the Virgin or another woman preaching or discussing philosophy with these men, as the noncanonical Gospel of Mary of Magdala did.[28] The evangelists did not report Mary's death or her assumption into heaven. They apparently did not anticipate her later career as a saint and Blessed Virgin.[29] Mary left neither a body to be enshrined and visited nor a record of where she may have been buried, although her childhood house, originally in Nazareth, supposedly rests inside a baroque church at Loreto, where angels deposited it intact in 1294.[30]

Mary's early history grew more detailed as generations of Christian thinkers puzzled out her role as Mother of God.[31] Early readers of the Book of Revelation associated the mother of Jesus with emblematic females mentioned in that narrative, especially the "woman clothed with the sun, with the moon under her feet and a crown of twelve stars on her head."[32] The identification became a favorite subject for Christian artists of the Apocalypse.[33] At the same time, more detailed stories of the Virgin's life and death circulated along with the canonical histories of Jesus' life. Over several centuries, as the religion that would eventually be known as Christianity took shape, theologians and church leaders assembled in one ecclesiastical council after another in order to articulate a doctrine of Mary. Bishops, abbots, and priests argued fiercely over the meaning of Mary's time on earth and its implications for Christian doctrines. One of their most taxing problems was how to reconcile humanity and divinity in a single historical figure born to a flesh-and-blood woman. By the third century, theologians were using Mary as a symbol of the new Eve, bride and partner of the new Adam (her son Jesus), who would eventually bring an end to the twin curses of sin and death. Whereas the first woman had tempted the first man to defy God and thus caused humanity's expulsion from Eden, Mary and her son would lead all Christians back to paradise.[34] Theologians created a logic of Marian intercession through which Mary became integral to the project of human salvation, both as a role model for Jesus followers and as a crucial actor in the drama of Christian history. Without Mary, there would have been no Jesus and no universal redemption. Still, she did not achieve official status as Mother of God until the meeting of church leaders at Ephesus in 431, more than four centuries after Mary had supposedly given birth.

The Virgin's cult flourished during the early Middle Ages, as European and Byzantine worshippers elaborated on theories of her divine motherhood and her position as the First Lady of heaven. Supplicants appealed to her as they would to an empress or queen, begging her to convey their pleas to her son, their Redeemer, Lord, and King.[35] Poets celebrated the Mother of God in hymns, while priests and bishops actively commemorated her role in the drama of Jesus' birth and death in liturgies composed for regular worship.[36] The Virgin was supremely suited to intercede on behalf of struggling humanity, churchmen reasoned, because by giving birth to Jesus she had made possible the singular moment of humanity's direct encounter with the living God. Since Mary alone among mortals was born sinless and utterly selfless, and since she gave birth without experiencing human lust or sexual intercourse, she was the only one noble and pure enough to channel God's mercy impartially to all his children.

The idea that Mary never really died was fundamental to her role as intercessor with the divine. Well into the Renaissance, writers and artists described the Virgin's death, although they called it the Dormition, as if she had simply nodded off and later awoken to find herself in heaven.[37] However, another doctrinal opinion, equally popular from as early as the fourth century, argued for the bodily Assumption of Mary. According to this opinion, made official dogma by Pope Pius XII, Mary was assumed body and soul into heaven at the end of her life on earth, rather than dying and returning to dust like the rest of us.[38] As the great Dominican theologian Saint Thomas Aquinas (d. 1274) put it in one of his prayers to the Virgin, anyone who desired "to obtain favors with God should approach this mediatrix, approach her with a most devout heart because, since she is the Queen of Mercy, possessing everything in the kingdom of God's justice, she cannot refuse your petition."[39]

Still, although premodern Christians prayed to the Virgin, they did not expect to see her. They learned what she looked like from statues, icons, or other simulacra. Some were lucky enough to glimpse an object that Mary herself had owned or touched, such as a bit of her cloak. Eastern Christians produced and venerated icons of the Virgin that spoke, moved, and bled in response to pious petitions and that defended good Christians from harm. Such spiritually charged objects and images were rumored to work many miracles for those who visited and admired them.[40] One holy picture of Mary allegedly saved the city of Constantinople from Persians in the seventh century, and a hundred years later, another staved off invading Avars from the Pannonian plains.[41] Western Christians, by contrast, relied more heavily on local miracle workers—saints whose bodies and images lay in nearby churches—than on the distant Queen of Heaven. When early medieval Christians had visions, they typically saw their favorite saints, angels, or demons rather than Jesus or his mother.

Mary began making regular European appearances only in the twelfth century, not long before Saint Thomas Aquinas, Doctor of the Church, took up his pen—at least, she began to show up in more stories of apparitions and visions around this time.[42] Historians have credited the increasing popularity of Marian devotion after the twelfth century to the flourishing of feudal culture, the development of medieval romance and courtly love, and widespread ecclesiastical reforms. Whatever its cause, bishops, abbots, and abbesses quickly learned how to profit from the Virgin's spreading reputation as a heavenly intercessor by rebuilding churches dedicated to Mary or by adding Lady chapels to their cathedrals. Christian scholars of the time fortuitously rediscovered ancient legends in which the Virgin had demanded that churches be built in her honor at Rome, Zaragoza (Spain), Evesham (England), and many other holy places. Most of the legends about these purposeful apparitions—lovely tales involving miraculous snows and supernatural transportations—were published almost a thousand years after the churches were originally constructed, and hence they reveal much more about concepts of Mary in the Middle Ages than about visions in the first few centuries of Christianity.[43]

The Blessed Mother became the patron of each shrine she commissioned, along with many that she did not. Some of her premodern churches were tiny and ordinary, rarely attracting many pilgrims. Each community preserved its stories of a dream, a speaking statue, or some other Marian miracle that inspired local devotions.[44] Witnesses' accounts suggest that the Virgin tailored her appearance for each shrine, changing her message, name, and title as often as her robes. Nonetheless, she remained the historical, singular Mary, mother of Jesus. The early sixteenth-century Litany of Loreto (the same Loreto that was home to the miraculously transported house) offers a typical invocation of the Virgin's multiple virtues and honorific titles. It calls her

> Mystical rose,
> Tower of David,
> Tower of ivory,
> House of gold,
> Ark of the covenant,
> Gate of heaven,
> Morning star,
> Health of the sick,
> Refuge of sinners,
> Comforter of the afflicted,
> Help of Christians,
> Queen of Angels,
> Queen of Patriarchs,
> Queen of Prophets,
> Queen of Apostles,
> Queen of Martyrs,

Queen of Confessors,
Queen of Virgins,
Queen of all Saints,
Queen conceived without original sin,
Queen assumed into heaven,
Queen of the most holy Rosary,
Queen of peace.[45]

The Virgin's requests for construction projects became a regular motif in early modern histories of conquests and religious conversions. Marian legends crossed the seas with French and Iberian Catholics sailing to Africa, Asia, and the Americas. Missionaries believed that the loving mother of the Christian God conveyed the religion's allure to ignorant savages who could not read scripture or grasp complex doctrines. Modern scholars have argued that natives of the Americas adapted the Virgin's traits and symbols to resemble attributes of local goddesses; indigenous iconography still features prominently in some Mexican and Latin American versions of the Virgin.[46] Colonial congregations built shrines to the Mother of God on sites that had long been sacred to other spirits. When the mother of Jesus purportedly appeared to a Nahua-speaking peasant named Juan Diego in 1531, she ordered him to erect a church at el Cerro de Tepeyac, a hill belonging to Tonantzin (the title of several local maternal/fertility goddesses.) At that location, the Virgin became Nuestra Señora, La Virgen de Guadalupe. In other places where she appeared, she became known as La Virgen de Luján, de Copacabana, de Ciudad de Los Angeles, and a thousand other designations in towns and villages across two American continents.[47]

Over the centuries, Mary's proliferating venues have earned her countless additional titles, some quite geographically precise and others more generously territorial. She now reigns, for example, as Our Lady of Africa, Altagracia, Altotting, Arabia, Beauraing, Bandel, Bandra, and Banneux, as well as Our Lady of the Valley, the Wayside, the Woods, Victories, Walsingham, and Washington. The Virgin has also collected symbolic and descriptive titles related to particular miracles, apparitions, and doctrinal attributes. She has become Our Lady Who Appeared (Nossa Senhora Aparecida), patron saint of Brazil, whose national shrine is in Aparecida in the state of São Paulo. She is also the Paradise Fenced against the Serpent and the Aqueduct of Grace. She is the Bride of Christ, Deliverer of Christian Nations, Dwelling Place of the Spirit, Eastern Gate, God's Vessel, House Built by Wisdom, the Immaculate Conception, and the Lady of Grace, Mercy, Perpetual Help, Sorrows, and the Rosary. She is Mary of the Hurons (Sainte Marie) in Ontario, Canada, where Jesuits briefly maintained a shrine on the banks of the river Isaraqui beginning in 1639.[48] In the diocese of Green Bay, Wisconsin, she is the Queen of Heaven and Our Lady of Good Help at the shrine established by the nineteenth-century Belgian immigrant Adele Brise; the site was formally approved by its bishop in 2010, becoming the first official Catholic shrine dedicated to a Marian apparition that took place in North America.[49] Elsewhere Mary is still the New Eve, Theotokos (God bearer), the Woman Clothed with the Sun, and everything else that believers have named her during two thousand years of veneration.[50]

Sensus Fidelium

In preparation for the summit of Catholic minds at Vatican II, Pope Paul VI issued a now-famous chapter of the 1964 Dogmatic Constitution on the Church, titled *Lumen gentium*, which directly addressed the Virgin's place in human history. Mary, the pope proclaimed, "is justly honored by a special cult in the church."

> Clearly from earliest times the Blessed Virgin is honored under the title of Mother of God, under whose protection the faithful took refuge in all their dangers and necessities. Hence after the Synod of Ephesus the cult of the people of God toward Mary wonderfully increased in veneration and love, in invocation and imitation, according to her own prophetic words: "All generations shall call me blessed, because He that is mighty hath done great things to me."[51]

Theologians refer to this inspired, grassroots consensus of believers with the doctrinal phrase *sensus [fidei] fidelium*, which means "ordinary people's sense of faith," or what church leaders presume to be Catholic popular opinion. As *Lumen gentium* also declared, "The entire body of the faithful, anointed as they are by the Holy One, cannot err in matters of belief. They manifest this special property by means of the whole peoples' supernatural discernment in matters of faith [*sensus fidei*] when 'from the bishops down to the last of the lay faithful' they show universal agreement in matters of faith and morals."[52]

However, Pope Paul cautioned, this does not mean that believers can negotiate with church leadership about the established dogmas of Roman Catholicism (the Magisterium). Marian adoration must, the pontiff ordered, remain within "the limits of sound and orthodox doctrine, according to the conditions of time and place." In 2012, during celebrations of the fiftieth anniversary of the Second Vatican Council, some church leaders and theologians lamented the decrease in Marian devotion that resulted from the council's decrees. Although participants in Vatican II had addressed the Virgin's role in the drama of world salvation, they did not generate a separate document on Mary but tucked their statements into *Lumen gentium*. This supposedly signaled the diminishing status of Mary's cult among Catholic intellectuals.[53]

The history of the Virgin Mary—her many personae, the doctrinal battles over her meaning for Christians, and rules about her veneration by Catholics—is a crucial context for understanding the pilgrims to Our Lady of the Rock. Very few of them have learned many details of Mary's long history. They are conversant with many Marys but probably have not heard about other shrines dedicated to a Lady of the Rock at, for instance, the

Benedictine monastery in Washington State, the fifteenth-century church in Montenegro, or the equally venerable hermitage in Portugal, all supposedly inspired by a purportedly sixth-century shrine to Santa Maria ad Rupes at Sant'Elia in Lazio. Leonardo da Vinci painted two pictures of the Virgin of the Rocks (plural), which now hang in the Louvre and the National Gallery in London; perhaps a few pilgrims have seen the pictures or copies of it.[54] But those are different rocks and other Ladies. The Virgin's past explains why the Lady who appears in the Mojave patronizes only that particular rock in that particular desert and responds verbally only to Maria Paula Acuña while attending to the prayers of Maria Paula's witnesses.

Pilgrims to the Californian Lady of the Rock sometimes advertise their loyalty to other manifestations of the Virgin from other famous apparition sites, for instance, by wearing Guadalupe T-shirts or Medjugorje medallions. They grasp the doctrinal principle of the one-and-many Virgins, with its implications of Mary's immanence in actual locations of both the past and the present. As one witness put it in December of 2009, the Lady of the Rock at California City is "La Roquera, she's not La Guadalupana." Pilgrims are not merely commemorating the historical Mother of Christ or the legend of her apparition in sixteenth-century Mexico City; they are also honoring the apparition occurring now, outside California City. Their multiple loyalties to multiple Marys signal their understanding of complex Catholic Mariology. When they shout "¡Viva la Virgen, Viva la Madre de Jesus, Viva la Reina de las Americas, Viva Nuestra Señora de la Roca!" devotees of Mary are saluting centuries of Marian encounters represented by the apparitions of Neustra Señora de la Roca.[55]

The Virgin's appearance in the Mojave is at once singular and familiar. Some Virgins look alike. In physical features and costume, for instance, the Lady of the Rock most closely resembles the pallid Lady who visited three children at Fátima. The visionary and the organizers of events at Our Lady of the Rock know about Fátima, and most of them firmly distinguish between the two Virgins. The Californian apparition "is *not* Our Lady of Fátima, she is Our Lady of the Rock," one devotee put it emphatically as pilgrims to the Mojave celebrated the feast day of Our Lady of Fátima (May 13) in 2010.[56] A few visitors to the Mojave vision site observe a more intimate overlap of Virgins, though. One pilgrim photographer who posted images taken at Our Lady of the Rock on that same May 13 of 2010 on YouTube entitled them "Apariciones de la Virgen de Fátima"—reasoning apparently that since it was Fátima's anniversary, it was Our Lady of Fátima who presided.[57] Maria Paula has admitted that she meets the Virgin on the thirteenth of every month because of Fátima's legacy, and La Roquera's messages to Maria Paula echo the advice that Mary whispered long ago in Portugal.[58] However, the Virgin's words also recall those she spoke at La Salette, Lourdes (1846, 1857, France); Medjugorje (since 1981); Conyers, Georgia (1990–98); and Phoenix, Arizona (1988), among hundreds of other places over the last two centuries.[59] One enterprising collector of twentieth-century apparitions who tried to index themes of reported Marian messages counted fifty-seven places where the Blessed Mother told audiences to pray the rosary (once or repeatedly), thirty-two sites where she demanded that a shrine be built, and eight where she emphasized purity or chastity.[60] Mary repeats herself regularly, according to her devotees, because her mortal children have failed to carry out her requests for repentance, prayer, and world peace. In thousands of messages, conveyed by almost as many seers, she has asked Catholics to pray the rosary daily.

Since only Maria Paula Acuña has laid eyes on the apparitional Lady who appears at the Rock (at least, according to Señora Acuña), pilgrims must rely on the visionary's description, along with whatever they have learned about the Virgin's many manifestations, in order to envision her and confirm her identity. For clues, they can study the statue kept at the grotto, copied after the Virgin of Maria Paula's visions. The statue's face recalls the Gospa of Medjugorje. Her posture resembles a particular Lady of the Immaculate Heart available for sale from web-based suppliers of Catholic statuary. The Virgin's pose—eyes downcast, one hand stretched out to those below and one slightly more elevated in the direction of her chest—recalls the doctrine of Mary's pure love for her son and all her other children, often also symbolized by a flaming or pierced heart.[61]

Maria Paula tells the story—actually, she tells several versions of the story—of the Virgin's first apparition. The visionary's young daughter was stricken with leukemia. One night the child dreamed of a "beautiful lady" who requested that Maria Paula visit a nearby mountain and "surrender herself to God and to His service." The toddler was too young to realize who spoke to her in the dream, but her mother recognized the Virgin. Maria Paula decided to pray on a lonely hillside in Lopez Canyon every morning from May 3, 1989—May is the traditional month of Our Lady—until July 24 of that year. According to one variant of the visionary's oral autobiography, she had been saying her rosary in the midst of a bright mist, typical of summer dawn near the southern California coast, when marvelous birds began to sing. Suddenly Maria Paula sniffed the scent of exotic blooms, as Saint Juan Diego reputedly did long ago when he stumbled upon the Virgin on a Mexican hill in 1531. The luminescent curtain of fog parted to reveal a lady wearing "white clothing, standing on a cloud, with a great rosary in her hands," according to Maria Paula.[62] The Virgin identified herself and announced that she and Maria Paula would "form an army" and "work together."[63]

Maria Paula returned to Lopez Canyon on the thirteenth of each following month to meet the Beautiful Lady. Since then, the Lady has always returned to Maria Paula in a cloud of light and a gown of white. In 1997, the Virgin looked "like a big ray of light coming from the sky very slowly . . . in front of me. She looks like a cloud. I see her very clearly. She's a very beautiful woman, very young. . . . Maybe 18 years old. About 5'5"."[64] In 2006, the visionary added that the Virgin's hair was blond, her eyes blue, and her voice "sweet, sweet." In that same year, Mary wore white and appeared, in Maria Paula's opinion, to be either twenty-five, thirty-five, or forty-five years old—"just like me," added the visionary, who was about forty-five at the time.[65]

Maria Paula's description of the Lady of the Rock's appearance and the Virgin's mode of transportation is familiar from reports of previous apparitions in other places, as well as from paintings, prints, statues, and written descriptions stretching back at least five hundred years or more. In medieval European depictions, the Virgin usually, although not always, wore blue.[66] In her many Italian and Spanish apparitions of the fifteenth and sixteenth centuries, she began to appear in gold costumes, as befitted her royal divinity, although she also appeared in visions as a little girl or small woman with long, veiled hair.[67] According to the 1649 version of his legend, when Juan Diego supposedly met Nuestra Señora at sunrise on Tepeyac, her clothing "was shining like the sun, as if it were sending out waves of light and the crag on which she stood seemed to be giving out rays; her radiance was like precious stones, it was like an exquisite bracelet (beautiful beyond anything else); the earth seemed to shine with the brilliance of a rainbow in the mist."[68] The self-portrait that the Virgin supposedly left on Juan Diego's cloak, or *tilma*, hidden now in the basilica of Our Lady of Guadalupe, actually depicts her in a gown of red and a blue-green cloak decorated with golden stars, surrounded by rays of light and supported by an angel holding a crescent moon. Her hair is dark, her skin light brown. The Virgin supposedly appeared again just ten years later on another Mexican hilltop at Tlaxcala, not far from Tepeyac, to a different Juan Diego; this time, though, she was wearing a blue blouse and white skirt in native style. Still, she radiated the familiar light—perhaps because she was perched in a burning tree.[69] It was La Virgen de Guadalupe, however, not the Virgin of Ocotlán at Tlaxcala, who became the premier icon of Mexican nationalism, historical identity, and what the scholar Davíd Carrasco has called Latino/a Catholic "difference."[70]

In the nineteenth century, thanks to the growing cult of her purity and the declaration of the doctrine of the Immaculate Conception, Mary began to favor a white dress. There are famous exceptions—she wore gray, normally reserved for her mournful aspects, at Medjugorje.[71] Since the Virgin's shift to pure white, however, modern visionaries have typically described her as young, petite, lovely, soft-voiced, and veiled, although sometimes crowned. Rays of light, luminous fogs, and shining clouds still herald her approach. Sometimes the sun whirls or dances in the sky, as it did several times over the Mojave in 2010, or thunder signals her coming as at Medjugorje, Garabandal (Spain), and Fátima.[72] The scent of roses wafts behind her.

Mary's light comes not from her clothing, however, but from within. Bernadette Soubirous first saw her in 1858 as a vague glow in a dark grotto but later described the apparition as "a lady dressed in white, [who] wore a white dress, and equally white veil, a blue belt, and a yellow rose on each foot."[73] In 1909 at Le Pailly, France, she came surrounded by "a brilliant furnace of light." At Fátima in 1917, when the three peasant children met her, the Virgin emerged from a ball of light from the east, preceded by lightning. She was clothed in a white tunic and mantle more brilliant than the sun, the edges of which glittered like gold. Her presentation was so bright that the young visionaries claimed they could not stare directly at its dazzle.[74] Often uncanny light precedes the Virgin, who emerged from it in Amsterdam (1945), Tre Fontane (Italy, 1947), Lipa (Philippines, 1948), Gortnadreha (Ireland, 1988), and Cuenca (Ecuador, 1988), among many other places.

At Akita (Japan, 1973), her wooden statue came to life while suddenly bathed in gleaming light. Elsewhere the Lady oozed light, shot multicolored light from her immaculate heart, or, as at Cuapa (Nicaragua, 1980), radiated light from her fingers. She often wears a crown or halo of shining stars and has also been spotted with rose-adorned sandals of splendid radiance.[75]

The Virgin generates light and, like the sun, moon, and stars, lives in the sky. She rarely stands or sits on the earth. At Fátima, as elsewhere, the Virgin hovered above the ground as she does when addressing Maria Paula. Mary glided down on a shining cloud at Medjugorje (Bosnia-Herzegovina) in 1981. Likewise, when Rosa Quattrini heard a voice summoning her to pray in 1964 in San Damiano, Italy, she hurried into her backyard, where she sighted gold and silver clouds floating over her plum tree. A red sphere emerged from the clouds and drifted down to her pear tree, out of which shone great light. As the Virgin emerged from the sphere, luminous rays shot from her hands, and rose petals showered Rosa.[76]

These visions of a white-clad shining Lady stepping from a bright flying sphere sound oddly similar to another famous scene: the entrance of Glinda, Good Witch of the North, as depicted in the 1938 film *The Wizard of Oz*. The comparison is not facetious or whimsical, for witnesses to the supernatural typically explain the looks and logic of inexplicable phenomena in visual terms borrowed from other media, such as art, photographs, and moving pictures.[77] In March of 2009, the Virgin came whizzing into the sanctuary at Our Lady of the Rock as a flash of light, according to one of Maria Paula's witnesses. The pilgrim may have been envisioning Steven Spielberg's aliens in *Close Encounters of the Third Kind*, or perhaps he recalled representations of the traveling Christmas star in films and television animations. Another pilgrim to the Mojave has seen the Virgin drift languidly upward into the sky after the day's events were done, which is also a common trope in vision reports. Mary's bodily ascent into Heaven, now known as the Assumption, has been a favorite subject of Catholic artists who crafted church decorations, books, and holy cards over the last thousand or more years. The Virgin's vertical mode of travel is famous. She never sneaks in and rarely melts away unnoticed. In July of 2010, as the Lady of the Rock slowly lifted into the sky (according to Maria Paula), pilgrims waved good-bye in rhythm and sang "¡Adios!" to her as if they were enacting the final scene of a musical play. When the apparition took an apparent right turn, so did the crowd, in unison, as if choreographed.

Maria Paula's dreaming daughter can be forgiven for failing to recognize the cues to heavenly apparitions, since visionaries often fail to recognize Mary at first glance. The dazzling lights, obscuring fogs, and morphing appearance of the Virgin must be startling; how much more shocking must be an encounter with the Mother of God, face to shining face? Visionaries and their audiences usually doubt their own eyes, as the apostles doubted their sight of the risen Christ. Modern seers frequently report that they initially mistook the Virgin for a trick of the light or an optical illusion. Visionaries and their allies always struggle for the right words to describe and substantiate their sightings.

Many scholars have criticized the formulaic descriptions that visionaries give of the Virgin's physical appearance, including her gestures and postures, but witnesses to vision events are grateful for Mary's regular habits. Throughout Christian history, seers and witnesses have relied on aides-mémoire such as statues, paintings, holy medals, and other evocative images of the Virgin to help them recognize the Mother of God and explain accurately what they have witnessed. They have inherited a visual vocabulary, the terms of which they only occasionally share with religious authorities and outsiders. When reporters or authorities interview visionaries, their questions tend to prompt familiar responses. "What was the Virgin wearing?" inquisitors might ask, anticipating right or wrong answers from a limited set of possibilities. Church inquisitors from the sixteenth to the twentieth centuries typically asked visionaries and witnesses for details of the apparition's clothing, footwear, and hairstyle, her gestures, and the objects she carried. However, like copies of a famous painting created from memory, responses to such questions have varied by territory, culture, and historical location. In addition, churchmen constantly compare new reports with older, already approved accounts of the Virgin's appearances.[78] If the Lady's looks were identical to those of a recent apparition, a vision report typically lost credibility. Yet if the Lady's presentation did not recall previous images, or if the apparition behaved in unexpected ways, ecclesiastical authorities doubted its heavenly origins. The Virgin is unlikely to appear naked, for instance, or ugly, dancing, armed, astride a camel, or stepping out of a spaceship. Visionaries, witnesses, and religious authorities all refer to reliable icons rendered in diverse visual media in order to communicate and authenticate the Virgin's appearances.

Models of Mary have varied marvelously over the centuries, but only at the dawn of the twentieth century and the advent of cinema could artists hope to reproduce the living drama of Mary's appearances. Before movies, though, Mary appeared in magic lantern shows—in fact, when news of an apparition at Knock (Ireland) spread in 1879, authorities considered the possibility of fraud perpetrated with a magic lantern.[79] Devotees also reenacted the drama of Jesus, Mary, and the apostles in Passion plays. Mary made her movie debut in 1897, played by the Austrian Anna Wenzieger, in a filmed version of the Horitz Passion play. Since then, Mary's celluloid apparitions have appeared to millions of cinemagoers in hundreds of films, made in at least ten languages (and probably dubbed into more tongues besides.) The most famous Spanish-language biography of the Blessed Mother is probably the 1948 film *La Reina de Reinas: La Virgen Maria*, which was shown in cinemas and aired on Mexican television.[80] The Virgin of movies often resembles her famous statues and painted portraits, except in determinedly "realistic" biblical epics such as Robert Altman's *Last Temptation of Christ* or purposely provocative films such as Jean-Luc Goddard's 1985 *Je vous salu, Marie*, in which Mary is an unwed, teenaged, pregnant basketball player living in contemporary France. But even Goddard's Marie has long lustrous hair, blue eyes, and a serenely enigmatic demeanor.

More recently, however, films, television, and the Internet have expanded the visual language of apparitions by offering a multitude of moving, talking models of the historical

Mary and the apparitional Virgin for global audiences. Films and websites creatively conflate the Virgin's historically reimagined appearances and her apparitional presences; the Virgins of visual media are also one and many. In a similar way, movies and modern novels treat many different visionaries but tend to depict them as a predictable type. Historical films, such as the Oscar-winning 1943 *Song of Bernadette*, have portrayed their heroines as dreamy, innocent, self-sacrificing young women from poor and otherwise marginal classes.[81] Like the Virgin herself, cinematic visionaries are generally divinely good-looking—their external appearance is, after all, a by-product of their inner beauty. They are humble and overwhelmed before the Virgin but passively stubborn before suspicious religious authorities.[82] Filmmakers model the looks and poses of their characters on famous artistic depictions of religious figures, hoping to convey the human reality of mystics and seers, ironically enough, with references to paintings and statues.[83] Many documentaries and educational films also mix static shots of Marian icons or painted scenes of apparition events with dramatic reenactments; yet those same docudramas often rely on cinematic special effects—derived from the very same religious iconography—to demonstrate the supernature of apparitions.[84] The Virgin glows and floats in movies as well as in visions. No matter the medium or intent of its maker, every depiction of visions and visionaries features some cross-cultural clue to the Virgin's identity so that the audience may recognize her.

Images of the Virgin pervade the Internet, too. The Web offers innumerable venues where viewers can reenvision the Virgin in cartoons, photographs, and abstract images as well as in text and music. Despite the artistic possibilities offered by easily available image-making and publishing technologies, a selective set of familiar attributes still dominates Mary's appearances on the Internet. As one blogger put it in the fall of 2009, commenting on the picture of a purported apparition in Ireland, everyone recognizes the Virgin Mary "because they all have holy cards with pictures of her on them! (You know, the blonde lady with the white scarf and the blue dress.)"[85] The writer assumed that his readers knew exactly which blonde and which white scarf he meant. Websites dedicated to Marian apparitions privilege a limited and repetitive set of visual and musical themes. Roses are a popular motif, for instance, and many sites include the strains of Schubert's "Ave Maria" or well-known classical choral pieces invoking the Mother of God.

Twentieth-century artists tested the limits of modern apparitional iconography with their portraits of Our Lady. In 1996, the British-Nigerian artist Chris Ofili made headlines and infuriated New York's mayor Rudolph Giuliani when his painting *The Holy Virgin Mary* appeared at the Brooklyn Museum. Giuliani, a Catholic, objected to the cutouts of genitalia and dried elephant dung that adorned Ofili's picture.[86] The artist Yolanda López and other twentieth-century feminists have commented on patriarchal politics and Latino culture with their updated representations of the Lady of Guadalupe dressed in a karate uniform, in modern work clothes, and without any clothes at all—apparently the Virgin can indeed appear naked. At least a naked woman can evoke the Virgin's iconography, as in Alma Lopez's *Our Lady* and the African American artist Renee Cox's 1994 *Yo Mamadonna and Child* and her 1996 *Yo Mama's Last Supper*.[87] A model wearing nothing but a veil posed as a nude Virgin on the sensational December 2008 cover of Mexican *Playboy*, timed to appear for the feast day of Guadalupe.[88] Still, even these controversial portraits depend on traditional elements of Marian iconography to provoke a response from self-identified Catholic viewers, who may not understand the long history of Marian iconography but know how the Virgin should look. As Yolanda López has said, "It is important for us to be visually literate, it is a survival skill."[89]

Mary's appearance has shifted in the context of evolving religious doctrines, social-political contexts, and historic trends in Christianity, such as the fracturing of the faith into its many modern denominations and sects. The Virgin has always adapted to new cultural and visual environments wherever proselytizers, conquerors, and colonizers have carted their micro-Christianities. She has assumed the visual dialect of each new culture that she has visited. In the same way, seers and witnesses to apparitions have always employed a hybrid language of historical Mariology and local visual culture while trying to meet the expectations of larger audiences and religious authorities in their reports of the Virgin. Scholars tend to frame the history of Mary and her iconography as a constant waxing and waning of her popularity, but many of them overestimate the influence of formal religious doctrines upon Marian devotees. Since late antiquity, Mary has remained directly accessible to her devotees in ways that God and his son are not.[90]

In the last 150 years, more people have claimed to see the Virgin—or, rather, more reports of apparitions have reached global audiences—than ever before. Since 1945, Mary has made hundreds of documented appearances, most of them beyond the premodern boundaries of Christendom. The percentage of all apparitions, reported worldwide, occurring in the United States increased from 10 percent just after World War II to more than 50 percent at the end of the end of the second millennium.[91]

Today's visionaries and pilgrims admittedly resort to well-tested terms and trusted models in order to identify the Virgin Mary. The evidence for Marian apparitions was built into Christianity from its start, then negotiated over the generations by believers, sympathizers, and critics. Mary's visual and behavioral clichés make her recognizable and render her apparitions authoritative. Her ever-expanding iconography offers collective homage to a two thousand-year-old history that began after her death, Dormition, or Assumption in the first century CE. To devotees of La Señora de la Roca, the glimmering Lady who faces Maria Paula Acuña is the very same Galilean who gave birth to Jesus. She is also the Mary of canonical New Testament scriptures. She is the Virgin of Vatican-approved feast days. She is the Virgin who appeared in Guadalupe, Lourdes, Fátima, Betaña, Cualpa, Clearwater, Conyers, Medjugorje, Phoenix, Windsor, Green Bay, and every other locale—each with its own visionaries, visual environments, and religious habits—where Mary has revealed herself.

June 13, 2006

Once a month, the theology, doctrine, and iconographic history of the one-and-many Virgins intersect with the expectations, religious literacy, and visual environments of modern pilgrims in the Mojave, thanks to the mediation of Maria Paula Acuña. Many pilgrims to Our Lady of the Rock wonder, though, about the Virgin's mysterious choice of venues and visionary.

The Desert Is Wide 2

Maria Paula Acuña had several good reasons for moving to the Mojave Desert in 1995. First, she had been evicted from the original site of her monthly visions in the San Fernando Valley. Second, the Virgin ordered Maria Paula into the desert. The visionary had asked the Holy Mother what to do after losing the canyon site. "The desert is wide," the Virgin responded enigmatically. Fortunately, the desert was also cheap. Property was available and affordable in exurban communities within two hours' drive from Los Angeles.[1] Meanwhile, the Virgin's motives for selecting the desert remain mysterious, although she had been known before to insist on unlikely points of rendezvous. Despite her name, La Señora de la Roca did not choose the property for its rocks; there were none at the site when she first arrived except the usual dusty pebbles. Members of the Marian Movement hauled in sparkling white boulders to signpost the site so that the Lady could retain her title at the new locus of her miracles.[2]

Still, the Virgin's cryptic command suggests the most compelling motive for relocating to the desert. Wilderness, real and metaphorical, is a traditional site of visions and apparitions in the Christian tradition. The Mojave may seem empty to those who speed through it on California freeways, but the desert's surface conceals the source of Maria Paula's prophetic authority. She and her pilgrims are invoking a model for extraordinary religion in barren settings that was built into Christianity from its start and inscribed in its earliest scriptures and cultic histories.[3] Revelation of the Savior's arrival came out of the desert with John the Baptist. Jesus himself supposedly entered the desert to battle Satan. Seventy generations of hermits, monks, ascetics, and pilgrims have left their homes and churches to follow Christ into the wilderness.

Today's hermits may not navigate the desert exactly as ancient prophets did, but they grasp the ancient custom of spiritual retreat and the sacral potential of uninhabited spaces. From a pilgrim's perspective, deserts must be remote from life's daily traffic but close enough to visit.[4] Believers arrive in the desert with all sorts of ideas about prophetic authenticity and visionary efficacy. It is easier to discern genuine prophets in a desert setting, absent temporal clutter and noise. The relentless sun amplifies messages from heaven; clouds and low rainbows also signal the divine presence. The Virgin sent Maria Paula to find and name a place for apparitions in the Mojave Desert. At the same time, the desert theater helped to authenticate Maria Paula's spiritual authority and secured a spot for her in the history of Christian apparitions. Even the dirt at Our Lady of the Rock is "holy ground," according to Maria Paula. Barren, baked earth offers the perfect setting for rebuilding religion from the ground up.[5]

History and Uses of the Desert

To casual visitors, the land around Our Lady of the Rock probably seems no different from any other patch of the Mojave. It is a mere speck on the geological map of California's three great deserts. The Mojave stretches over seventy-eight thousand square miles of California, Nevada, Arizona, and Utah. Our Lady of the Rock sits in its southwestern corner, at the extrasuburban edge of greater Los Angeles. Pilots from nearby Edwards Air Force Base can glance down at the vision site as they rocket through the skies. Real estate developers still envision the territory around Our Lady of the Rock as a zone of private properties, linked by roads and water lines to the small town of California City (population approximately 12,700).[6] The Marian Movement of Southern California—a nonprofit, tax-free religious organization with headquarters in the nearby town of Mojave—acquired the acreage in the 1990s. Tortoises, coyotes, rabbits, lizards, and roadrunners have it to themselves most days and nights of the year.

Certainly nothing marks this particular corner of the desert as especially religious, although an occasional billboard along the highway quotes Bible verses popular among evangelical Protestants. Travelers descending from the San Gabriel Mountains to head northward through the desert must pass through miles of low scrub sparsely punctuated with Joshua trees and one-stoplight towns. The landscape's monotony is deceptive, though. Environmentalists would never call this a wilderness. They claim that the desert's lively diversity lies in barely visible details of geological history measured by shifting plates and vanishing seas. The Mojave basin has altered considerably over the centuries. Millennia ago, long before scribes composed the Bible, the shifting surface of the earth thrust up ridges that prevented the basin's rivers from emptying into the ocean; inland lakes once covered much of what is now desert. When the last of the glaciers melted around ten thousand years ago, the region dried out and warmed up. Creatures and plants appeared in this arid land that now exist nowhere else on earth. Temperatures commonly top one hundred degrees Fahrenheit in the summertime when the Santa Anas blow. Just enough rain falls in winter and in sporadic summer storms to keep the yuccas,

Joshuas, and ancient clusters of creosote alive. Flora and fauna survive by storing water or going dormant in the hottest months.

If religion flowered in this desert long before the Virgin arrived—say, when some of the ten thousand-year-old creosote cores were born—not much evidence of it remains. In the prevailing arid climate of the last five hundred years or so, humans have tended to move through the Mojave as efficiently as possible without pausing to pray. Before Europeans and their descendants appeared, indigenes preferred to live near hills, springs, and rivers, venturing into the desert only to hunt, not to worship. They left religious tokens and carved petroglyphs on rocks in the surrounding hills but not typically on the desert floor.[7] Spanish intruders later entered the Mojave on their way elsewhere. The intrepid priest Francisco Tomás Hermenegildo Garcés journeyed through the region near modern Mojave in 1776, preaching to the indigenes. "I showed them the picture of the Virgin," he wrote in February of that year, meaning the people he called Jamajabs (Mohaves), "it pleased them much."[8] Neither Garcés nor his Franciscan colleagues built churches in this desert, although they encouraged—or forced—natives to move to missions established along the coast.

As Euro-Americans headed west in search of gold, wagon trails and, later, railroad lines helped move them speedily through the wilderness. Cowboys herded livestock in the highlands and miners dug ore out of the surrounding hills, but still no one tarried in the Mojave until the twentieth century.[9] The region remained mostly unpeopled in the 1940s when U.S. Army troops practiced tank maneuvers there. Today military bases still claim much of the southwestern deserts. Filmmakers from Los Angeles use the Mojave for movie scenes of apocalypse, perhaps drawn by the desert's history of practice battles or by rumors of ancient giants, buried ships, and alien encounters in the region.[10]

In 1958 a different kind of visionary landed in the Mojave, promising water lines, sewers, and electricity to the new pioneers who would settle there. Nathan Mendelsohn allegedly envisioned a city greater than Los Angeles as he surveyed the undeveloped lands beyond the railroad terminus at Mojave. Mendelsohn never delivered, but the midcentury population boom that washed over southern California eventually spread inland.[11] By the 1980s, at least half a million people had built small communities across the California deserts, including California City, founded in 1965. Just a decade before Maria Paula and company arrived, around 90 percent of permanent residents in the Mojave still admitted to having been born elsewhere.[12] Between 2000 and 2010, California City's population grew by more than 68 percent—the second-fastest-growing population center in the state until the economic collapse of 2008. About one-fifth of the town's houses were empty in 2010.[13]

Despite a halt to the demographic expansion, residents have finally built enduring monuments to religion in the desert. Today California City boasts eighteen churches, including the Our Lady of Lourdes Roman Catholic Church.[14] Still, Christians have not yet fully exploited the Mojave Desert's potential for spiritual retreat. No monasteries or meditation centers have sprung up to receive pilgrims, as they have along the more

June 13, 2006

welcoming lands of the California coast. Instead, locals retreat to the lonely wilderness and its seemingly static landscapes for other kinds of relaxation. On any given day, for instance, off-road vehicles (ORVs) zoom across the property of the Marian Movement. When Maria Paula Acuña speaks with the Virgin, the angry buzz of bikes and buggies often makes it hard to hear her prayers. California City hosts an annual ORV rally that attracts between fifty thousand and eighty thousand drivers of the monstrous, roaring contraptions.

It seems that many people who do not dwell in the desert are nonetheless eager to face its challenges to the body and the inspiration of its perceived emptiness. In 1980 the U. S. Bureau of Land Management issued a warning against recreational pursuits that endanger the Mojave's rare plant and animal species, which are sustained by the "delicate crust" of its soil. However, the bureau's report also repeated the typically American maxim that wide-open "natural lands . . . satisfy a basic need in the American character." The Mojave, according to these environmentally minded bureaucrats, must retain "open space," which is a "basic requirement for activities such as soaring, target shooting, hand gliding, sand sailing, and, using the obstacle nature of the desert as a resource, recreationists who challenge terrain and distance on motorcycles, dune buggies, and four-wheel drive vehicles."

One citizen told the bureau that "activities we do in the desert can only take place in the desert. Where else can we find open space? Not at the ocean beaches or in the mountains."[15] The bureau did not plan for or render an opinion on religious uses of the desert.

Like the sports enthusiast who craves open space, Maria Paula and her followers cannot carry out devotions to the Lady of the Rock anywhere but in the Mojave. Pilgrims' longing for religious refuge in the desert clearly conflicts with the aims of other wilderness enthusiasts. Like off-road vehicle races, religious traffic is still fairly new to this corner of the Mojave. It remains, in many senses, virgin turf. The effects of religious use on desert resources remain unmeasured. If the congregations of California City's many churches have ventured beyond city limits, they have left no signs. The town's religious institutions have no official connection to Our Lady of the Rock. Nothing else human-made rises from the lands surrounding the Marian Movement's shrine, although houses have been planned in the vicinity. The visionary and her witnesses are building from the ground up to meet the Virgin on her way down.

The conceptual tabula rasa of this desert has rendered Maria Paula's chosen site ideal for visionary religion. No previous history or competing faith impedes her practice. At the same time, more prosaic and local features of the space have also prepared the plots on Lincoln Boulevard for miracles and pilgrimages. The real estate was cheap. Water lines and roads already snaked beneath the soil, thanks to Mendelsohn. Tracks on the surface have proper street names, signed and registered with the county. At the same time, the nearest Catholic priest preaches about ten miles away. Vandalism is rare, partly because the shrine is invisible from the nearest paved road. For almost fifteen years, nothing stood at the site but a large shed about a mile off the highway. During those years, a permanent shrine to commemorate the Virgin's appearances and Maria Paula's visions remained little but a heavenly request and a property deed.

Today a six-foot wire fence encloses a low, rectangular building with a circular windowed chamber on its western end. Inside the rounded chamber, an almost life-sized statue of the Virgin poses on a pile of imported rocks for which the site is named. Maria Paula and the pilgrims call the structure a grotto. The building's western facade confronts an intricate system of walkways, young trees and struggling rosebushes, and occasionally functional fountains. The building is too small to accommodate congregational services, but the shrine is not intended for the priestly rites of Catholicism. The place still lacks simple shelter for visitors, but at least the grotto features toilets marked for *damas* and *hombres*, which is an improvement over the portable potties that used to line up behind the sanctuary. Construction and landscaping continue whenever donations flow to the Movement. Construction halted briefly in 2009, when a rumor circulated that one or more of the builders had made off with the Movement's funds. At another point, the city forced the Movement to replace the grotto's roof because it did not meet California City's building code.[16] The Marian Movement continues to make improvements to the site, expanding the garden with trees and rosebushes and lining the grotto's approach with four-foot crosses. Pilgrims who work in the construction business often help out.

Desert Traditions

Our Lady of the Rock exists in a desert both real and symbolic, which has its roots in biblical wildernesses. Hebrew scriptures have at least four different words for the various places that English-language Bibles call "deserts," all of them rich with multiple meanings. Latin translators understood *desertum* as a place of solitude, with both negative and positive connotations. For instance, Israelites fleeing Egyptian slavery sought asylum in the deserts of the Arab peninsula and made a covenant with their God in the Sinai. In theological terms, their journey through the wastelands transformed the Jews from refugees into the chosen people of Israel, inscribed forever in the Torah (the Christian Old Testament.) On a desert mountain, according to the Book of Exodus, Moses spoke to God "face to face as one man speaks to another"—although Moses did not actually look upon his Creator's face for, as God pointed out, "humans cannot see me and live."[17] Those who clung to Moses and accepted the desert's austere lessons eventually reached Canaan. Yet other scriptural passages expressed ambivalence about deserts, which lacked the comforts as well as the torments of civilization. "I wander far off, I would lodge in the wilderness," lamented the psalmist, "for I have seen violence and strife in the city" (Ps. 55). Proverbs 21:19 famously advised that "it is better to dwell in a desert land than with a contentious and fretful woman." Scouring winds blew in from the desert, bringing caravans but also fearsome armies. But God also lurked there in the burning bush, the whirlwind, and in still, small voices heard only in lonely caves.

Desert symbolism was crucial to the first generations of Jesus followers. According to New Testament scriptures, John the Baptist emerged from the desert to proclaim the advent of the Messiah. Jesus himself went into the desert for forty days to prepare for his mission, according to three of the Gospelists. Like his ancestors, who had endured the Sinai for forty years, this son of David faced trials in the wilderness. He is said to have emerged from the desert to form a new religion, as Moses did centuries before him, based on a covenant with the Creator. Catholic pastors still routinely make this connection in their sermons for Lent, which are now easily available online as well as in churches.[18] The Exodus also remains a central theme in Latin American liberation theology, which identifies the oppression of native peoples and working classes with the suffering of the Israelites in slavery.[19]

For centuries, the desert has offered symbolic refuge to Christians seeking spiritual solitude and provided a haven for rebels (religious or other) eluding disapproving authorities. The very first Christian monks left Egyptian towns for isolated caves in the desert beyond the Nile. Stories of their visions, miracles, and extreme asceticism, collected by pilgrims who trekked to visit them, reaffirmed the ancient relationship between self-denial and visionary ability. Writers of late antiquity admired desert-dwelling hermits who easily subdued wild beasts and demons with prayer and were so holy that their flaming fingers could serve as torches. "The cell of a monk," proposed one Christian cave dweller, "is the furnace in Babylon where the three young men found the Son of God;

and it is also the pillar of cloud from which God spoke to Moses."[20] By the fourth century, then, the desert had become more than just an arid physical environment or site of religious observance; it was a devotional method as well as a metaphor for ascetic sanctity. Deserts might look desolate, but genuinely holy men and women could spot devils lurking among the dunes and in the dark ruins of pagan temples, ready to tempt pious Christians. Whatever form demons took when attacking the desert fathers—dreadful lions or irresistible dancing girls—it was easier to discern their deceptions when undistracted by gentler settings and ordinary comforts.

The early Egyptian ascetics inspired subsequent generations of Christians everywhere to withdraw into local deserts or equivalent wildernesses. In the sixth century, Saint Benedict, now celebrated as the father of Western monasticism, chose a mountaintop for his community at Monte Cassino. A century or so later, hardy Irish monks sailed out to the rocky island of Scéilg Mhichíl off the coast of Kerry, where they perched like seabirds on the barren cliffs. Other men and women disappeared into permanent exile and pilgrimage, monastic cells, or anchorholds, from which they prophesied and reported ecstatic visions, as Hildegard of Bingen did in the eleventh century and Teresa de Ávila in the mid-sixteenth.[21]

Since then, the inspirational trials of reclusive saints and desert fathers have continued to motivate modern seekers of religious solitude, such as Thomas Merton, the famous twentieth-century Trappist monk. Merton found periodic sanctuary in his Kentucky monastery as well as in his written meditations on ascetic withdrawal, including his retelling of the desert fathers' stories.[22] Today's hermits more often dwell in lonely urban flats or remote rural houses than on mountaintops or desert floors. For instance, among the new wave of Catholic hermits is a cluster of vowed Catholic women who inhabit cottages scattered around the snowy woods of La Crosse, Wisconsin. More than one Christian recluse inhabits the wastelands of southern California, too.[23] Meanwhile, Catholic retreat centers around the world are doing a booming business, as one pilgrim to Our Lady of the Rock recalled in March of 2009. He visited just such a place in Malibu along the California coast, where he experienced the miraculous cure of an eye injury.[24]

The Mojave Desert offers this same traditional refuge to pilgrims every month. The desert is clean of architecture and ready for the latter-day rendezvous of the Virgin and her chosen messenger. If churches dotted the desert, it would not seem nearly as wide, nor would its sight lines to heaven be as clear. Our Lady of the Rock's location at the edge of California City, beyond town and parish boundaries, was crucial to its selection, especially given the visionary's disagreements with local bishops and with the owner of her first vision site in Lopez Canyon. No one can evict her now. No canonical decrees direct Maria Paula's devotions, and no church roof obscures the view. Churchmen cannot bother worshippers with questions or rules, although priests sometimes turn up in civilian dress in order to participate in the vision event as ordinary witnesses.

Maria Paula and the pilgrims are at liberty to gaze wherever and however they wish. They can imagine themselves as heirs to ancient desert religion. They can even remain respectable Catholics so long as their devotions do not violate doctrinal dictates and they refrain from performing sacraments that, according to Catholic tradition, must be conducted by an ordained priest inside a church. Many witnesses belong to churches in Mojave, Bakersfield, or Johannesburg ("Joburg," as some locals call it) or to congregations in Los Angeles and its suburbs. Maria Paula and her monjas regularly attended Mass at Our Lady of Lourdes in California City until 2009. In the desert, believers are free to call themselves both Catholics and something else—charismatic, Pentecostalist, agnostic, or humbly curious.

The desert also offers a place in the sun for conscientious worshippers dismayed or dismissed by their pastors or churches. Many scholars have suggested that Latino/a Catholics of the American Southwest have always been uncomfortable with *norteño* Catholicism, which has traditionally been governed by bishops and priests of European origins. Mission records and burial vaults at California missions chronicle the generations of German and Irish men who led California's Catholic congregations through the nineteenth century and most of the twentieth. The first Hispanic to become archbishop of Los Angeles was José H. Gomez, elevated to his position in February of 2011.[25] For many years before that, however, Mexican emigrants fruitlessly searched American parishes for the vibrant Catholicism of their people's past, according to experts in Mexican American culture. The Pew Forum reported in 2007 that Latino/a Catholics still prefer Spanish-speaking liturgies and choose congregations that observe traditional holidays familiar from Spanish-speaking countries. However, some sociologists and historians also blame Mexican clergy for the alienation of Mexican American believers, because many priests played a conservative role in the revolutions and civil wars of the last century and a half.[26]

Over the last thirty years or so, theologians of Latino/a religions have worked hard to situate Marian devotions in this complicated context of cultural discontent and historical oppression, social dislocation, and racial hybridity.[27] Both sociological and theological studies of Marian devotions in Mexico, the American Southwest, and as far north as New York have emphasized the efforts of Catholic communities to maintain traditional cults of Our Lady of Guadalupe, along with various other local Virgins and saints, including the new saints and heroes of *la frontera*.[28] Many scholars of religion and Latina studies, as well as Chicana feminists, have argued that devotion to La Señora de Guadalupe and other local manifestations of Mary has periodically raised the prestige of motherhood among Mexicans and hence increased the authority of individual mothers within their families and in society generally.[29] Historians have shown how La Guadalupana evolved from patroness of the Conquest to a protectress of the indigenous oppressed and eventually became the symbol of both Catholic and Mexican identity. The Lady of Guadalupe remains a mutable figure, signifying mainstream religion to many Mexicans, but functioning in the United States as an icon of social justice for diverse immigrant groups, social activists, and workers.[30] Guadalupe's feast day on December 12 occasions festivals and performances in every major Catholic church of Mexico and the American Southwest; her shrine in Mexico City draws millions of worshippers on that single day.[31]

However, as pilgrims to the Mojave constantly point out, Our Lady of the Rock is not La Virgen de Guadalupe. Maria Paula Acuña is no San Juan Diego either, although at least Maria Paula is verifiably real; many modern historians assume that Juan Diego is fictional. Although the largest contingent of Spanish-speaking pilgrims to Our Lady of the Rock is of Mexican descent, not all of her followers are. What is more, not all Mexican and Mexican American Catholics in the greater Los Angeles area share exactly the same religious beliefs or equate their faith with *mexicanidad*.[32] Regional loyalties and devotions remain influential among emigrants' children and grandchildren, similar to the deeply felt rivalries that formerly pitted Irish, Italian, Polish, and French Canadian Catholics against each other in eastern and midwestern cities of the United States. Still, the small shrine in the Mojave does not bear the weighty nationalist and ethnic symbolisms built into the cathedrals of Chicago or Detroit or the basilica of La Virgen de Guadalupe in Mexico City. Nothing at this emerging vision site near California City explicitly evokes European conquests, the enslavement of Indians, racialized colonialism, the furious anti-Catholicism of the Mexican civil wars, or more recent border conflicts precipitated by transnational population movements. The shrine is equally remote, in spirit, from the deadly wastelands of the U.S.-Mexican border and the urban wilderness of Los Angeles, with its fraught racial history of barrios, riots, and protest marches.

Pilgrims may be more or less conscious of religious, ethnic, and national pasts when they visit the desert sanctuary, but politics do not drive this vision event—apparitions and visions do. Although a voyage into the Mojave may recall other difficult passages in individual pilgrims' lives, Our Lady of the Rock's purposeful isolation from contemporary politics is one of the shrine's most important qualities in the eyes of pilgrims, who enter the desert to escape past injuries and injustices. When Maria Paula shouts out to visitors from far away, they proudly identify as natives of Sacramento, La Jolla, Guadalajara, Tijuana, Oaxaca, Nicaragua, Bolivia, Venezuela, the Philippines, and more distant locales, such as England or India. Pilgrims join together on the thirteenth of the month to celebrate their multiple origins at this singular spot. The Marian Movement of Southern California maintains that the site's greatest attraction and value lie not in the shrine but in resources concealed deep below its surface. Maria Paula's references to holy ground come straight from scripture. "Take off your shoes," God called to Moses from the burning bush, "for the place where you stand is holy ground." (Ex. 3:5)[33] The earth at Our Lady of the Rock can scorch the feet of any sinner who treads upon it, the visionary says. On many days of the year, the surface is hot enough to roast pious soles as well.

Yet pilgrims are well aware that fellow travelers have helped convert this place to religious use, not only by their attendance and their willingness to treat the site as sacred but also with hard labor. They have watched the grotto rise slowly from foundations, month by month, thanks to the donations and labor of other pilgrims. They have waited patiently for the roses to bloom and the new fountains to flow. They know that *las rocas* from which the Virgin gets her title are transplants like themselves and like the Lady herself. "I don't know where the rocks are from . . . they brought those rocks," Tom, a regular pilgrim to the site, told me in 2009. Juan Rubio says that it took several years before Maria Paula named the first vision site in Lopez Canyon "Our Lady of the Rock."[34] Although the name migrated north with Maria Paula and the Virgin, the visionary has not yet revealed the full significance of the boulders.[35]

Exile, migration, and refuge are appropriately complex metaphors for pilgrimage to this particular landscape, especially for those who have arrived in the Mojave after perilous journeys from other countries. Even the Virgin Mary commutes regularly through a heavenly portal, leaving signs in the sky when she returns to paradise, like a jet tracing vapor trails. As Bible writers knew and many anthropologists of religion have reminded us, the desert of pilgrimage changes the identities of all who pass through it. Prophets and heroes emerged from the wastelands as if reborn. Metaphorically, passage through the wilderness transforms believers' understanding of the places they have left behind— be those seemingly secular cities, ethnic homelands, or conventional churches—and prepares them to arrive in a better place. Pilgrims may regret leaving the comfort of familiar contexts, as the newly released Israelites complained about leaving the safety of their slavery in Egypt, but they also believe that the desert's rigors improve their lives, heal their bodies, and may help save their souls.

October 13, 2006

Modern desert pilgrims continue to reinvent themselves as worshippers instructed and influenced, but not directed or restricted, by the customs and iconographies of holy places in much earlier times. Some believers carry their new spiritualities home to living room shrines and kitchen tables, to share with family and friends. Others consider their desert religion a private matter unrelated to their overlapping identities as workers, parishioners, or residents of modern nations. As Saint Augustine, great Doctor of the Church, put it sixteen centuries ago, all Christians of this earth are merely travelers en route to the City of Saints in heaven. That heavenly city, he wrote, "gathers together a society of pilgrims of all languages . . . recognizing that, however various these are, they all tend to one and the same end of earthly peace."[36] For pilgrims to Our Lady of the Rock, the road to meaningful religion and the way to heaven cross in the Mojave.

The Model Visionary

3

Christians have been wondering about the reliability of their alleged visionaries since the religion began. "Beware of false prophets who come to you in sheep's clothing," Jesus purportedly preached in his Sermon on the Mount, "but inwardly are ravenous wolves."[1] The earliest Christian authors, beginning with Paul in the mid-first century, wondered how to identify dependable prophets and sort true from false revelations. Neither Paul nor the other writers of what became the New Testament proposed a foolproof method for distinguishing divinely wrought visions and apparitions from other kinds of supernatural encounters. Throughout the centuries, theologians, clergy, and ordinary believers struggled to categorize and define human perceptions of the divine, and to differentiate these from the misleading or delusive visions of sinners, fools, demoniacs, and heathens. The enlightened Pope Benedict XIV (1675–1758) analyzed the opinions of many renowned thinkers who had tried to distinguish among the prophets and the spirits that impelled them. He quoted Bible, Roman history, Thomas Aquinas, and Savonarola to demonstrate that God had sent accurate prophecies to pagans, such as the Sibylline oracles, as well as to Satan, while respectable biblical prophets had sometimes mistaken human imagination for divine illuminations or vice versa.[2] Discernment remained a problem for church councils, other pontiffs, and Vatican commissions up to the present day.

Today's priests and pilgrims, like yesterday's apostles, base their judgments of alleged visionaries on external criteria perceptible to all. The modern discernment of an alleged visionary's spirits begins, per the oldest strategies in the Good Book, with the assessment of visible signs of the visionary's character and abilities. At Our Lady of the Rock, witnesses ask themselves and each other not only what Maria Paula sees but whether she looks, behaves, and speaks like a historically approved Catholic visionary (a group that, for them, includes pre-Reformation Christian visionaries.) They have models in mind.

Observers who have never before attended a modern vision event nonetheless arrive in the Mojave with mental pictures of prophets in Bible illustrations, saints in church windows, and visionaries from religiously themed films. They compare Maria Paula with women depicted on holy cards and statues who gaze serenely upward from beneath veils and wimples. Maria Paula in full regalia resembles an old-fashioned nun, the kind who might have taught middle-aged pilgrims in school. Visitors to Our Lady of the Rock expect her to look the part of holy woman, just as they expect priests to wear cassocks and collars.[3]

Witnesses measure Maria Paula's authenticity on the basis of three different kinds of evidence. First, they study her visionary performances, including her sermons and her ritual use of the shrine. Second, they gauge the efficacy of her prayers on behalf of her pilgrims. Third, they examine her dress, her facial expressions, gestures, intelligence, conversation, and character at the vision site as well as other, more mundane places. Maria Paula Acuña has striven to meet their expectations for at least twenty years now by crafting a persona based on the same models of visionary authority familiar to pilgrims. The tale of her first apparition varies a little each time she repeats it, but the plot and meaning follow a formula familiar to Catholics and many other Christians.[4] Her personal history references visionaries of the last two centuries, such as the children of Fátima and Bernadette of Lourdes, as well as the most famous Catholic visionary of the early modern Americas, Juan Diego of Tepeyac. Those earlier seers and the people who told their stories relied on even earlier exemplars—medieval mystics, Spanish missionaries, local saints, healers, and shamans—to demonstrate visionary authenticity. Ultimately, all Christian visionaries have taken cues directly or indirectly from the seers and prophets described in the Hebrew Bible and Christian New Testament, including Jesus Christ.

Maria Paula Acuña's appearance has changed gradually since her first meeting with the Virgin Mary. The woman who went to Lopez Canyon one summer morning has disappeared, leaving behind the visionary captured each month by Sister Thelma's digital video camera. Maria Paula has increasingly come to resemble the female visionaries of nineteenth and early twentieth-century Europe, made familiar the world over by postcards and holy cards. She presents herself as a vowed woman. She rarely mentions her children but instead presides as Madre Maria Paula to all pilgrims. For years, she has lived with Sister Thelma and sometimes other monjas in humble housing. The women survive on the donations of pilgrims and supporters, according to members of the Marian Movement. Maria Paula spends her days in a monastic routine of prayer, visits to the sick, and other charitable deeds. "I'll be sleeping sometimes, sometimes I'll be kneeling, praying, the phone rings, there is an emergency," she told a reporter several years ago. "I am at the mercy of the needy, where God tells me, look here, look there, look over there, I go in the company of Mother Mary."[5] Sister Thelma reports that Maria Paula works so hard to care for others that she has several times imperiled her own health.[6]

Still, every day Maria Paula follows a script set down centuries ago by other visionaries and their chroniclers, which has been passed along in visual, textual, and oral forms across generations of believers. Every month her self-presentation is as crucial to her reputation as the messages she receives from Mary. Maria Paula has worked hard to meet her audience's expectations of someone specially selected by the Mother of God for the communication of heavenly messages.

Visionary Orthodoxy

By traveling to the desert, pilgrims tacitly agree that Mary, the Mother of Jesus, could appear in the Mojave. Otherwise, why bother to drive so far to a place with no obvious signs of religion? They also accept the Mojave as an appropriate venue for apparitions or at least the right place for some sort of extraordinary spiritual experience. They believe that a pious Christian woman might see the invisible. They also assume that there probably is a meaningful invisible to see. They understand, as most people do, the distinction between individual perception and its multiple possible interpretations. Yet they further suppose that the Virgin's devotees, with the Lady's help, have a potential for spiritual agency lacking in less engaged Christians. Pilgrims recognize that what they do together in this desert is religious and more specifically Catholic, but it could never take place in a priest's church.

The local Catholic pastor has admitted that Maria Paula and the pilgrims are pious but religiously illiterate. "You're talking about uneducated people," he explained in the fall of 2010, who are "overly fervent" and "used to carrying statues around."[7] If he meant that pilgrims to Our Lady of the Rock are driven by a historical accumulation of beliefs and images of revelation, visions, and prophecy as old as Christianity itself, then he is correct. They might differ with the priest, though, about what exactly they have learned or should learn in order to be educated. Except for the occasional visiting nun or cleric from Latin America, most pilgrims have not formally studied Catholic doctrine or visionary history at any length, although many profess to be Bible readers. They learn in other ways.

Even the worst-informed participants at Our Lady of the Rock know that Catholics can ask Mary to influence her son, Jesus Christ, on their behalf and, further, that a bona fide visionary can convey petitions to the Mother of God. They cull other pertinent data for evaluating Maria Paula's communicative powers from the scenes and stories of their individual and collective pasts and from their diverse visual environments. They derive visionary models from Gospel readings and church rituals, in conversation with clergy or teachers, in gossip with other believers, and in both institutional and popular reports of vision events. They learn, too, from the responses of Catholic leaders and the news media to vision events, as well as reports on the Internet. Some have traveled to see visionaries perform or attended shrines commemorating vision events elsewhere, or have heard stories of local visionaries. Many pilgrims have grown up with home shrines, in which tiny statues dedicated to apparitional Virgins stood among candles, rosaries, and other decorative sacred objects.[8] Scholars and philosophers refer to the collective knowledge of pilgrims as their religious imaginary or their implicit understanding of a visionary heritage.[9] Pilgrims use all available interpretative tools, along with some commonsense psychology, to assess Maria Paula's appearance and behavior.

Maria Paula shares that same heritage and tool kit. Basic doctrinal themes and broad Catholic references, rather than theological argument, inform her sermons and conversations with pilgrims. She has spoken frequently about sin, penitence, and the importance of prayer to the Blessed Mother and God. Her sermons have often chided witnesses in simple metaphors of light and darkness, sight and lack of it. "We are dying in our blindness, Our Lady," she told the Virgin in a 2007 sermon, while to pilgrims she declared, "I want to continue with you all to take the veil from your eyes, so that you do that which God asks of you, that you walk with the weak of the world, bringing the light of heaven to each person, that you take them out of darkness."[10] The visionary sees more clearly than her witnesses, she has often implied, but they too can learn to guide sinners into the light.

Maria Paula did not need any training to discuss the moral dimensions of religious vision. The dialectic of light and dark is equally obvious to her witnesses and to believers across faith traditions. "Happy are the pure in heart, for they shall see God," Jesus was reported to have promised his followers (Matt. 5: 8), but the biblical Savior was not the only religious founder to articulate his theology in metaphors of light and dark, good and evil, sight and blindness. From the start, Christian writers understood religious ways of looking in moral terms. Early church leaders argued about the emerging doctrine of divine revelation, as well as about visionary and prophetic practices, but Christians across the generations have always agreed on one crucial point: a hierarchy of sight exists among God's creatures. Some people see better than others. Some also have more visionary potential than others, not because their eyes work better but because their virtue enables them to perceive more profound truths.

Gospel writers, for instance, were keenly aware that only a tiny cohort of humanity had been privileged to look upon the actual Incarnation of God during the three brief decades of Jesus' life on earth. According to the evangelist John, Jesus reminded his companions that they were privileged with a theophany that subsequent generations of Christians would never experience. "If you know me," he explained, "you know my Father too. From this moment you know him and have seen him" (John 14:6–7). Even among the apostles, only Peter, James, and John gained a glimpse of Jesus' godly nature. Shortly before Christ's execution, according to all four Gospels, the three men watched him rise into the sky and hover in the company of the long-dead prophets Moses and Elijah. Christ shone like the sun, according to John; like pure light, according to the evangelist Matthew (Matt. 17:1–13). Luke compared Jesus' radiance to lightning (Luke 9:28–36), while Mark declared the Savior's dazzling clothing to be brighter than any human-made bleach could ever achieve (Mark 9:1–13). The episode, which draws on Torah precedents, represents some of the earliest attempts of Christian authors to articulate the experience of seeing God. In exchange for witnessing the living Incarnation, his followers—and those who recorded the testimony—bore the responsibility of informing other Jesus followers, who never had the chance to gaze upon Jesus, about what they had seen and heard from the Savior.

The Gospels promised that every follower might eventually receive a revelation of Christ. Visionary doctrines and practices developed in dialectic with records of Jesus' life, death, and resurrection and his demonstrations of divinity. Yet as scriptural stories also made clear, theophany and prophecy did not come easily to ordinary folks. It was not just a matter of looking in a particular direction or of being in the right place or pondering visual evidence in any special way. In fact, concerns about the visual illogic of Jesus' resurrection pervade the canonical Gospel narratives. All four Gospels, as well as Acts, describe the confusion of eyewitnesses to Jesus' reappearance after his execution. The texts puzzled over the illogical visibility of the resurrected Christ. John wrote that Mary Magdalene initially mistook the risen Jesus for a gardener (John 20:11–18). According to John, other companions could not recognize the Savior when he approached them a few days after his crucifixion and burial. Even after Christ identified himself verbally, his followers were wary of his authenticity. "They saw him and worshiped him," wrote Matthew, "but some of them doubted" (28:17).

The story of Thomas, who was absent during Jesus' first visit to his followers, provided the most famous trope for visual doubt and the fallibility of human sight. Not only did he reject his colleagues' eyewitness testimony to the resurrection, but he also distrusted his own eyesight and insisted on touching Christ's death wounds to make sure of what he was seeing. Jesus gently rebuked his incredulous disciple, suggesting that "blessed are those" who believe without demanding sensory evidence (John 20:24–29).

However, the lesson of Thomas also proposed a new way of perceiving the created world that defied human reason as well as perception. How could it be that a dead man—prophet, messiah, son of God though he might be—actually rose, walked, spoke, broke bread, and was tangible? Christ's claims to resurrection and his promise of universal revelation necessitated a new kind of looking. Just as near-sighted humans may squint and dyslexics mentally rearrange letters on a page, the first Christians had to constantly adjust their visual perceptions. This story is familiar to scholars of the New Testament, Christian patristics, and late antiquity, but it is easy to underestimate the effects of such a paradigm shift on the first generations of believers. From the start, as Jesus followers organized themselves, Christian ways of looking were far more complex than merely laying eyes on something and understanding it according to a simple set of precepts articulated in sacred texts. It was not enough to imitate Jesus and his apostles. It took lifelong practice of body and mind and help from a community of more experienced believers, to look like a Christian.[11] Collective self-training in discernment coevolved with individuals' expertise in vision and prophecy.

As early as 50 CE, groups of Jesus followers began to develop formal criteria for evaluating visionaries and prophets. The disciple Paul wrote to warn fledgling congregations about people who claimed to receive new revelations long after Christ's death.

Paul demanded more from putative prophets than simple reports of what they had seen. "If I speak in the tongues of men or of angels, but do not have love, I am just a resounding gong or a clanging cymbal," Paul explained to the people of Corinth. "If I have the gift of prophecy and can fathom all mysteries and all knowledge, and if I have a faith that can move mountains, but if I do not have love, I am nothing" (1 Cor. 13:1–2) Paul asked for evidence—not necessarily visual—that visionaries and prophets genuinely embraced Jesus' teachings, as mediated by him and other mutually recognized disciples.

Paul and other intellectuals of Christianity's first few centuries also worried about conflicting interpretations of Jesus' life and words, each opinion supported by claims to vision and revelations, within communities of Jesus followers. The anonymous author of Second Peter, probably writing in the second century, elaborated on the continuing dangers posed by dissenting visionaries:

> But false prophets also arose among the people, just as there will be false teachers among you, who will secretly bring in destructive heresies, even denying the Master who bought them, bringing upon themselves swift destruction. And many will follow their sensuality, and because of them the way of truth will be blasphemed. And in their greed they will exploit you with false words. Their condemnation from long ago is not idle, and their destruction is not asleep. (2 Pet. 2:1–3)

Christians needed reliable methods for discerning the spirits and motives behind revelatory claims lest they follow the wrong prophet and lose sight of Jesus' teachings. The *Didache*, a fragmentary tract about proper Christian practices probably produced in the second century, offered some practical guidelines. Anyone who taught ideas contradicting Jesus' preaching was untrustworthy. So was any self-identified prophet who cadged lodging, food, or money from fellow Christians. "Let every apostle who comes to you be received as the Lord," the text advised, "but he shall not remain more than one day; or two days, if there's a need. But if he remains three days, he is a false prophet." Besides posing moral behavior as a criterion for prophetic authority, the *Didache*'s author also suggested comparing visionaries in order to measure their relative orthodoxy. "Not everyone who speaks in the Spirit is a prophet," he wrote, "but only if he holds the ways of the Lord. Therefore from their ways shall the false prophet and the prophet be known."[12]

Not every Christian read the *Didache*, but the document reflects a mind-set of Jesus followers in the Roman Empire. Congregational leaders and, later, politicians regularly debated major doctrinal issues in the years before 600 CE, including the question of Christ's nature (fully divine? fully human? one nature? two natures?), the timing of universal salvation, the relation of grace to free will, and the role of the Virgin Mary in history. Christians also chewed on the meaning and practice of divine visions and prophecies. Almost every important theologian of the medieval and early modern period had something to say about the possibility of seeing God, the Virgin, saints, angels, or demons—and how to prove it.[13] In fact, today's Catholic rubrics for personal and prophetic revelation rely partially on the Neoplatonic topology of Christian vision proposed by Saint Augustine of Hippo, composed fifteen hundred years ago. This was Augustine's famous division of human sight into bodily, imaginative, and visionary categories. The relation between these three modes of seeing, however, was unstated. Thomas Aquinas, the twelfth-century fan of Augustine, wrote, "For vision is made actual only when the thing seen is in a certain way in the seer." As Aquinas put it, believers had to agree that they had all seen something astonishing, and that they shared an appropriate vocabulary to describe it; in the same way, a soul in genuine union with God had to describe the experience of that union to other Christians in order fully to experience it.[14]

However, neither Augustine nor Aquinas could explain how to be sure of what he perceived. Augustine had experienced visions, or so he claimed in his retrospective *Confessions*, among other works. He described his own supernatural encounters in both dreams and waking visions, and those of his mother and friends, for the benefit of all Christian readers.[15] In several learned treatises, Augustine also considered philosophical and psychological aspects of human sight and vision, positing his threefold hierarchy of visual and visionary experience. The lowest sort of seeing, according to Augustine, is simple eyesight of material phenomena. This includes phenomena within nature, such as dogs, rocks, and thunderstorms, as well as entities and events outside it, such as apparitions or burning bushes. The second kind of seeing is interior visualization, similar to acts of memory or imagination. One might close one's eyes and envision a friend, an event, Jesus, or the Virgin Mary. The third and highest mode of "vision," achieved by few mortals, is the profound, bodiless, unmediated consciousness of God—what William James, psychologist and a founding father of modern religious studies, famously labeled transcendence.[16] Just as the eyes depend on light to see, so each soul relies upon God for the illumination that results from the third, mystical way of seeing.

Augustine's hierarchy, along with the Neoplatonic philosophy that suggested it, continues to influence modern academic constructs of visual experience. Scientists and humanists alike typologize visual perceptions, differentiating among physical eyesight, visualization, memory, and more complex mental states such as ecstasy or transcendence.[17] Nonetheless, contemporary biologists and brain surgeons use terminology for elevated forms of knowing that sounds like reductive essentialism to many humanists; meanwhile, scholars of religions rarely appreciate the body's role in mystical and visionary experience.[18] William James summed up the postmedieval dilemma concerning religious ways of looking and knowing in relation to the sensation of supernatural contact: "Of course, such an experience as this does not connect itself with the religious sphere. Yet it may on occasion do so."[19]

When believers confront problems of discernment, they appreciate evidence for orthodoxy and visionary authenticity communicated in the local lingo. A claimant to Christian visionary experience who speaks in biblical terms or refers to saintly exemplars is more likely to be deemed authentic than someone who reports an unintelligible or inexplicable vision. Church officials generally ignore news of Marian manifestations in food products, for instance; popular media, too, make fun of Virgins sighted in cheese sandwiches or Jesuses found in crunchy snacks. The language of fungible apparitions may amuse today's Catholics but does not win their approval. Seers who adhere to religious rules are more likely to seem authentic than supposed visionaries who reject the community's behavioral standards. The bishop of Fresno and archbishop of Los Angeles disapproved of Maria Paula for one of the same reasons mentioned by the *Didache*'s author: they accused her and her supporters of "financial irregularities," that is, seeking payment for visions in the form of pious donations.[20] A few pilgrims have noted that the Movement used to charge money for blessings.[21] It is a common accusation aimed at modern prophets who appear financially comfortable.[22]

Twenty-first-century ways of Christian looking evolved in identifiable historical circumstances, including twentieth-century "secularization," the explosion of digital technologies, and the escalating fracturing of Christianities. Nonetheless, across denominations, believers have learned how to practice Christian looking in ways personal, communal, analytical, devotional, and reciprocal. They have not yet mastered revelation, though. Although Jesus promised every believer the chance of theophany, the difficulty of establishing revelatory authenticity has probably deterred most Christians from advertising prophetic or visionary experiences.[23] Fear of ridicule, censure, or even persecution inhibits visionary claims. The documents and visual record of Christian history preserve mostly clerical accounts of visions and visionaries. When medieval chroniclers or Renaissance inquisitors noted heretics or deviants, witches, or practitioners of magic, they may well have meant people who considered themselves quite respectable Christians with meaningful revelations to share. The process by which other witnesses assessed local visionaries is rarely evident. What is more, the records lump together many different kinds of spiritual experiences as visions and prophecies and also use multiple terms for the same kind of visionary phenomenon. In the premodern world, some dreams were "visions of the night," and apparitions were routinely visible to the naked human eye.[24]

To make things even more complicated, the experience of revelation, vision, and prophecy has varied widely across periods of Christian history and regions of Christendom, so far as historians can tell. Visions, like other religious phenomena, tend to follow cultural trends and fads.[25] In the early Middle Ages, European Christians saw all sorts of strange things—flying ships, rains of blood, demons disguised as dancing girls, armies of angels, mysterious flames—that later medieval or modern believers would never consider religiously meaningful; yet famous churchmen, such as Gregory of Tours (d. 534) and Bede (d. 735) interpreted such phenomena as signs from heaven.[26] The late medieval meld of theology and the sciences, followed by the Protestant Reformation, realigned the boundaries of orthodox theophanies.[27] The expansion of Christendom beyond the Old World to other continents led to countless new kinds of revelations in myriad local idioms for witnesses' discernment. Sixteenth- and seventeenth-century paintings and drawings from New Spain, for example, reveal images of apparitional Virgins that could never have won favor in earlier Europe but which became icons of devotion for ethnically and racially diverse residents of Latin American communities.[28]

Still, throughout the twenty centuries since Jesus supposedly lived, died, and reappeared—and despite momentous historical shifts that separate his first followers from believers of the twenty-first century—Christians have continued to ponder the problem of authentic revelations. Official Catholic criteria for authentic revelations and the proper methods for discerning them have remained largely unchanged since the Council of Trent (1545–63), when church leaders gathered to reframe their practices in response to Protestant challenges, particularly devotions to Mary and the saints. Trent authorized local bishops to investigate and rule on reports of visionary experience.[29] Two centuries later, Pope Benedict XIV codified the procedures for evaluating personal visions, insisting that all private revelations be proved beyond natural explanation before they were assumed to offer religious messages.

Trends in visions and visionaries have shifted with the times, as has the policing power of Catholic clergymen, but the leadership's responses to visionary claims have not altered much at all. According to the latest revised Catechism, "No new public revelation is to be expected before the glorious manifestation of our Lord Jesus Christ." Nonetheless, the Catechism continues,

> Throughout the ages, there have been so-called "private" revelations, some of which have been recognized by the authority of the Church. They do not belong, however, to the deposit of faith. It is not their role to improve or complete Christ's definitive Revelation, but to help live more fully by it in a certain period of history. Guided by the Magisterium of the Church [the collective authority of bishops], the *sensus fidelium* [the consensus of believers] knows how to discern and welcome in these revelations whatever constitutes an authentic call of Christ or his saints to the Church.[30]

Bishops and lay believers still share the responsibility of evaluating reported visions and apparitions. Church leaders cannot prevent apparitions or monopolize discernment. Neither ecclesiastical office nor religious education is required to tell a charlatan from a visionary saint. However, the discerners of spirits can and do disagree. They have been doing so ever since Paul first complained of false prophets.

How to Discern Authentic Spirits

Today's Catholic Catechism is readily available through parish offices and on the Vatican's website, as are the public decrees of popes regarding visions and apparitions.[31] However, the updated guidelines for discernment, issued by the Congregation for the Doctrine of the Faith (CDF) in 1974 and approved by Paul VI in 1978, remained unavailable to the public until spring of 2012. They were first published *sub secreto* because,

Impressions

Our Lady of the Rock, 2006–2011

December 13, 2006

December 13, 2011

December 13, 2007 (morning rosary)

December 13, 2009

December 13, 2009

July 24, 2007

October 13, 2006 (Mustang and family)

December 13, 2009

November 13, 2006 (talking to the Virgin)

May 13, 2007

May 13, 2007

August 13, 2006

May 13, 2007   December 13, 2008

October 13, 2006 (Virgin in the clouds)

November 13, 2006

June 13, 2006

March 13, 2009

October 13, 2006

July 24, 2010

July 13, 2006

November 13, 2006 (Ada Luz)

April 13, 2008

July 24, 2010

August 13, 2006

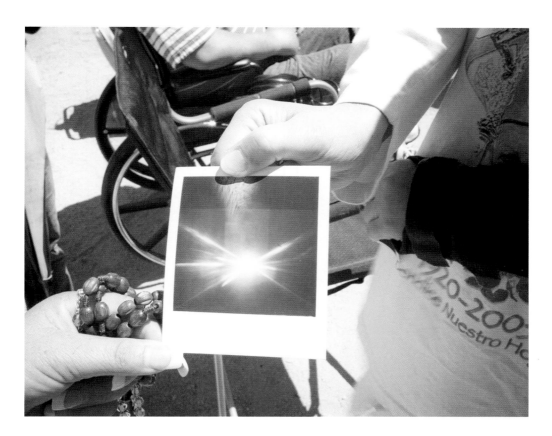

June 13, 2006 (The Gates of Heaven)

December 13, 2011

July 24, 2011

July 13, 2006

according to Monsignor Angelo Amato, former prefect for the CDF, they were intended exclusively for bishops and heads of religious orders, and "thus it was never felt necessary to disseminate them further."[32] Nonetheless, an interview with Amato, along with unofficial translations into French and English, could be found in print and electronic forms before the official Vatican official electronic publication of the guidelines.[33] The CDF's guidelines echo the standards of one, two, and five centuries past, aiming to reduce the significance of individual visions and laying responsibility for discernment on the local bishop's shoulders. When news of an apparition, prophecy, or some other vision surfaces, the local bishop may choose "either on his own initiative or at the request of the faithful" to investigate, according the CDF. Of course, the report of visions never reaches him at all if the visionary chooses not to disclose what she has seen or if friends and neighbors have not already vetted her.

If the bishop learns of an alleged visionary, he must decide whether to investigate further. He should first consider whether the visionary is causing or may cause any kind of harm, either to others, to herself, or to the equilibrium of the diocese. According to a deacon in the bishop of Fresno's office, for instance, their bishop annually receives at least half a dozen letters or e-mails about visions or apparitions, two or three of which may "raise concerns about mental stability or possible threat of violence." The deacon was unsure about the number of reports, because the bishop kept his correspondence private; besides, he added in interview, "it's nothing we trained about."[34] Once alerted to possible trouble, the bishop should proceed to observe the visionary or interview her. He might send a diocesan official to do the job. At any time, the bishop may also invite episcopal colleagues, local or national assemblies of bishops, members of the CDF, or other offices within the Holy See to intervene, and those offices may also do so at will.

Left to discern a visionary's authenticity on his own, though, the bishop's next task must be to impose silence on the alleged seer. Saint Paul inspired this visionary discretion. "I know a man," he wrote, who "was caught up to paradise and heard inexpressible things, things that no one is permitted to tell. I will boast about a man like that, but I will not boast about myself."[35] If a modern visionary refuses, unlike Paul, to keep quiet, the bishop must take this as evidence against her authenticity. Humility characterizes the genuine seer, in addition to "mental balance, honesty and integrity, sincerity and habitual docility to church authorities," according to the CDF's guidelines.[36] The bishop must also determine whether the visionary or her followers promote doctrinal truth and whether the visions inspire "healthy" devotions, such as prayer and religious conversions. Evidence of error, attempts to profit from visions, and any hint of immorality disqualify a supposed visionary for church approval.[37]

The bishops should also check on the visionary's physical and mental health. If he has initiated a formal investigation, he is required to send physicians and psychologists to observe the seer; they must be atheists or Catholics, not adherents of another faith tradition. Doctors should consider whether the visionary may suffer bodily ailments or "psychic disorders or psychopathic tendencies . . . which would exert an unquestionable influence on the allegedly supernatural facts, or indeed psychosis, mass hysteria, or other factors of the same kind."[38] Church leaders have long worried about the effects of mind, body, and environment on eyesight and perception. They have summoned the assistance of physicians to determine the boundaries of vision and delusion since at least the fourth century, when Saint Jerome recommended that any enthusiastic ascetic who claimed to have visions should visit a doctor. There are some dedicated believers, Jerome commented, who "from the dampness of their cells and from the severity of their fasts, from their weariness of solitude and from excessive study have a singing in their ears day and night and turn melancholy and mad, so as to need the poultices of Hippocrates more than exhortations from me."[39]

By the late Middle Ages, church leaders were routinely advising medical examinations to ascertain the cause of ecstasies. Renaissance church authorities drew up increasingly narrow lists of the observable symptoms of genuine revelation, derived from the latest research in health sciences. Influential academic theologians such as Jean Gerson (d. 1429) worked hard to reconcile medical discoveries about the physical and mental causes of hallucination with firm belief in the possibility of theophany and also devilish deceptions.[40] Today's medical textbooks interpret claims to religious vision as symptoms of mental defects, diseases, and psychoses, as does the current Catholic leadership. For instance, trance states characterized by lack of voluntary movement and diminished awareness of the environment—traditional conditions of prophets and shamans across cultures—can be signs of illness and mental defects or of epiphany. In either situation, the subject loses track of what others perceive as reality and experiences a reality that others cannot actually perceive. To determine whether a purported visionary is in a genuine religious state, generations of learned clerics and ostensibly objective physicians have poked, pricked, kicked, and slapped entranced subjects in order to discover whether they are faking their ecstasies. The young seers at Marpingen (Germany) were sequestered in an orphanage for five weeks of intensive medical examination.[41] The children who saw the Virgin at Garabandal in 1961 apparently never flinched when observers shone flashlights directly into their dilated pupils, poked, and even burned them as the girls engaged with the Blessed Mother. Likewise, in the 1980s, the six teenaged seers of Medjugorje were similarly unmoved by any visual or noisy distractions while they gazed raptly upward at the Gospa, as they called the Virgin. Medical experts approved by the Catholic Church timed the seers' rapid eye blinks, checking for perceptual responses to Mary's presence. The six visionaries fluttered their lids in total synchronization.[42]

Both medical and Catholic professionals recognize that trances may be symptomatic of any number of conditions, including hypnosis, meditation, catatonia, conversion disorder, delusive disorder, and use of hallucinogens. The subjects' description of their experiences can sometimes help determine what has spurred their visions. "Delusions are deemed bizarre if they are clearly implausible," notes the latest *Diagnostic and Statistical Manual of Mental Disorders*, "not understandable, and not derived from ordinary life experiences." Grandiose delusions are obvious in a patient "when the central theme of the delusion is the conviction of having some great (but unrecognized) talent or insight or having made some important discovery. . . . Grandiose delusions may have a religious content (e.g., the person believes that he or she has a special message from a deity)."[43]

Catholic leaders are aware that the science of psychology helps them sort visions from delusions, but they hesitate to embrace a strictly scientific approach that also rules out supernatural influence—including the will of God or the presence of the Virgin—as a possible cause of visions. As Joachim Bouflet, who participated in the CDF's committee on visionary discernment in 1974, noted, "Because of current instruments of knowledge, the contributions of science, and the requirement of a rigorous criticism, it is more difficult, if not impossible, to arrive as speedily as previously at judgments which conclude, as formerly happened, investigations into this matter (*constat de supernaturalitate, non constat de supernaturalitate*); and because of that, it is more difficult for the Ordinary [church leaders] to authorize or prohibit public worship or any other form of devotion of the faithful [related to visions and apparitions.]"[44]

In addition to the insights of science, the CDF has recommended that bishops also consider the local circumstances of visions and apparitions and the community in which they take place. As Bouflet and his colleague Philippe Boutry put it, writing on the congregation's behalf, "The contribution of the social sciences makes it possible to locate the apparition in the historical and sociocultural context where it finds at the same time its roots and its application." Bishops must ponder the alleged visionary's community, congregation, and the larger culture and society of which she is part so that "the parish [and] the communion which is the diocese, becomes the place and the test bench of the mariophanies." In other words, religious customs of the region, visual environment, and the visionary's social networks influence her or his potential for revelations and their disclosure. Not only the alleged seer but also her family, friends, neighbors, and witnesses are subjects for scrutiny, for they function as both audience and collaborators in the vision event.[45] This approach to discernment, which the CDF refers to as "calmer" than canonically based inquiry into visionary claims, acknowledges the role of communities in shaping religious visions. To maintain congregational equilibrium, Catholic authorities should aim "to strike a happy medium between vain credulity and sterile skepticism."[46] This measured approach also allows bishops to diagnose the "popular Christianity" of entire communities as a partial cause of visions, just as doctors might pathologize an individual seer's behavior in relation to her family members.

Still, just because a particular bishop or priest disapproves of a vision, his decision does not necessarily determine its orthodox religious value. Other regional or national groups of bishops may intervene even if the local prelate never invites them. Groups of faithful laypeople may also contact other church authorities, including the CDF, regarding a possible vision or apparition. Neither a bishop, the CDF, other offices of the Vatican nor the pope can prevent a vision event, although they can refuse to permit such activities on church properties. The Marian visionary Veronica Lueken drew witnesses to apparitions on the grounds of St. Robert Bellarmine Church in Bayside, New Jersey, between 1970 and 1975. When the parish evicted them from church property, Lueken and her followers simply moved to Flushing Meadows-Corona Park in Queens, where prayer meetings continue despite denunciations from the diocese of Brooklyn and the visionary's death in 1995.[47]

Vatican guidelines suggest that broader cultural influences may also help prove or disprove a seer's claims to heavenly vision. Veronica Lueken admitted that her first vision of Saint Theresa, the Little Flower, was inspired by a radio appeal for prayers on behalf of the dying Robert F. Kennedy in 1968. During that period of political assassinations, riots, and Cold War politics, Lueken's subsequent visions of the Virgin Mary conveyed threats of world war, the Antichrist, and cosmic apocalypse. The Virgin's messages to Lueken, as one supportive website explains, "recapitulate and update Jesus' and the Virgin Mary's messages at past true apparition sites."[48] Like pilgrims to Our Lady of the Rock, witnesses to Lueken's visions also took photographs of the sky during vision events, although mostly at night. They decoded these images by direct reference to the Book of Revelation.[49] Hence, political events and social anxieties of the late 1960s, modest Catholic literacy, and acquaintance with visionary practices elsewhere contributed to Lueken's visions and her followers' discernment of the same; the same circumstances motivated the local bishop's condemnation of Leuken.[50]

Bishops are also supposed to consider the purported visionary's educational background to find out what she has learned in the past and has been reading lately and whether she may have stumbled across obvious models for pretended or misguided visions. If she has been preparing for or practicing visions, she is likely a sham. Perhaps, the clerical logic runs, a pseudovisionary has been studying politics before predicting international conspiracies involving the Antichrist or reading theology when she claimed to receive messages about doctrinal issues. She may even have had some secret source of data about the pilgrims whose personal problems she seems to intuit. Interrogators of Bernadette Soubirous, for instance, were suspicious of the teenager's claim that the Virgin at Lourdes had announced "I am the Immaculate Conception." The doctrine was much discussed in French churches during the 1850s. Authorities were uncertain, though, how an uneducated peasant girl could have learned the complex theological concepts under debate.[51]

Finally, the CDF recommends that the bishop probe the seer's domestic and social life for possible motives to visionary claims. Could she be seeking admiration and love outside her home? Could she be she trying to assert authority and influence upon coreligionists? Was she disliked or revered by her neighbors before she had visions? Is she reacting to local political situations or social tensions? Does she go to church? Is her family supportive? Did she ever do anything unusual or remarkable before?[52]

Ironically, the discussion of visionaries by clerical investigators helps educate local communities in church policies, Christian doctrines, visionary history, and traditional modes of discernment. Public news media help spread this information by interviewing visionaries, witnesses, and religious officials and publishing in print, photographic, audio, and video formats. In the process of transmission, reports of vision events often multiply and change.[53] Catholic guidelines insist that the investigating bishop compare the supposed visionary's accounts of her experiences with witnesses' testimonies about the seer's words, appearance, and behavior. Catholic leaders also consult published news of vision events. If the visionary has offered different versions of her story or if her evidence conflicts with witnesses' stories or if witnesses offer contradictory accounts, then somebody is misremembering, imagining things, or lying.

The Catholic leadership maintains further that if, like Veronica Leuken, a visionary directly criticizes the clergy or Catholic institutions or in any way contradicts official doctrine, she is not having authentic visions. No genuinely Catholic visionary seeks to diminish the institutional authority of the one holy and apostolic church. As Pope Benedict XVI put it when he was still Cardinal Ratzinger, "To all the curious, I would say I am certain that the Virgin does not engage in sensationalism; she does not create fear. She does not present apocalyptic visions, but guides people to her Son. And this is what is essential."[54] But Leuken and other Marian visionaries have not been so sure about the Virgin's position on spectacle and apocalypse—or on the priesthood, for that matter. "You will not receive a kind ear from the clergy, for man can be wise but stupid," the Virgin supposedly told Leuken in 1971. Leuken advised her followers to pay no attention to the bishop of Brooklyn, who denounced her visions as contrary to Catholicism.[55]

If somehow a visionary passes all the required tests of authenticity, the bishop must still send demonologists and exorcists to examine the seer. If the devil is behind such business, it would not be the first time; even Jesus suffered demonic trials in the desert. Fables of demonic deception and possession have circulated around Christendom for as long as tales of divine vision.[56] The dancing girls who tempted Saint Jerome, the evil spirits who tempted medieval mystics from their prayers, the Satan whom nuns have always warned schoolchildren about are one and the same entity denounced by the modern CDF.[57] Visionaries, witnesses, and church authorities have been famously misled in the past. In the sixteenth century, the visionary Magdalena de la Cruz (d. 1560) convinced almost the entire order of Spanish Franciscans, the archbishop of Seville, and the inquisitor general that she had received messages directly from God; yet eventually, after a life-threatening illness, Magdalena confessed that it had all been a hoax instigated by Satan.[58] Cases of collective demonic possession, such as the hysterical visions experienced by an entire convent of nuns in seventeenth-century France (and made famous by Aldous Huxley in his novel *Devils of Loudon*), showed how easily sinners could be deceived by what they saw. As a parish priest at Medjugorje remarked, "Look, sometimes the devil says these things, he pretends and says 'I am Jesus' or 'I am the Gospa' or 'I am this or that' in order to trick people. We read all these things in the lives of the saints." In fact, one of the six seers at Medjugorje claims to have encountered the devil disguised as the Gospa.[59]

These days, bishops and their congregations trying to determine the legitimacy of visionaries' claims must deal not only with Satan's wiles, ambiguous medical evidence, and a vast canon of doctrinal opinions about religious visions but also with an ever-expanding body of reported visions and apparitions. Public claims to extraordinary sightings of the Virgin, as well as saints, Jesus, angels, and demons, multiplied exponentially after 1969, when Pope Paul VI lifted the ban on publishing visionary experiences without church approval (previously imposed by canon law in 1917.) The Catholic leadership's embrace of lay devotions after the Second Vatican Council pleased some Catholics, but it has made the task of discernment that much harder for more skeptical members of the church. As a spokesman for American bishops declared in 1996, "The multiplication of supposed 'apparitions' or 'visions' is sowing confusion and reveals a certain lack of a solid basis to the faith and Christian life among her members. On the other hand, these negative aspects in their own way reveal a certain thirst for spiritual things which, if properly channeled, can be the point of departure for a conversion to faith in Christ."[60] More recently, the CDF has dismissed popular Marian devotions that lack a solid historical and doctrinal basis, such as the repetition of rosaries during the Mass (on the grounds that rosaries are for private devotions, not the collective celebration of the Eucharist led by a priest in church). The congregation has also undertaken a full reinvestigation of the famous ongoing apparitions at Medjugorje, which draw millions of witnesses every year.[61]

Popes on either side of Christianity's third millennium have expressed contrary opinions about religious visions, particularly Marian apparitions. Pope John Paul II (d. 2005) eagerly embraced apparitional devotions, particularly at Fátima and Medjugorje. John Paul apparently attributed his survival of an attempted assassination in 1981 to the Virgin's intervention.[62] His successor, Benedict XVI, took the opposite approach, cracking down on the profusion of apparitions and visions reported by the faithful, including those at Medjugorje.[63] It is with good reason, argued one spokesman for his pontificate, that the church has acknowledged only 11 of the 295 appearances by the Virgin Mary reported between 1905 and 1995.[64] Even when visionaries' credibility survives the lengthy verification process, their reported experiences "do not add to the Revelation given to the Church in Sacred Scripture." Or, as Pope Benedict put it back in 1985, when he served as prefect of the CDF, "No apparition is indispensable to the faith. . . . The Revelation ended with Jesus Christ."[65] The current pope, Francis I, has not been in office long enough to register his stance on apparitions, although his affection for and theological approach to the Virgin Mary seem fairly traditional.[66]

Many pilgrims to Marian apparition sites are aware of papal and episcopal disapproval but not obviously deterred by it. A subtle hostility toward the higher echelons of Catholic leadership permeates popular websites devoted to visions and pilgrimage, as well as the blogosphere. By comparison, Pope John Paul II and local priests supportive of visionaries are touted as role models of Marian devotion. "Many apparitions are not accepted by the Catholic Church," wrote blogger Nancy47 on the Catholic Answers Forum in February of 2008, "Even the visitations to the 6 visionaries in Medjugorje which is observed and witnessed by thousands, also recorded and video taped by people of all denominations. . . . Sooner or later Mother Mary will have the church so infiltrated; the church will not be able to deny her, and her visits. . . . John Paul II said before he died that he would go to Medjugorje to witness if he were not Pope. I believe Her plan is to infiltrate, to be accepted; and not be denied."[67]

Still, if that is the Virgin's plan, she has not made much headway with the last two popes or with the higher clergy of greater Los Angeles. After the office of Archbishop Mahony of Los Angeles completed an investigation of Maria Paula and Our Lady of the Rock in 1995, the archbishop circulated a pastoral letter warning Catholic priests in his archdiocese about doctrinal and canonical errors (as well as the financial irregularities mentioned earlier) of the Marian Movement of Southern California.[68] As a result, he urged pastors not to endorse Maria Paula's visions. Gregory Coiro, spokesman for the archdiocese at the time, referred to Our Lady of the Rock as "that fraud going on in the desert." Maria Paula, Coiro added, was a "free-lancer. . . . The sham she's running has no affiliation with the Catholic Church."[69] Apparently, although pilgrims to Our Lady of the Rock during the 1990s shared with the archbishop a faith tradition, a visionary history, and techniques of discernment, they disagreed about Maria Paula's religious authenticity. Catholics and other believers continued to attend Our Lady of the Rock on each thirteenth of the month, where they exercised—and still exercise—their doctrinally approved powers of discernment as they observe and listen to Señora Acuña. Regular pilgrims to the Mojave already knew a lot more about Maria Paula than the cardinal and his staff, because many of them had observed her closely for months or even years in order to decide whether she looked like a visionary when she saw the Virgin. Her appearance, her story, and her performance at the vision site persuaded them that Maria Paula was the real thing, notwithstanding discouragement from church leaders.

In the Beginning

Maria Paula Acuña's public persona—the way she looks and behaves—is the first and most important body of evidence for her visionary powers. Her self-presentation, including the story of her visions, has evolved over the two decades of her prophetic ministry in response to her critical audiences. In a 2010 interview, Maria Paula described once more how she had first encountered the Virgin in Lopez Canyon. "My girl was the first one who spoke with her," she explained, referring to the toddler who was suffering from childhood leukemia around 1990. In this narrative, Maria Paula's five other children and their father(s) have no role. The story does not reach as far into her past as her birth and childhood in Sonora or her marriage and migration to California. It begins at that moment in 1990—or 1989 or 1987 (she has offered different dates for this event)—when Maria Paula saw the Virgin.

This later version of Maria Paula's introduction to the Virgin Mary begins the same way as her original account, told to reporters in 1997. According to the visionary, her ailing child declared that "a very beautiful girl" had come in a dream and ordered Maria

Paula to visit the mountain beside Lopez Canyon to pray. "But she never told me that it was the Virgin Mother," Maria Paula added. She did not presume that the Mother of God had visited her daughter. Such a thought would indicate to other Catholics a lack of humility. "I am nothing," she still tells her witnesses. "I am dirt." She is *un trapo viejo*—an "old rag" that the Virgin "uses to clean those who are filthy and to fill with flowers those who are ill."[70] Instead, the visionary stumbled across a series of mysterious clues before actually setting eyes on what turned out to be the Blessed Mother. "I left to the mountains outside of the city to pray," Maria Paula recounted. "And on the twentieth of July, I was praying at about five in the evening, and I turned towards the top of a peak, and I saw how the trees moved with the wind and I was able to see in a corner, something like a table, I was curious enough to climb and I found a basin of cement with fourteen crosses [*pila de cemento con 14 cruces*]."

A few days later, she returned to the same site to pray early in the morning. She stepped on a "big serpent," which she feared would bite her foot. She was terrified, alone, and defenseless, yet she also sensed a reassuring presence behind her. "Focus on me and you will be safe," a voice advised her.

> Before I knew it, I turned forward and she was standing on a very white cloud, and the trees that were surrounding her had roses, very big red roses. I saw a haze in their midst, and in it was the Virgin Mary. She told me: "Maria Paula, my daughter, God has sent me to this place, to give you the peace and the love that so many need. I will end the tribulations of the young people, do not have fear, I am the mother of God for whom we live, [and of] Jesus Christ for whom we live. You must come every day at six in the morning; later on, I will tell you what it is that God wants with this place."

"That was the first time," Maria Paula recalled in a sermon of 2010, "that Mother Mary presented herself in front of me, telling me her sweet words."[71]

Mary's sweet words were a paraphrase of something she had said five centuries earlier to Juan Diego at Tepeyac, as recorded in the *Nican mopohua*, an account of the apparitions of la Virgen de Guadalupe. Published in church Nahuatl by Luis Laso de la Vega in 1649, it is not the earliest history of Juan Diego's visions but the source of their enduring legend. Spanish translations are ubiquitous in both print and electronic versions. "Sábete que yo soy la siempre Virgen María," the Virgin asserted in printed Spanish, "Madre del verdadero Dios, por quien se vive" ("I am the eternally Virgin Mary, Mother of the true God for whom we live.")[72] Scholars are still arguing about whether Juan Diego heard these exact words in the sixteenth century, when he supposedly met the Virgin on a hill near the modern Mexico City. Nonetheless, this familiar pronouncement of Mary's identity has been repeated by bishops, priests, and multitudes of believers across Mexico for centuries, especially between 1987 and 2002 while the Vatican canonized Juan Diego.[73]

Maria Paula's story directly recalls the legend of Juan Diego, who reportedly told the Virgin, "I am a nobody, I am a small rope, a tiny ladder, the tail end, a leaf." Maria

Paula's accounts of her first vision echo other features of the vision at Tepeyac, too: the dawn setting, the dazzling haze from which the Virgin emerges, the scent of roses, and the Virgin's promises of protection for her downtrodden children. Maria Paula does not always include the snake in her story of the vision at Lopez Canyon, although it is a common feature of Marian iconography elsewhere, including depictions of the Immaculate Conception. The iconography of the snake or dragon derives originally from Bible verses in Genesis (3:15: "She shall crush thy head") and Revelation (12:17: "And the dragon was angry against the Woman: and went to make war with the rest of Her seed.")[74] Depictions of La Virgen de Guadalupe feature the same visual motif. Popular copies of the image imprinted miraculously on Juan Diego's tilma often show the Virgin stomping on a snake.

Maria Paula's contest with a serpent suggests that she, like the Virgin, is fighting Satan on behalf of fellow believers. As for the pila with fourteen crosses, Maria Paula has not divulged its significance or where to find it. Lopez Canyon's trails are littered with the remnants of minor industries, now failed, and of its days as a landfill. At several turn-offs from Lopez Canyon Road, broken concrete blocks and cylinders lie in piles, some chunks scratched with what could conceivably be any number of crosses. Presumably, the pila in her story harbors iconographic evidence as yet unexplained, just like the mysterious white rocks at La Señora de la Roca.

Since that initial apparition in Lopez Canyon, Maria Paula has increasingly come to resemble other visionaries too, particularly the female seers of nineteenth- and twentieth-century Europe. The Lady of the Rock, as we have seen, has more in common with the Ladies of Fátima and Lourdes, in looks and messages, than with La Guadalupana or any other Latin or Northern American manifestations. Photos and videos from the last fifteen years show that Maria Paula has altered her uniform to look less like an emigrant mother and more like an old-fashioned nun in formal orders. When she appeared publicly in the 1990s, she wore simple dark civilian dress with a veil draped loosely over her dark hair. She usually clutched a rosary. Today she wears a full-length, bone-white monastic habit that covers everything but her face and hands. A wimple conceals every hair on her head, leaving only her expressive facial features exposed to view. As her eyesight declined, Maria Paula added enormous round sunglasses to her uniform, thus obscuring any messages conveyed in her glances. In 2010 the shades covered an eye patch that she replaced in 2011 with a glass eye. Maria Paula now completes her uniform with sparkling white sneakers.

The monjas who live and work with her wear identical nun-like tunics with capacious sleeves, aprons, wimples, coifs, and veils. Each sister's costume bears an iron-on image of the Lady of the Rock, copied from the statue that occupies the grotto. The statue wears the same habit, complete with a smaller iron-on image of herself, suggesting her intimacy—if not identity—with the visionary and the monjas. Every month, rain or shine, in blustery winter or on blazing summer days, the monjas flutter around the vision site in their spotless, old-fashioned draperies.

Maria Paula has refined her performance as a visionary, preacher, and healer with the same care given to her appearance. Repeat visitors have come to expect her liturgical routine: vision days begin with the congregational procession, during or after which Maria Paula receives one or possibly two visions of the apparition, followed by an explicatory sermon, and finally the visionary's interactions with individual members of the crowd. Maria Paula shifts voice and gestures for each phase of the ritual, arranging her facial expressions to match the drama of each moment. During her conversations with the Virgin, her voice is soft, high-pitched, and often tearful as she gazes raptly upward. On most vision days, Maria Paula would switch tone to match moments in the desert liturgy, however, sometimes bellowing commands at her audiences of thousands. She would reprimand them fiercely for their sins and, in the next instant, offer solace to men, women, and children. She would often lead the audience in rallying shouts of "!Viva la Virgen!" At other times, she might moan hoarsely into her microphone about the dangers of contemporary society and the many sins of Mary's earthly children. Once in a while, she stage-whispered to the faithful crowd of pilgrim photographers, as if the hovering Virgin could not hear her, "Taking the pictures now of the Blessed Mother. . . . Take it now!"[75]

The visionary has a dynamic smile and a volatile temper and can alter abruptly from beaming and blessing to sharp scolding. As she circled the sanctuary in May of 2007, greeting and laying healing hands on members of an enormous audience, one woman seemed to suffer ecstatic convulsions. Maria Paula pointed a finger at her and snapped, "Control yourself!" The visionary is usually reserved with skeptics and glares at obvious outsiders. When she discovered a group of university students in the crowd one month in 2006, she aimed her gaze and her diatribes at them: "Don't be drinking, dancing, taking drugs, or making sex," she commanded sternly.[76] In April of 2008 she pleaded tearfully with the crowd to avoid the devil: "It's never too late!" she reminded them.[77] Her lectures on behavior have a gendered edge; she frequently harangues her audience about the evils of consumerism and debauchery, harangues women about wearing too much makeup, and begs parents to preserve traditional households where mothers remain at home with their children.

Maria Paula's performances also evoke old-time healers, both ancient saints and latter-day *curanderas*. Local healers have long helped sufferers in towns and villages of Mexico and Latin America, as well as the streets of east L.A. They are celebrated in Chicano/a literature, have been thoroughly analyzed by anthropologists, and are sung about by popular bands.[78] In rural districts of Mexico, healers typically work from home. In the great cities of the borderlands, however, they run storefront *botánicas* where Spanish-speakers, mostly women, seek cures for body and soul, as well as for bad karma and misfortune. Curanderas too claim revelatory dreams and sightings. Like Catholic visionaries, they garner inexplicable knowledge from beyond the perceptible world. Some pray and light candles to Jesus and La Virgen de Guadalupe, along with a roster of saints, would-be saints, and protectors from other faith traditions such as Santería. Like Maria Paula, they tend to afflictions that neither medical doctor nor priest can alleviate: bad energy, desperation, broken hearts, and long-term pains of muscles, bones, and spirit.[79]

Maria Paula could have learned to look like a healer from another cultural source, for many modern Catholic visionaries also tend ailing patients. In fact, this is one of the main purposes of established Marian shrines, which claim to extend an original visionary's powers of intercession to later generations at the place where she first saw the Virgin, often through waters blessed by the apparitions.[80] Pilgrims to Our Lady of the Rock recognize in Maria Paula a religious healer who supplements medical and pastoral care. When the visionary lays a hand on a disabled pilgrim's forehead or dabs a patient's eyes with special oil, no one is surprised. These gestures are ancient tropes in Christian culture. Newcomers come to the grotto in search of cures. Even if they have never laid eyes on a curandera or Marian visionary before, they are prepared to recognize and evaluate Señora Acuña's thaumaturgic powers. Recovered patients testify to the efficacy of Maria Paula's prayers and the Virgin's involvement in their personal health (discussed at length in the next chapter.)

Most days of the month, Madre Maria Paula and Sister Thelma visit petitioners who have requested special prayers or interventions for themselves or family members. Maria Paula prays the rosary, discusses her revelations, and begs the Virgin to help heal bodies and souls. The Marian Movement's brochure reports that Maria Paula and the monjitas also keep busy ministering to the homeless and visiting hospitals, prisons, and juvenile detention centers. They also make rosaries and then put them to good use. The Marian Movement advertises weekly rosary recitals with the monjas. Occasionally the women practice other handicrafts too. Because the visionary's health is declining, though, she sometimes has to pray for her many supplicants from afar. Thelma takes down telephone numbers and e-mail addresses from clamorous pilgrims at the vision event so that Maria Paula can carry out long-distance prayers on their behalf.

Thelma, a genial Filipina and former nurse, is devoted to the visionary, and helps with Maria Paula's self-presentation. She credits Maria Paula's prayers with saving her aged mother's life and has testified publicly about it before pilgrims and on video. Her evidence contributes to Maria Paula's credentials as a traditional Marian visionary whose innocent, unlearned piety inspires educated believers to renewed faith. "The first time I met her," Thelma says, "I felt something different . . . like my heart opened up." Thelma realized then that "there's another life that's waiting for me." She had considered becoming a nun when she was young, but it was only after meeting Maria Paula that she took religious vows. Her decision proved the right one. "I have seen a lot of manifestations of our Blessed Mother. I myself have received miracles from our Lord and our Blessed Mother through Maria Paula," she attests. Maria Paula "has a special gift of healing. So many have recovered from terminal illnesses, and that's confirmed by doctors; we have the doctors' proof, the documentation from the hospital."[81]

Thelma worries about Maria Paula's health, though. The visionary is an advanced diabetic, which she often mentions in sermons. She announced in July of 2007—on a day when the desert's temperature rose well over 100 degrees—that "I am a little sick, I've had diabetes sugar levels at 550." Thelma explains that Maria Paula suffers on behalf of the ill and needy, absorbing their pain for her own. "I know that for a fact," the monja observes, "because I take care of her."[82] Throughout the centuries, putative visionaries have presented physical symptoms of religious revelation, such as fatigue, vomiting, various pains, fever, glowing, incurable disease, coma, and inexplicable bleeding, including stigmata (the incurable wounds of Christ on the head, hands or wrists, feet, and torso.) Increasingly over the last two centuries, women have become the primary victims of these afflictions, whose symptoms resemble those of nineteenth-century neurasthenics and twentieth-century psychiatric patients. Christians still expect sick, wounded, and disabled believers to offer up their physical suffering as a sacrifice on behalf of others, based on the model of Christ, who died in pain on behalf of humankind.[83] The same saints who miraculously healed pilgrims themselves endured appalling health problems during their lives, which paradoxically further authenticates their curative powers.[84]

Modern physicians have retroactively diagnosed premodern visionaries (as well as false prophets of the past) with various physical and psychological illnesses. Hildegard of Bingen, a famous medieval mystic and theologian, is suspected by historians and physicians alike to have suffered from migraines.[85] Historians have similarly accused late medieval mystics of eating disorders, rejecting claims that these saintly women subsisted solely on communion wafers in order to maintain visionary purity.[86] Scholars have also mocked the dramatic public fits of Margery Kempe (d. 1438), the English visionary, who disrupted Mass and badgered her bishop until he listened to her vision reports.[87] Nonetheless, these and many other ailing women retain their visionary reputations.

Most pilgrims are probably not familiar with medieval exemplars such as Hildegard and Margery, but pamphlets for sale at the vision site advertise the Chilean girl Blessed Laura Vicuña (1891–1904), who died of a combination of injuries from beating and tuberculosis and was beatified by Pope John Paul II in 1988.[88] Maria Paula has not offered up her pain to benefit other sinners, like more famous holy women—Thérèse of Lisieux or Maria Goretti, for example.[89] However, she keeps the crowds updated about her health. She suffers from a debilitating affliction, diabetes and its complications, common among Americans. When she sees the Virgin, Maria Paula seems to lose strength as she drops limply to the ground and her voice dwindles to whispers. During the vision event, she frequently retreats to a trailer when overcome by heat or battered by cold winds. She regrets that "very soon I will be taken, and you will stay in darkness, and you won't hear my voice anymore." Nonetheless, she has promised her followers, "I will continue doing this until my eyes close and my tongue cannot speak words."[90] Thelma worries, too, about what will happen after Maria Paula dies: "Who's going to tell us what God wants of us through the Blessed Mother?"

Maria Paula presents herself as a woman from the working class. Most publicly discussed visionaries of the nineteenth and twentieth centuries have come from groups disenfranchised by ethnicity, race, or sudden shifts in national politics.[91] The majority have been female; of that majority, most were either children or postmenopausal women when the Virgin first came to them. Maria Paula displays the naïveté expected of a people's visionary. Like the desperately poor Bernadette Soubirous and the three young peasant visionaries at Fátima in 1917—Jacinta, Francisco, and Lúcia—Maria Paula has no pretensions to education. She calls herself illiterate. Like those earlier visionaries, too, Maria Paula claims ignorance of her selection by the Virgin Mary. Why, she asked one interviewer, did the Blessed Mother not choose a lawyer, doctor, or teacher to convey her messages instead? Visionaries typically pose this rhetorical question. Witnesses expect the Mother of God to choose untutored innocents as her mouthpieces. They would distrust a well-educated, clerical, or prosperous prophet. As bloggers commenting on a website dedicated to Medjugorje pointed out, in reaction to news about the Lady of the Rock, the California visionary could not possibly be legitimate if she came from Beverly Hills, Hollywood, or some other well-to-do part of Los Angeles, but her stays in Pacoima and California City were appropriate for a genuine visionary.[92]

Inexpressible Things

A long scriptural tradition of humility permeates orthodox stories of Christian visionaries, emphasizing the need for secrecy and the intensely private nature of authentic visions. Saint Paul set the model, writing to the Jesus followers of Corinth in the mid-first century, "I know a man in Christ who fourteen years ago was caught up to the third heaven. Whether it was in the body or out of the body I do not know—God knows" (2 Cor. 12:2). Most readers assume nonetheless that Paul was actually the visionary in question. In Paul's mind, visions were "inexpressible things, things that man is not permitted to tell." To relate a personal vision was to diminish its case for authenticity. A meaningful account of visions could be repeated only by someone who witnessed the visionary's experience or trusted the seer's confession of visions. "I will boast about a man like that, but I will not boast about myself," wrote the apostle. "Even if I should choose to boast, I would not be a fool, because I would be speaking the truth. But I refrain, so no one will think more of me than is warranted by what I do or say" (2 Cor. 12:5–6).

Over the centuries, a visionary's required reticence has also signified her or his obedience to church leaders, who still frown upon those too eager to tell their own stories. The young seers at Fátima in 1917 famously kept secret the three major prophetic visions granted by the Virgin, as well as their own interpretations of what they saw. The surviving visionary, Lúcia dos Santos, revealed news from the Virgin only in 1944 when she put her written account in a sealed envelope, which she sent to the Holy Office. Her written revelations remained unread until 1981, when Pope John Paul II finally opened the envelope; however, he did not make the message public until 2000.[93] Likewise, the former teenagers who saw the Virgin at Medjugorje beginning in the 1980s also claim to have received secrets from the Virgin. However, they have been more eager than Lúcia to explicate their personal experiences, with resulting damage to their credibility among church officials. Local Croatian bishops, whose job it is to evaluate events at Medjugorje, have consistently complained about inconsistencies in the visionaries' numerous reports. For instance, the six visionaries announced in 1981 that the apparitions would continue only for three days, yet they continue to reveal new messages from the Virgin to this day.[94] To date, the Blessed Mother has delivered more than thirty thousand bulletins to the Medjugorjeans, which is one of the major reasons that Cardinal Vinko Puljic of Sarajevo announced in summer 2006 that a newly formed church commission would reinvestigate the events. Critics refuse to believe that Mary would repeat her messages so relentlessly.[95]

Relative silence and invisibility are savvy strategies for a Marian visionary. Maria Paula has rarely granted interviews during her twenty-year career as a visionary. She will not disclose details of her personal past or speak about herself except to emphasize her unworthiness as a visionary. Even longtime witnesses claim ignorance of Maria Paula's biography and cannot answer such basic questions as where the father of her six children has gone, when and where she was born, and what happened to the child with leukemia. Thelma and the other monjas who attend Maria Paula also refuse to discuss the visionary's personal past or her family. They will only repeat the story told by Maria Paula of her first vision. Maria Paula turns to her closest companion, Sister Thelma, for the confirmation of such details. The monjas and members of the Marian Movement prevent individual witnesses and other visitors to the shrine from pestering the visionary, who is never left alone during a vision event. Her handlers accompany her everywhere, patrolling the sanctuary and controlling the crowd during processions. While Sister Thelma conscientiously copies down the names and phone numbers that witnesses will not yield to reporters, she also efficiently intervenes between enthusiastic believers as Maria Paula greets and blesses them. As the vision event has matured and the grotto has progressed, Maria Paula and the sisters have become more elusive. They no longer live at the edge of town en route to the vision site, where lost pilgrims used to stop for directions to the shrine. Their increasingly formal costumes shield them too.

As a result, it is almost impossible to compare Maria Paula's story of herself with any other biographical data. She was probably born around 1940 in Sonora. She migrated with her children sometime before 1990, "for the same reason everyone comes," she has explained, "to look for a better life for my children."[96] Although she has offered different dates for her first vision, in July of 2009 she celebrated its twentieth anniversary.[97] She currently lives with the monjas in a house near California City, supposedly supported by donations to the Marian Movement of Southern California.

Meanwhile, members of the visionary's family live somewhere nearby. A little old lady used to arrive at vision events in a Lincoln Town Car and occupy a lawn chair in the shade, right next to the old stage, while Maria Paula preached. She was supposedly Maria Paula's mother. Informants have also reported that the visionary's family runs the concession stand selling fresh tamales and soft drinks at vision events. Other members of Maria Paula's family are involved in the monthly operations of the shrine. Her daughter maintains contact with her by cell phone during the vision liturgy.[98] Maria Paula's son-in-law was one of the contractors who helped build the grotto. However, the man who claimed to be that son-in-law denied it in a later conversation. Although he once shared gossip about local priests, on another occasion he ordered me away from Maria Paula's trailer and, in response to a question about the family, told me, "That information is restricted, ma'am."[99]

The Movement's members are somewhat mysterious too. They resemble many other groups of lay Catholics attached, more or less formally, to lay organizations such as the Legion of Mary (founded in 1921 by an Irish layman), the Blue Army (founded in the United States in 1947), and the Marian Movement of Priests (founded by Father Stefano Gobbi in 1972.)[100] All these movements claim as inspiration the apparitions at Fátima. Members of the Marian Movement of Southern California also refer to Fátima, and Maria Paula has mentioned both Gobbi and "mariano" armies.[101] At vision events, only a handful of Movement members wear the special T-shirt of their organization. There's Ron, the tall elderly Anglo who leads the rosary and makes official announcements; Rolando, who organizes prayer sessions and sometimes drives Maria Paula in his car; and Pat, the woman who minds the information table.

Movement members manage the logistics of the vision event, which used to take place on a temporary stage but now focuses on the grotto. They operate the sound system, security, and cleanup. They also arrange hospital visits, prayer interventions, and cenacles (prayer sessions with rosaries) in private homes. They have a post office box and a public telephone number, which is sometimes answered by the monjas or Maria Paula herself but more often rings unanswered. There is a humble office in Bakersfield, locked and seemingly unused, but the Movement has little presence on the Internet and hardly any official literature. A photocopied brochure is the only official testament to the group's origins and history. Tax documents filed with the IRS, available online to the public, claim exemptions for the Movement as a nonprofit religious organization. The IRS forms feature names of two or three Movement officers, which seem to change annually.[102] However, Maria Paula and Sister Thelma have several times been listed as president and vice president of the Marian Movement of Southern California. The Movement's annual revenues, which ranged from $20,000 to $200,000 between 2002 and 2010, consist entirely of donations to Our Lady of the Rock. Their main assets seem to be the property and grotto in the desert.

Maria Paula is wary of personal interviews with strangers and consistently refused me an interview for two years. Finally, after Matt and I had made many regular appearances at the vision event, and with the sympathetic intervention of Sister Thelma, the visionary consented to sit down with us in April of 2008. Maria Paula was exhausted by a long day of spiritual labor in the desert heat. She was also distracted by departing friends and pilgrims who called out to her as they trudged to their cars. Her attention wandered. She resisted eye contact. She greeted Matt, whom she had seen taking photographs for the book. It had taken a year for her to recognize him and allow him entry into the sanctuary during the actual vision event. Members of the Marian Movement had chased other photographers out of the sanctuary and shooed them away from the procession but had come to welcome Matt. He snapped many close-ups of Maria Paula.

After preliminaries, I smiled and asked my first question: "The first time you saw the Blessed Mother, were you alone?" "Yes," she replied and then abruptly declared that she was unable to answer any more questions until she had consulted her spiritual adviser, who was then traveling in Spain. She had no idea when he might return or how to send him a message, Maria Paula explained. She would be happy to discuss her visions but had made a vow not to speak about herself without his permission.[103] "I am for everyone," she said. "I am dirt." If she divulged anything more, though, she would get into trouble with her adviser. She promised to telephone after she had spoken with him. She also suggested that her lawyer might be displeased with our publication of a book about the vision event. She hoped that Matt's photographs would not cause him any legal trouble. When I explained that we were academics and did not expect to profit from the book, she congratulated us on our professional status. Then she reminded us, "This is holy ground. If you step on it, your feet will burn if you're a sinner, your ears will burn." She added, "Many miracles happen here." Thus ended the interview.

Her discretion, her disguise, and obscure history seem to be both performance and a plan. Maria Paula is conscious that personal information detracts from the timeless role of Christian visionary, which she has so carefully constructed over the years. She knows, too, that her appearance and behavior are criteria by which pilgrims, interrogators, and clergy measure her visionary abilities and religious authority. The less individuality she displays, the more she resembles formulaic visionaries from Catholic history and saintly legend, and thus the more authentic she becomes. She keeps a diary of the Virgin's messages, she claims, but shows it to no one. Other visionaries publish their messages for the benefit of other believers, sooner or later, but not Maria Paula.[104]

In 2011 one of my student research assistants, Jake Bloch, secured an interview with Maria Paula, which he was allowed to record with a digital video camera. He did not mention that he worked for me. The evidence from Jake's five-minute conversation, along with his interviews of Sister Thelma and several pilgrims, is cited throughout this book and its footnotes. Maria Paula did not reveal anything that she has not already said publicly, except to mention that the Virgin had assured her a place in heaven. "It would be the greatest happiness for me and that many go with me, including the two of you," she informed Jake and his cameraman.[105] Other videographers have not shared the visionary's esteem, however. On the same afternoon that she shunned me in 2008, Maria Paula also refused to converse with a reporter and photographer from the *Los Angeles Times*, although she commiserated with them about her spiritual adviser's restrictions.[106] Likewise, an independent film producer who telephoned me last year seeking contact information for Maria Paula and members of the Marian Movement despaired when neither Movement members nor the monjas would talk to him. He had hoped to film the vision event for a new television series about miracles and apparitions. He called me a second time some days later. "Have you yourself ever seen any visions or miracles?" he asked me forlornly, but I would not admit to anything. He eventually gave up on the project.

Maria Paula does not work to satisfy outsiders, but she labors tirelessly to meet the expectations of pilgrims to Our Lady of the Rock. They share criteria for the discernment of authentic visions. It would never occur to believers to ask the visionary whether anyone witnessed her first encounter with the Virgin or to request more details about the apparitions. They gratefully receive the words that she grants them and the comfort of her hugs and touches. One of the men who helped build the grotto spoke of the visionary as his "spiritual mother": "I care for her as if she were my mother, how she is attentive with us, she respects us. And, when she has a meeting or a gathering, sometimes it is so that we can discuss what is going on here, what more can we do, how can we motivate others."[107]

Like a parent, Maria Paula speaks to her flock with love and also disappointment, encouragement as well as annoyance, but she consistently reminds them that she shares their perspective of the world outside the desert. She can tell who believes and who does not. "I know who has faith in this moment," she declared during a sermon in 2010,

> because I see . . . in your heads a light, a crown of light, and there are others who have little black dolls. Who will it be, as Jesus said during the Last Supper? Will it be me? . . . Judas was the one who was going to betray him and he posed as if he did not know. Jesus knew. Today, I have seen her, I am not a saint, and I am not comparing myself to a saint. But God has given me the vision to know who loves him and who does not love him, thanks to God. Therefore, he has given me this vision to help the one that does not love him and to increase the faith in that person, in the person that loves him.[108]

The Virgin shares that special language of discernment with Maria Paula and the pilgrims to Our Lady of the Rock. The Virgin is dismayed, according to the visionary, when observers do not trust her appointed interlocutor. In the midst of a sermon in 2007, Maria Paula reported that the Virgin had "moved away and marked with her finger certain persons that come to ask for proof, for proof of our mother, and she says with tears in her eyes, I forgive you, and I trust you will keep the word of God in your heart. She has moved away and is lost in the distance."[109]

Only the visionary is able to see those crowns and haloes hovering—or not—over the heads of pilgrims. Maria Paula has addressed unbelievers among the crowds both directly and indirectly. In 2010 she chastised reporters and filmmakers (including Jake) as vipers because she anticipated popular misunderstanding of her visions and bad publicity. "You can say what you want about me but cannot misrepresent the word of Mary," she warned camera-wielding outsiders.[110]

Still, even veteran pilgrims seem to have no more information about Maria Paula than newspaper reporters do. They too lack answers to basic questions about the visionary's past and vocation, although Maria Paula has apparently passed their tests of authenticity. Even by comparison with other contemporary Marian visionaries, Maria Paula's comportment is unusually secretive. Unlike the Medjugorje seers, she does not travel much; although she has mentioned a trip to Rome and pilgrims have talked about her visits to Mexico and the Philippines, it remains unclear whether these trips actually took place. Instead she has pursued a semicloistered nun's life. Unlike other visionaries in the United States over the last few decades, Maria Paula has never articulated explicitly unorthodox or apocalyptic doctrines or openly reviled the clergy, although she has occasionally sniped at priests. Still, like Stefano Gobbi, the Italian priest who experienced Marian locutions and founded a worldwide Marian movement—and whom Maria Paula has mentioned as a role model—Maria Paula and her witnesses are usually respectful of traditional priests.[111] Most of the time, though, she simply ignores the existence of the clerical hierarchy of Catholicism. Proof for the archbishops' complaints about financial irregularities remains secret, although pilgrims have mentioned that the Marian Movement used to sell photographs of the vision event for $5 each.[112]

Pilgrims show no obvious signs of popular resistance or dissatisfaction with Catholic orthopraxis. Each vision day's events resemble the ordinary negotiation of rituals carried out continuously by Catholic congregations everywhere. Pilgrims rely on the catechism, papal pronouncements, and conciliar decrees—as communicated by parents, pastors, and teachers and harvested from news media and religious publications—as guidelines for orthodoxy. They also copy the devotional habits of fellow Catholics. For instance, rosaries are ubiquitous at Marian shrines approved by the Vatican as well as under-the-radar shrines, such as the one at Our Lady of the Rock. Many pilgrims grew up with relatives who carried rosaries in their pockets or hung them on bedposts as a sign of special devotion to the Virgin Mary. They may have heard a priest preach, as Bishop Steinbock of Fresno did in May of 2004, urging his Californian congregations to pray the rosary every day. "The family that prays together stays together. . . . A break of fifteen minutes from the TV to pray the rosary each evening in May can work miracles in our Christian families."[113]

Rosaries abound at Our Lady of the Rock. They hang from the monjas' necks and slip from the grasp of pilgrims. A variety of crystal and plastic beads sparkle from the table of the Marian Movement where they are displayed for sale. Rosaries also adorn the grotto, where they are left for Maria Paula's blessing. Pilgrims wield this five hundred-year-old devotional tool of the laity in order to prepare themselves for the Virgin's arrival and Maria Paula's performance. They selectively employ other ritual objects, iconographies, and rituals to celebrate the monthly holy day too. They do not hesitate to perform familiar liturgical dramas in the desert rather than in clerically approved Catholic spaces. Do they wonder why some seers, such as the Medjugorje visionaries, are allowed to meet the Virgin in churches all over the world, while Maria Paula must meet them in the middle of nowhere? I did, after watching Ivan Dragicevic—one of the six original teen seers at Medjugorje—speak to the Virgin in the parish church of Saint Monica's, in Santa Monica, California.[114]

Yet there could be no Maria Paula without Dragicevic and his friends at Medjugorje or the American seers at Scottsdale and Phoenix, who carried reports home from

Medjugorje to inspire a whole generation of visionaries in the 1980s and 1990s. The six teens would never have recognized the Gospa on Vision Hill if other children at Garbandal, Fátima, Lourdes, and La Salette had not spotted her first. Likewise, Maria Paula passes on visionary etiquette to her observers (as we shall see in detail in the next chapter.) To paraphrase one expert on Marian apparitions, witnesses have jointly configured the devotions at Our Lady of the Rock, using the rosary and other useful tools from the Catholic devotional kit.[115]

Maria Paula Acuña has been rewarded for her patience and twenty years of service, her followers claim, with additional miraculous signs of her intimacy with the Blessed Mother and Jesus Christ. The visionary claims that she has three times received holy communion from the hand of an angel. One time she caught sight of a whirlwind of tiny white birds, which morphed into an angel bearing a chalice and host; the angel laid a communion wafer on her tongue. Another time she was at the vision site with the grotto's construction crew. Rolando, one of her team of helpers and a member of the Marian Movement, witnessed the strange incident of the bouncing Eucharist: when an angel descended to give the visionary communion, the wafer boomeranged off her tongue and rolled away. Maria Paula chased it to the foot of the giant steel cross, where the host landed, she says, standing on its edge. "Therefore, first it was deposited on my tongue and then it jumped to be on the cross; these are very marvelous wonders," she explained to interviewers.[116]

In 2010 new wonders further established Maria Paula's visionary status, according to reports from the visionary, her monjas, and pilgrims. She saw Jesus Christ inside the new grotto. A life-sized blotch on an interior wall indicates where he stood to bless Maria Paula. He imprinted his bodily shape in holy oil on its painted surface. Then, in early 2011, blood began to drip from the blue-painted ceiling of the shrine. Pilgrims are not normally allowed inside the building, but word spread. Soon after, city officials ordered the Movement to rebuild the grotto's roof because it did not meet legal standards and always leaked during rare desert rainstorms. No further blood has appeared, but later in the same spring another sign of the Virgin's favor manifested itself inside the shrine: the shape of Mary's face appeared on the wall. Shortly after came the most amazing miracle of all: Maria Paula's feet began to bleed with the stigmata, the same wounds suffered by Jesus when nailed to the cross. Sister Thelma apparently exhibits photographs of Maria Paula's feet when asked politely, although I have not seen the pictures or the lesions. Other visionaries and miracle workers have manifested the same signs, but they rarely appear to a single seer all at once.

The timing of this recent proliferation of miracles is mildly puzzling. Although many pilgrims have testified to the power of her intercessory prayers, Maria Paula never previously offered material proofs of her visionary status. The sensations of peace and comfort that wash over witnesses at the vision event, the evidence of healed bodies, and Maria Paula's sermons provided pilgrims with enough proof of her spiritual authority. On the other hand, the completion of the grotto at Our Lady of the Rock forced the visionary to

October 13, 2006

share pilgrims' attention with the monument and the statue inside. The grotto is nothing special as far as religious architecture goes. The magnificent and costly Cathedral of Our Lady of Los Angeles puts it to shame, as does the Crystal Cathedral, a megachurch acquired by the Roman Catholic Diocese of Orange (County) in 2012. The seventeenth-century missions that dot the California coast, built and rebuilt in adobe over the centuries, are more charming than the desert grotto. Still, this humble marker of invisible wonders will last for many years if the new roof holds and pilgrims continue to come.

Maria Paula may endure as long the grotto if she is able to lodge herself in the collective memories of pilgrims as the copatron of this place, along with the Lady of the Rock. The same witnesses who have worked with Maria Paula to discern her spirits will also help determine her place in visionary history. As just another middle-aged woman in a Catholic cathedral or parish church, Maria Paula might fade into the pews and queues for Holy Communion. In the desert, though, she shines as brilliantly as her spotless white garments. Where the wind scours witnesses clean and the sun illuminates their prayerful faces, pilgrims can see the visionary more clearly than under the artificial lights of a church. The Virgin knew what she was doing when she sent Maria Paula to this very spot in this wilderness.

Looking Like Pilgrims

4

In July of 2008—but not on the thirteenth day of the month—pilgrims discussed how they first came to Our Lady of the Rock. It was the anniversary of Maria Paula Acuña's first vision in Lopez Canyon. Every year on July 24, the Virgin arrived in the desert and hovered low enough that pilgrims could touch the hem of her garments. As usual, no one but Maria Paula claimed to see La Señora de la Roca, but the visionary indicated where pilgrims should aim their eager fingers. Members of the Marian Movement of Southern California had prepared for the anniversary by laying a plank across two sawhorses at one side of the stage, near the lone tree of the sanctuary; there was as yet no grotto with decorative plantings.

It was high summer in the Mojave, and the temperature rose above one hundred degrees that afternoon. Pilgrims who had forgotten umbrellas or tents could not escape the relentless rays of the sun. Most pilgrims had arrived early in the morning to await the Virgin. Some had camped out and kept vigil during the previous night. It was a smaller crowd than the monthly apparitions typically drew, consisting mostly of veteran visitors to the vision site. The procession was especially decorative on the anniversary. A pickup truck, swathed in white sheets and strewn with roses, rumbled slowly down Lincoln Road carrying Maria Paula, a life-sized statue of the Lady, and two monjas in the flatbed. Behind the truck, marchers toted flags of the many pilgrim nations: besides the American countries, India and the Philippines were also represented. Hundreds of silky banners of white and celestial blue lined the road where two devotees had planted them the previous day. It had been just as fiercely hot on the twenty-third.

After the Virgin's statue was parked in the sanctuary, front bumper facing the stage and tailgate open for easy access, pilgrims settled down to wait. They kept as still as possible and hoarded their drinks. They drowsed, sipped, and recounted personal encounters with supernatural phenomena. Several regular witnesses, including members of the

December 13, 2009

Marian Movement, rose by prearrangement to address the crowd through the portable microphone. One by one, a chosen few stood by the pickup in the sanctuary, surrounded by a circle of panting pilgrims, and testified. A man well into his seventies named Juan recalled his grandson's horrifying accident in Sacramento. A train had partially crushed the young man's skull. The family had argued about whether to pull the plug on his life-support mechanism. Juan had consulted with Maria Paula, and at her suggestion, the family had prayed relentlessly until a nurse spotted the patient's slight movement. After five or six weeks, the grandson recovered consciousness; after a year of therapy, he could walk again. When Juan finished speaking, other witnesses recounted bouts with terminal cancer, broken bones, heart attacks, dialysis, and coma.[1] Each story ended the same way: the visionary's pleas to the Virgin had helped them live. Maria Paula listened to the witnesses while wandering around the sanctuary, examining objects left for her blessing, and drinking a Coke.

Shared suffering of the brutal desert led to confessional intimacy among longtime pilgrims, newcomers, and even academic observers. Even after someone turned off the microphone and the visionary retreated to an air-conditioned trailer for her siesta, pilgrims continued to whisper their histories. They told how they had first heard of the

May 13, 2007

Lady of the Rock and Maria Paula and what their first trips to the desert had revealed. Some had followed Maria Paula to the Mojave from Lopez Canyon. A young woman also named Maria explained that this was only her second visit. When she had arrived with family members on the previous June 13, she had captured an image of the Virgin on her cell phone. That was surprising enough, but when she examined the image afterward on her computer, something else lurked in the margins: a devil was caught in the pixels. At least, that is how her brother read the photo. She tried to display the image to fellow pilgrims, but the phone's screen was too small and the sunshine too bright to reveal the Prince of Darkness.

Some pilgrims had given up the vigil by late afternoon, when Maria Paula finally emerged from her trailer and announced the Virgin's approach. Movement members helped hoist the visionary onto the temporary reviewing stand that they had built, where she perched for the entire duration of the hem touching. Meanwhile, pilgrims queued up to pass by Maria Paula and under the Virgin. The visionary pointed; the pilgrims stretched, grabbed, and waved hankies or long-stem roses (for sale at the site) in what they assumed to be the direction of the Blessed Mother's toes. Some hopped a little to gain altitude. The witnesses were solemn, but Maria Paula chuckled and enjoyed herself.

March 12, 2009

She borrowed a camera and took photos of the pilgrims and of the apparition's airspace. Young Maria moved through the queue to touch the Virgin's robe but reported afterward that she "didn't feel anything, to be honest." Still, she giggled and decided to give it another try.[2]

All first-time visitors to Our Lady of the Rock do the same thing: they give this desert, its rituals, and its visionary a try. Potential witnesses make an initial decision about the revelatory potential of Maria Paula and the Lady of the Rock before they begin that first drive into the Mojave. Some are determined to discover a holy woman in converse with the Blessed Mother. Others come in desperation, willing to try anything after medical doctors have failed them. Many visitors have less precise expectations of Maria Paula and the Lady. No one comes to disprove the vision; unbelievers never return. "She has the blessing of God and the privilege to have communication with the Holy Virgin," explained one pilgrim in 2010, "and we cannot doubt her because if we doubted her we would not be here, with all our hearts."[3] Kids complain of being dragged to the shrine by devout parents, but except for babies and the mentally disabled, everyone arrives prepared to see something rare and astounding, perhaps even moving and transformative, and to assess its causes and meanings.

December 13, 2009

They begin the day as ordinary citizens of the twenty-first century—people who go to work, have families, watch TV, and participate more or less successfully in the society that surrounds them. When they hit the road to the Mojave, they become pilgrims. When they turn off the highway at Lincoln Boulevard, follow the dust trails to the shrine, park the car, and put their feet on the desert floor, the pilgrims become witnesses. As soon as they lay eyes on this place, they begin the discernment of spirits.[4] They may be uncertain as to what they believe about miracle cures, whirling suns, or apparitions of the Virgin Mary, but they hopefully scrutinize and construe everything they see, including fellow pilgrims. Meanwhile, they process, pray the rosary, sing hymns, and accept blessings just as congregants do in churches around the world. Like most contemporary American Catholics, pilgrims to Our Lady of the Rock assume the right to select and practice only the religious customs and rituals that are meaningful to them.[5]

Our Lady of the Rock is not a church, though. As one witness put it, at Sunday Mass, "you only attend for one hour and everything depends on the devotion we bring to church; many people go only to chat."[6] The pilgrims' most important ritual could never take place in church because priests would not permit it. Besides, one cannot stare at the sun or take photographs of the sky when under a roof. At Our Lady of the Rock, pilgrims

August 13, 2006

aim their eyes and other lenses upward, all day long. They stare directly at the sun, the clouds, and the dome of turquoise sky that stretches to the desert's rim. None can perceive exactly what Maria Paula sees, although a surprising number of witnesses have admitted that they, too, have gazed upon the Blessed Virgin, angels, or other heavenly emissaries at the vision site or elsewhere. Most pilgrims, though, deploy the latest visual technology to capture evidence of the Virgin's presence in the Mojave. Men, women, and children wield cameras and cell phones as instruments of discernment and devotion. They teach each other how and where to look for signs, and how to capture these signs for keeping. They share and exchange the resulting pictures, debate the encoded meanings of the images, and carry them home for further inspection and display.

Taking pictures, like reaching for the Virgin's hem, is an affirmation of faith at Our Lady of the Rock—faith in the Virgin and in the visionary but also in the decision to come to this place instead of another. Pilgrims believe in their ability to make legitimate, meaningful religion together. Their scrapbooks and shoe boxes full of printed photos serve at once as confirmation of the desert's numinous qualities, proof of Maria Paula's authenticity, visual instruction in Marian devotions, and relics of personal mariophany. Their pictures testify, as do their memories and sometimes their very bodies, to their collective achievements. Everyone has some kind of visions at Our Lady of the Rock.

Protocols of Pilgrimage

The solemn parade that officially begins each vision event at Our Lady of the Rock looks much like other processions at Catholic shrines and parish churches from Sacramento to Puntas Arenas. Pilgrims sing and intone the "Ave Maria" in Spanish. They honor the statue of Our Lady carried at the head of the procession. Four lucky men or women share the prestige of bearing the litter upon which the statue of Nuestra Señora de la Roca perches. Everyone follows Maria Paula Acuña and the monjas down Lincoln Boulevard to the sanctuary. At crucial points in the march, pilgrims choose the same postures that Christians have long used when addressing God, his Mother, and his saints: the drop to the knees, the *orans* stance (eyes directed upward, hands raised with palms up), or the hands bound tightly by a rosary. When Madre Maria Paula or one of the Movement members issues instructions about pilgrims' collective progress ("Please stay behind Mother Maria Paula!" or "You may be taking the pictures now!"), they obey. They sing when Maria Paula sings, pray when she prays, and hush briefly when she sees the Virgin.

The layout and iconography of the vision site are familiar, too. Christian shrines everywhere feature a few architectural elements that have remained the same for almost two millennia. The holiest space—the church altar, the shrine's sanctuary, the saint's tomb, the holy well, or whatever sacralized object signifies resident spirits—must be clearly marked. The sanctum sanctorum is surrounded by less holy and less formal spaces where pilgrims prepare themselves for ritual, interact socially, and recover from events within the sanctuary. Often a series of approaches brings pilgrims only gradually to the sacred core of the shrine, as in the ultimate model for Christian structures, Solomon's Temple.[7] The Church of the Holy Sepulchre, built by the Emperor Constantine and his mother on the suspected site of Christ's tomb in the fourth century, lured visitors through an atrium, into a basilica, out into a courtyard, and finally into a rotunda that contained the aediculum, or tiny building that housed the actual tomb (as they supposed.) Each step of a pilgrim's approach through successively holier spaces enriched the experience of the divine immanence hidden within.

The Holy Sepulchre and its multiple portals offered a model for major pilgrimage centers of later centuries. Christians who followed the medieval route to Saint James's tomb at Santiago de Compostella in northwest Spain, for instance, were supposed to visit a lengthy itinerary of churches—each with its own traffic pattern for devotions—until they finally arrived at their planned destination.[8] The same pattern of successively holier spaces organizes modern shrines, too, whether they are internationally famous or local retreats. At Lourdes, an elaborate system of parking lots, shuttles, shops, and toilets, labeled in multiple languages, guides visitors to the grotto where Bernadette Soubirous first glimpsed the Virgin Mary so long ago. Arrows and signs also send pilgrims to purifying baths, spots for private meditation, and sheds full of devotional candles to purchase and set alight. Still humbler are the roadside pull-offs and smaller glass boxes that house tiny roadside shrines

December 13, 2008

to Mary and the saints throughout European, American, and Latin American country-
sides.[9] Still, the protocols of the slow approach are much the same everywhere.

Until 2010 and the completion of the new building, the desert itself set the pace of pilgrimage and protected the sanctuary at Our Lady of the Rock. Today the grotto remains
invisible from the nearest paved road, as well as from orbiting satellite cameras. The site
is one mile and two dirt roads away from the two-lane highway running between the
towns of Mojave and Randsburg. The land's rocky surface still controls the flow of traffic

August 13, 2006

to the shrine. The chain-link fence merely reinforces the symbolic markers that mark the sanctuary's boundaries, such as the giant steel cross rising just outside the fence. Before the grotto was finished, colorful streamers crossed the air above the sanctuary; banners still flutter around the site's edges for the anniversary. Religious objects and flowers litter the pavement before the grotto, as they used to carpet the temporary stage. In addition, Maria Paula's assistants and members of the Marian movement ceaselessly patrol the sanctuary while she is present, maintaining contact by cell phone as well as exchanged glances.

June 13, 2006

The mile-long procession from highway to sanctuary emphasizes the shrine's isolation from the ordinary world. Although the Lady has finally found a permanent home in the new grotto, she too remains mobile. The Blessed Mother's statue still begins each vision event at the junction of the Randsburg-Mojave Highway and Lincoln, just like every other participant. Icons have been known to migrate from one shrine to another, and Virgins have journeyed with migrants to new homes. Our Lady of the Rock began her career in Lopez Canyon, as we know, before arriving in California City and entering the desert. Now she commutes on the thirteenth of each month, leaving her grotto showcase early on the morning of the thirteenth and riding in a truck to the highway. Later in the morning she processes back to her sanctuary, borne on a litter held aloft by pilgrims.

Unlike more venerable Marian shrines, the grotto at Our Lady of the Rock has no posted behavioral guidelines or directions. Newcomers must search for clues about where to park and stand, when to march, and how to behave. A single handwritten, misspelled sign tacked to the telephone pole at the junction of the highway and Lincoln sends pilgrims to the shrine. Other instructional signs have appeared briefly at the sanctuary. In 2006, a cardboard poster nailed to a fencepost listed the costs of building the grotto, presumably to inspire donations to the cause. In 2008, a wooden poster at the sanctuary's entrance pleaded with its readers:

BIENVENIDOS AL LUGAR SANTO PROHIBIDO ESTA POR EL PADRE Y EL HIJO INVADIR ESTA LUGAR SANTO DE MI MADRE NO HAGAS NADA QUE PERTURBEN TUS CAMINOS SI TU QUIERES VISITAR ESTE LUGAR DE MI MADRE. TIENES QUE BUSCAR LA GRACIA DEL ESPIRITU SANTO Y RESPETAR ESTE LUGAR Y RESAR CON MI MADRE.[10]

Welcome to the Holy Place. It is forbidden by the Father and the Son to trespass in this holy place of my Mother. Do nothing that disturbs your ways if you want to visit this place of my Mother. You have to search for the grace of the Holy Spirit and respect this place and pray with my Mother.

Whether these instructions were meant to reprimand potential trespassers and owners of the ORVs buzzing by the shrine or were intended as instructions for unruly pilgrims, however, is unclear. For advanced tutoring, observers must rely on announcements by Maria Paula's handlers or fellow witnesses.

Fortunately, the liturgy of the shrine and of devotional witnessing is familiar and easily learned. The liturgy of the vision day makes sense to pilgrims raised as Catholics, whether in Oaxaca, Los Angeles, or Medjugorje—there is nothing too unorthodox or surprising to a seasoned believer in the actions of either visionary or witnesses, except that everything happens in the desert rather than in a church. Much of what they do on the thirteenth is also familiar to anthropologists, historians, and scholars of religious literature. The Virgin's reputation for championing the poor and powerless and her willingness to convey petitions to God are well known to witnesses, whose mix of ethnic identities and religious backgrounds mirrors the social situation in southern California and the borderlands more generally. Most pilgrims have previously sought her protection when they traveled, migrated to new homes in unfamiliar places, sought work, or raised families. As children, they learned the same routines for solace in times of trouble: pray to the Virgin or a favorite saint before her statue, repeat extra rosaries, visit a shrine to light candles, or kneel before a wall of brightly painted ex-votos, each commemorating successful miracles of assistance.[11] These habits of body and mind are venerable, reproducible methods for invoking supernatural support.[12]

The pilgrims' religious habits—and those of their parents, grandparents, friends, and neighbors—surface in processions and prayers at Our Lady of the Rock, where pilgrims reconsider and revise established liturgies in order to facilitate direct contact with the Virgin. They watch Maria Paula in hopes of benefiting from her mediation with Mary, but this is not their main purpose in coming. They also anticipate joy in the Virgin's presence. They come to witness and worship as Mary herself witnessed the crucifixion. Their pilgrimage is, as a Univision reporter enthused in 2009, a story that "transcends borders." They come to the desert in order to participate in Christian history, no matter what sacrifices or extreme temperatures they must endure.[13] Each time pilgrims arrive at Our Lady of the Rock, they find additional proof of the Virgin's miraculous powers and Maria Paula's prophetic authenticity.

Witnesses draw upon their collective visionary heritage as they celebrate the present moment in the Mojave, recalling previous meetings in the desert in order to make

May 13, 2007

sense of this one. "We invented the thirteenth of the month," declared one man at the anniversary celebration, "to come here, to listen to prayers, to listen to the mother, and to feel in this . . . in this little box, no?" He pointed to his chest. "Do you see this little box? The heart, no? To feel . . . there in the temple of Jesus, in the temple of the Holy Spirit, and also of Mary, [to] feel it here. That is why we are here, sunning, very pleasant, very nice. And before the Mother arrived, we had already, here, prayed the Holy Rosary." Every gathering in the Mojave extends the history of Marian apparitions and Christian visionaries a little further into the future. Maria Paula and her many witnesses have built their grotto as a monument to the Virgin but also to their own hard work, so that future generations may continue to recognize the Lady of the Rock.[14]

From Pilgrims to Witnesses

At first glance, the congregation at Our Lady of the Rock looks identical to any crowd milling in a southwestern small-town plaza or an East L.A. neighborhood for a rally or fiesta. Unlike historical vision events and most modern ones, too, the monthly gathering at Our Lady of the Rock did not originate within an existing community in a single location but as a destination for self-selected men and women from across southern California and beyond. Although most pilgrims live within a few hundred miles of the vision site, they come from a sizable territory—from San Diego to Sacramento and from the sea to Las Vegas. Los Angeles and its suburbs are well represented. Also, while the majority of visitors to the shrine are Hispanic, primarily Mexican residents of the United States or Mexican Americans, Spanish-speaking pilgrims come from a variety of nations and cultures, each with its own Catholic habits. A little conversation reveals immigrants from Nicaragua, Ecuador, Guatemala, Bolivia, and Peru.

The Virgin always uses the tongue of her chosen seers—Serbo-Croatian at Medjugorje, for instance, Rwandan at Kibeho, and Lingala at Kinshasa, Zaire.[15] Maria Paula and the Virgin speak in Spanish, but the visionary manages a little broken English with the crowd, especially when she wants to hammer home a point or aim her rhetoric at specific pilgrims. For example, when she denounced abortion in July of 2007, she switched to English: "You understand what Mary said? She stand up in the white crown, and she see a lot of dark inside, and a lot of children, very small babies in pieces, the head, the hand, the hip, the stomach, I see this vision, and she say this is the human pieces, what the people say is garbage in the earth."[16]

Usually, everything that comes out of the electronic sound system at Our Lady of the Rock is in Spanish except for announcements made by Ron, a member of the Marian Movement who leads the rosary on vision days. (Ron admits that he cannot say much in Spanish, although he also makes announcements to the crowd: Maria Paula is delayed, please help clean up the trash, please kneel.) Only a small number of pilgrims have no Spanish, like Ron. A tiny group of foreign-born witnesses, most of them over sixty years old, cannot speak English. Most pilgrims are bilingual. Those who lack the lingo still find ways to understand Maria Paula's reports as well as Ron's instructions and to share their impressions with the rest of the crowd. They read the visionary's tone and gestures or seek assistance from fellow pilgrims.

Not all pilgrims are Hispanic, though. Attendees at the vision event are as nationally, ethnically, and culturally diverse as the flags that fluttered over the hem touching of July 2008. Roughly 15 percent of witnesses at any given vision event are Americans of European or Asian descent, including religious tourists from such exotic lands as Britain or Hollywood. An important contingent is originally from the Philippines; witnesses murmur about a Filipino contingent that has loyally supported the Marian Movement since its founding and has supposedly financed the grotto.[17] About four hundred thousand, or close to one in four Filipino Americans, live in greater Los Angeles, and 85 percent of these are self-identified Catholics, well known for their fervent devotion to Jesus, Mary, and the saints.[18] As audiences began to dwindle at Our Lady of the Rock in 2009, one pilgrim blamed the Filipino/as for deserting the shrine.[19]

June 13, 2006

Pilgrims call themselves Catholic or admit to being raised in that faith tradition, but plenty of people in the audience belong to other denominations instead or in addition. Charismatic Christian churches and prayer groups became very popular among Latino/a Catholics in the wake of the Second Vatican Council. According to a national survey of Hispanic Churches in American Public Life funded by the Pew Charitable Trusts (1999–2003), more than 20 percent of U.S. Latino/a Catholics identify as "born-again and Pentecostal, Charismatic, or spirit-filled." About half of them admit to being "charismatic Christians," which is to say, they feel a direct, emotional connection with the divine. Latin Americans are also more likely than other Catholics to pray daily, keep religious objects at home, attend church regularly, and believe in modern miracles.[20] Marian devotees and fundamentalist Protestants in Spanish-speaking cultures tend to get along better than those groups do in the United States, where Protestants from European-based cultures find Marian icons and liturgies distasteful, if not blasphemous.

Although no one talks openly about it, Pentecostalism and other forms of evangelical Christianity have infiltrated the crowd at Our Lady of the Rock. Pilgrims hint that they are familiar with non-Catholic denominations or participate in more than one congregation simultaneously. Denominational identities seem less important in the desert. "It's all one God," shrugged a construction worker from Big Bear at the annual hem touching

July 24, 2008

in 2010.[21] Juan Rubio, a regular witness and a visionary in his own right, samples Christian churches around his home in Hemet, California, basing his selection on the quality of sermons and availability of free food. He reads his Bible daily, highlighter in hand, because a door-to-door evangelist taught him to do so. The influence of non-Catholic doctrines lurks in his increasingly ambivalent comments about the Virgin Mary's role in salvation. All the pilgrims, he points out, pray directly to Mary, "asking for miracles to *her*—not asking please, your son, ask your son [to make] this miracle—no, straight to *her*." Juan thinks "it's not the way."[22] Maria Paula seems aware of evangelicals' challenge to Catholicism. She has grumbled occasionally about reclaiming Catholics, although whether she means souls lost to Satan or stolen by other Christian sects is not clear.[23]

Whereas the pilgrims' buffet-style approach to religious selection is typically American, the crowd's demographic differs from that of American Catholic congregations in that witnesses are fairly equally distributed across age and gender categories.[24] At weekday vision events, retirees, unemployed adults, and young mothers with babies predominate. Unlike medieval pilgrims, it seems that modern travelers to the desert are not willing to abandon their jobs and lose income in order to visit a shrine.[25] But if the thirteenth falls on a weekend, working adults with teens and toddlers accompany parents, grandparents, and other relations to the vision site. One twenty-something informant named Carolina

April 13, 2008

recalled how her parents had nagged their kids gently for a week before finally persuading the whole family to take a Sunday outing to Our Lady of the Rock.[26] Young adults often roll their eyes when asked why they've come, affecting nonchalance or shrugging curiosity, and claim that friends or relatives compelled them. Still, teenagers have consistently attended Maria Paula and the Lady, and also snap photos.

Smaller children often scramble outside the sanctuary, occasionally getting lost or causing a minor ruckus. In April of 2008, a small boy stumbled and broke his ankle—only the second accident to occur at a vision event in her twenty years, according to Maria Paula. She chided the entire crowd for inattention to their devotions, which had permitted the Enemy (the devil) to approach the shrine and attack the boy.[27] Most parents keep an eye on toddlers as they play in the dust, eat snacks from coolers, and nap under umbrellas. There are usually a couple of dogs to tease with pebbles.

Pilgrims' clothing and cars offer additional visual clues about their lives. Few appear either wealthy or distressingly poor. The informal parking lot always contains a variety of gleaming vehicles, including SUVs, vans, RVs, large sedans, economy cars, and hybrids. Clothing is mostly middle- and working-class casual, although a few older women wear conservative skirts and cover their heads with scarves or shawls. T-shirts boast assorted slogans, mascots of school sports teams, Barbie and Hello Kitty themes, and characters from television shows ("No contaban con mi astucia!!" read one, referring to a popular

March 13, 2009

Mexican television comedy show).[28] Tattoos and baseball caps abound. Every sensible witness wears a hat to ward off the desert sun. Some adolescent girls flaunt tight or scanty tops and studded jeans, and some young men sport *cholo* apparel: drooping pants or long gym shorts paired with tank tops, gold jewelry, basketball shoes, and caps. Bright Hawaiian shirts dot the crowd. Older pilgrims, such as our informant Juan Rubio, turn up in cowboy attire (boots, belts with silver buckles, hats). Shirts and jewelry, as well as tattoos, umbrellas, and blankets featuring La Virgen de Guadalupe are ubiquitous. However, Our Lady of the Rock appears only on the official T-shirts of Movement members and on the habits of Maria Paula, the shrine's statue, and the monjas—at least until fall of 2010, when the T-shirts briefly went on sale to the crowd. Reporters and student anthropologists mark themselves as outsiders with their clothing, such as khaki vests with pockets, sensible shoes, and sweatshirts with university acronyms.

One costume invisible at Our Lady of the Rock is that of a Catholic priest. The crowd there is both politically and nationally diverse, so no single ideology can explain the absence of priests at the shrine. The twentieth-century history of Mexican and Mexican American disaffection with the clergy is visible at the shrine. To pilgrims from other places, such as Nicaragua, priests are untrustworthy because they supported leftist governments and reform movements.[29] Still others distrust Anglo clergymen. The former pastor of Our Lady of Lourdes apparently had frequent disagreements with Maria Paula

April 13, 2008

and the monjas, while the current priest seems determined to eliminate any unorthodox devotions to the Virgin practiced by Catholics in his parish.[30] The disregard of tradition-ally European Catholic clergy for the traditions of Spanish-speaking flocks in the south-west United States is legendary among Latino/a Catholics and the scholars who study them. Although the archdiocese of Los Angeles has been more welcoming to Latinos/as in the last few decades, during the nineteenth century many men and women baptized as Catholics found warmer welcomes among evangelical Protestant communities in L.A. or in private worship before home shrines.[31] The first native Spanish speaker to become archbishop, José H. Gomez, arrived only in 2011.

Still, Latino clergymen have also earned suspicion from pilgrims to the Mojave. At the start of her career, Maria Paula seemed to get along with local priests. In a 1995 video report by Paranormal TV, she appeared in scenes recorded at Our Lady of Help Church with Father Juan Santillan, a native Angeleno born in Chavez Ravine before it became the site of Dodger Stadium. Santillan was a community activist, gang counselor, and charismatic healer who worked in East Los Angeles from the 1970s through the 1990s. He also became a well-known leader of Renovación Carismática, then the largest Latino/a lay movement within Catholicism. Santillan reputedly spoke in tongues and maintained

MARZO 13, 2011

December 13, 2011

a reputation as a miracle worker and priestly *brujo* who could cure anyone of anything. In the 1995 video, Santillan discusses the curative power of prayer as he watches Maria Paula praying silently before a statue of the Virgin of Fátima; she looks on as Santillan lays healing hands on Edward Martínez, a cancer patient. At the end of the sequence, however, Santillan reveals a typically clerical opinion of Maria Paula: "I can't say whether I believe it or not believe. . . . On a truthful basis, I don't need visions. I don't need to see angels, I don't need to see the Blessed Mother, I don't need to see Our Lord. My faith is already set. That's all I need to see."[32] Apparently, Maria Paula did not need Santillan either. In the late 1990s he left for an indefinite stay in Bolivia; in 2002, he was charged with molesting a child in his former congregation of Saint Teresita over the course of five years during the 1970s. For a year or two he was rumored to be traveling in Europe, although his home is still in Bolivia.[33] Perhaps Santillan is the peripatetic "spiritual adviser" whom Maria Paula has mentioned but whose name she has refused to divulge.

Nowadays, if priests attend the vision event, they do not reveal themselves, probably fearing the antagonism of pilgrims as well as the disapproval of diocesan authorities. A priest in vestments appeared briefly on May thirteenth of 2007, which was also the anniversary of apparitions at Fátima. He admitted that he had come that morning from

Jo'burg (Johannesburg, about thirty-five miles to the northeast) but nervously refused to tell his name or parish. He emphasized that he would not be conducting Mass in the desert, which would be against church rules, but just taking confessions. Then he hastily disappeared, only to reemerge later beside Maria Paula in the processional march to the sanctuary, yet slipping away again during her sermon.[34] Adelia, who has lived in California City for years, reports that the former pastor of her church, Our Lady of Lourdes, was warned not to be seen at the grotto.[35] Several pilgrims insist that local priests still attend the vision event disguised in civilian clothing, confident of avoiding their bishops' reprimand.

Yet the presence of priests seems to have little effect on pilgrims' attendance or their self-identification as Catholics. Even without encouragement from the pulpit, large contingents of pilgrims from the same parish or neighborhood often arrive together at the vision event. Take, for instance, the woman I met while standing in line for the portable toilet on an April day in 2008. She had come with enough relatives and friends to fill eight cars. Her brother's mother-in-law had told them about Our Lady of the Rock, so they had driven up from Los Angeles on a Sunday morning to investigate. She thought it might be fun to go in a group. Pilgrims rarely come solo. One local Asian woman attended alone in May of 2010 because, she informed me, she was tired of begging her family to pray with her at home every evening. At Our Lady of the Rock, she found a more sympathetic cohort. Adelia always comes alone too, although she has a husband and at least one son in the area. Usually, though, only academic observers and independent photographers attend by themselves. Even newspaper reporters and film crews appear in small squads of three or more.

They don't need priests in the desert. Pilgrims arrive confident that they will find a welcoming religious community. Family groups hurry to stake their customary places near the grotto. Devoted veterans of the vision event look forward to seeing each other. They speak of following Maria Paula for ten years, fifteen years, or more. Most witnesses will smile at strangers, but they do not readily volunteer full names or other intimate information to newcomers unless the latter demonstrate proper observance of the shrine's liturgies. This, ultimately, is the lowest common denominator of their shared identity: after choosing to come, they are ready to participate, instruct each other, and make religion together.

What They Say

Most pilgrims are open to questions about the vision events, protocols for the day, and the strange phenomena that other people have seen or felt at Our Lady of the Rock, but they rarely speak of intimate religious experiences in first-time conversations. When responding to questions about their purpose in coming to Our Lady of the Rock, they stick to a few formulaic answers. They came out of curiosity, they say. Like Juan Rubio, they wanted to see whether Maria Paula is what she claims to be. Some claim it was a coincidence—something to do on an empty Sunday, like the young woman who came in a caravan of relatives. Others admit openly that they have come in search of consolation, advice, or healing for themselves or for someone they know. Only a brave few pilgrims describe the sorrows and difficulties that have driven them to this last resort in the Mojave. My daughter is sick, they say. My wife has cancer. I lost my way because of drugs and alcohol. I once stabbed a man. This is how pilgrims brusquely summarize episodes of pain and need for interviewers who have come to the desert for less personal reasons.[36] Yet these same individuals do not hesitate to testify publicly and at length before huge crowds of witnesses during the annual hem touching. When they stand safely surrounded by the sanctuary's barriers, they tell parables of life-changing transformations triggered by Maria Paula's visions and prayers.

Only the occasional pilgrim speaks in terms of spirituality. Larry, a hippie-ish, fifty-something Anglo from Orange County told me he had been attending the vision event for years, but on the thirteenth of March in 2009, he was still trying desperately to "get the message." He needed someone to carry out a simultaneous translation of Maria Paula's words. Alejandro, a pilgrim of about the same age, generously volunteered to jot down a quick English summary of the visionary's sermon. He summed it up for Larry: The Virgin said Jesus is praying for everyone, he will be here soon, you should avoid the things of this world—women should stay away from cosmetics—and you should say the rosary every day.[37] Alejandro was eager to share his first experience of the Virgin's loving care. Larry was not interested in sharing stories, though. His problem was not a lack of Spanish but a lack of empathy. When Alejandro started to tell how he first came to the desert, Larry lost interest and wandered away to mutter over the meaning of the Virgin's message.

Alejandro told me his story, though. A few years ago, he had been diagnosed with prostate cancer. He had shrunk to a mere 110 pounds, he explained, and was "75 percent" dead when his cousin asked that he accompany her to Our Lady of the Rock. She thought it would alleviate his misery to visit the site, be part of a group, and pray. Alejandro admitted that it had been difficult for him to participate, as he had not been a religious man at the time and did not believe in apparitions. Nonetheless, on the thirteenth of the month he found himself kneeling in the dirt and crying. He asked the Blessed Virgin to cure him. He also begged to see the Virgin as Maria Paula did, but he was not granted an apparition. He had to be content with taking pictures of the sky.

It became clear to me that Alejandro was not making a personal confession but teaching a lesson in piety. After that first disappointing pilgrimage he had returned to his doctor for radiation treatment. Suddenly he felt the Virgin holding on to him and comforting him. He left the clinic, went home, took a single pill, and banished his pain. Two months later, he was completely cured of his cancer. His doctor had never seen anything like it, he insisted, and could not explain the recovery. Now Alejandro prays the rosary every day. He is serene, he said, and nothing bothers him. To substantiate his miraculous recuperation, Alejandro suggested viewing a brief video segment about Our Lady of the Rock that had aired on television station Channel 62 (KTNV from Las Vegas) and had featured his own miraculous photo of the Virgin. "You won't believe it," he declared, although he meant the opposite. "And that is proof that I give you. OK? You got enough?"[38]

Alejandro had offered a neatly constructed and yet moving narrative to me when he saw that I was armed, as Larry had been, with paper and pen. He had given the same story to reporters from Channel 62. He knew he was providing evidence to a critical academic observer who moved around the vision event studying pilgrims rather than examining the heavens like everyone else. He insisted on using English, although he knew that I had some Spanish. He expertly organized his story to suggest that Maria Paula had indirectly initiated his recovery from cancer, although she did not feature in his account. Yet the moral of his story was that his own willingness to participate in the vision event had led to his renewal of faith, thus accelerating his cure, which was completed by the grace of the Blessed Mother. Alejandro also felt compelled to offer the visual proof of his own body—he clearly weighed more than 110 pounds now and seemed healthy. For extra assurance, he had volunteered the irrefutable (to him) confirmation of a television news report about his recovery.

Alejandro's tale was a more succinct version of the tearful testimonies offered by witnesses on each July anniversary. Every experienced pilgrim to Our Lady of the Rock can tell a similar tale, if not about him or herself, then about a parent, spouse, child, or friend. Christians have repeated similar narratives about miraculous healing since the beginning of their religion. Writers of the Christian Gospels told stories of men and women with permanent disabilities and incurable diseases healed by Jesus. The story was already old when they inherited it from other faith traditions of the ancient world. Multiple versions are readily available now online.[39] Like the promise of revelation—and as a metaphor for epiphany—healing narratives are built into historical Christianities.[40]

When Maria Paula signals the presence of the Blessed Mother, pilgrims exploit the moment by petitioning for all sorts of help and healing. They submit requests to the visionary, who relays them to Mary. Many, like Alejandro, journey to the vision event only after receiving a dismaying medical diagnosis. Others hope that their presence and participation at the shrine, along with the visionary's prayers, will prove generally efficacious for a variety of complaints. The first time a pilgrim named Dora journeyed to the desert, for instance, she brought five nieces and a mind full of worry for her diabetic nephew. She was haunted by two recent family suicides and desperate for any kind of consolation.[41] Pilgrims like Dora are clearly comforted—and some claim healed—when Maria Paula pauses to say a word or lay a tender hand on their foreheads. Everyone competes to touch the visionary and gain her attention as she passes. "When Maria Paula placed her hands on me, I felt that they were the hands of the Virgin," a witness told a reporter from Univision in 2009. "For the glory of God here I am alive and healed."[42]

Sometimes one of the monjas encourages pilgrims with petitions to come forward for special consideration. "Sick, please come forward so you can be touched. . . . If you want to leave a *petición*, you can leave it with your number and we'll call you with the Virgin's answer."[43] Believers whisper their names and numbers to Sister Thelma as she trails behind Maria Paula, who records them. Witnesses purchase roses or water blessed by Maria Paula and sanctified by the Virgin Mary's presence, which they take as both relics and tonics.[44]

The benefits of Maria Paula's prayers are as inexplicable to most pilgrims as the chemistry of cancer drugs, but they trust in both methods. The unseen Virgin offers as much to helpless invalids as the surgery that occurs while they sleep or chemotherapy carried out in closed rooms hidden inside medical clinics. Ailing pilgrims and their caretakers move between clinics and the desert, seeking second and third opinions about their pains and diseases. They ponder Maria Paula's visions and invocations as they mull the diagnoses of doctors, searching for meaning in technical terms for suffering and death. This is how Christians have always read their prophecies. Each verse of holy scripture contains multiple meanings, some explicit and others hidden in

April 13, 2008

October 13, 2006

allegory and complex symbols. Every written passage recalls ancient history and at the same time poses models for individual religious understanding; each case of cancer or some other incurable affliction harks back to other earlier cases and their miraculous cures. Eager interpreters return to their favorite lines to uncover all layers of meaning. Patients revisit the desert shrine and pray harder. As a news feature about Our Lady of the Rock put it some years ago, "Whether it's real or not, people leave convinced that they have felt the presence of the Virgin and that God has promised to cure all their ills."[45]

Still, they do not really expect to be healed right there in the Mojave. Invalids and patients who arrive in wheelchairs or on crutches do not depart without them—there is no fundamentalist-style faith healing at Our Lady of the Rock, although a couple of stories about instantaneous cures have circulated. Ron claims that he saw a boy arrive in a wheelchair and walk away after Maria Paula laid hands on him. Ron also says that in spring of 2008, someone discarded a back brace at the vision site.[46] Nonetheless, medical equipment is too expensive for most pilgrims to abandon in the desert. Instead, they take responsibility for their own health and arrive at the shrine ready to fight for recovery. They appeal to the Blessed Mother in prayers and hymns. They consult with Maria Paula

May 13, 2007

and ask her to pray too. The healer and her patients invest in long-term relationships that eventually, God willing and the Virgin abetting, may yield a mutually beneficial outcome. A pilgrim must often make many trips into the Mojave in order to accomplish his or her goals. Fortunately, the Lady of the Rock appears predictably on the thirteenth—"like clockwork," according to one pilgrim or, as Paolo Apolito writes of other Marian apparitions, with the regularity of a favorite television show.[47]

If their petitions are sincere, if the visionary's pleas on their behalf are persuasive, and if the Virgin wins her son's intervention for sufferers, they might conquer their pain, as Alejandro did. They might eventually regain their health. When that happens, they return to the grotto once more in order to testify to the astonishment of their flabbergasted oncologists and surgeons. A twentyish young man named Brian, who first arrived at the shrine bound by drips and tubes to a stretcher, appeared four months later on his slightly unsteady feet. He came out of the crowd to hug Maria Paula as witnesses clapped and cheered.[48] The visionary allows only the most spectacular cases to stand before the entire audience and exhibit newly healthy bodies as proof of the power of prayer properly channeled by someone with the Virgin's ear.

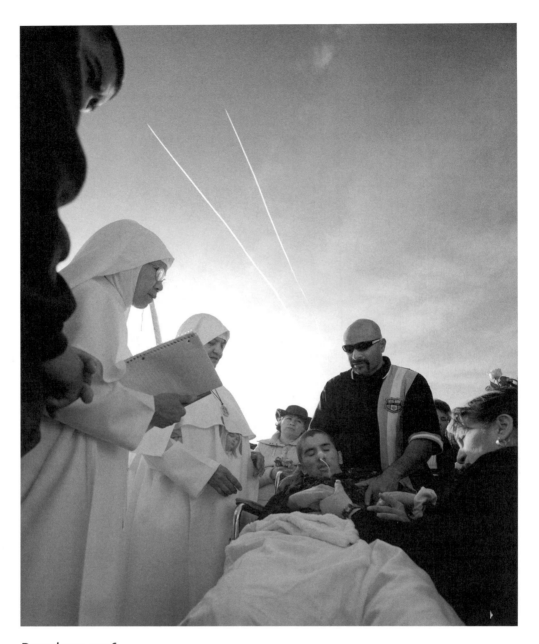

December 13, 2006

How They See

Although pilgrims journey to Our Lady of the Rock for a variety of confessed and secret motives, their main occupation at the grotto is vigilance. At any given moment, they are watching Maria Paula, observing their fellow witnesses, or searching the skies. Their inspection of the visionary helps them assess her abilities and the information she offers,

May 13, 2007

as well as her powers to intercede with the Virgin and her son. Their observation of other pilgrims teaches them how to evaluate Maria Paula but also how to behave during the event and, most important, how to read the skies. All this watching and looking requires a devotional state—what the billboard at the vision site called variously "searching for the grace of the Holy Spirit," "respecting this place," and praying. To interpret signs in the heavens, however, pilgrims also need cameras and lessons in using them.

As at other apparition events of the last thirty years, witnesses use electronic technology to capture signs of the Virgin that their eyes cannot. The practice is not part of the regular routine of Catholicism. Congregants do not usually carry cameras to weekly Mass. The skills must be acquired elsewhere. Juan Rubio has explained how he learned to take pictures of heaven. He had been a professional portrait photographer in his youth, before he moved to the United States, but he never trained to shoot the sun. "We should start at the beginning, the day I went over there. The first time I go to the desert, I go, I don't have a Polaroid camera," said Juan, a dapper, white-mustachioed man in his nineties. "They say, 'Look at it! It's here!' . . . I go around, try to see something and I can see nothing. I say, these people is crazy. Well, then I saw three little clouds, one two three, and I don't know why I think, but I come and—psht! psht! [clicking noises like a camera]— each little one. I start taking pictures everywhere over there. . . . The next time . . . they come to me and say, what [do] I see in the pictures, they don't see nothing."[49]

Now everyone asks him to help take pictures and interpret them. "Everybody say, 'Only Juan can take those pictures! You're the man that can read this?' Hey wait a minute! I can *try* to see what is in your picture and tell you." As he told his story, Juan grinned mischievously. "The only thing, it's simple, I try to see a picture right there, you don't see a picture?" he demanded. The first time I met Juan at the vision site in 2006, he silently shot a photo, waited for the Polaroid paper to slide out of the camera, and handed the filmy image to me. He had captured a ragged globe of blinding white light pierced by crossed diagonal lines on a field of deep blue-black. Gamely, I pointed to a lens flare that formed a cross in middle of the image. He chuckled as he indicated instead a vaguely triangular shape at the bottom of the photo. That, he explained, was the Virgin. Since then, he has tested me every time I have met him. He offered similar guidance to other puzzled newcomers to the Lady of the Rock.

New pilgrims come to the Mojave with cameras and the conviction that photography somehow enhances human vision of the unseen. Like Juan, they have already learned from friends or public media about the ritual of the photographs before they arrive at the vision event. None of the amateur videos or photo collections created at Our Lady of the Rock seem to have appeared on the Internet before 2006, but televised reports may have publicized the site earlier. The scanty printed news about Maria Paula and her Lady of the Rock has consistently emphasized the ritual of the photos. "They come with lawn chairs, rosaries and religious pictures to this stark, scrubby desert," began the 1997 piece in the *Los Angeles Times*. "Polaroid is the camera of choice—the better to see immediately if the Virgin Mary has appeared in the sky and allowed herself to be captured in some earthly form, if only on film." In 2008, Channel 13 from Las Vegas reported, "People say, if you look into the sky when the sun is shining you can see the Virgin Mary, her angels, and the gateway to heaven. Through pictures, believers say they can capture what is gleaming among the clouds."[50] The Internet preserves these earlier reports for aspiring pilgrim photographers. On the website of the American Festivals Project, the caption beneath one shot of pilgrims aiming cameras in different directions reads, "Taking pictures of the sky is a common activity during worship."[51] Photographers—both believers and religious tourists—also post their images of the vision site and events there on public websites such as Flickr, Photobucket, and Vimeo. An enterprising realtor in California City even posts images of photographers at Our Lady of the Rock as a lure to property buyers.[52]

Pilgrims who come to Our Lady of the Rock grew up using cameras and other image-making technology to commemorate all sorts of important private and public events, such as birthdays and holidays, and to preserve ephemeral events such as graduations, parades, speeches, or journeys to exotic places.[53] Even those who lacked cameras commonly looked at their products. These days, anyone who has a cell phone is ready to document history or miracle—a touch of the button and evidence exists for anyone's personal sighting of a rock star, a car crash, or the Virgin Mary. Visual proof of the unseen has become ubiquitous on television, in films and still images, and on computer screens. For those who have not personally enjoyed visions or visited apparition events, pseudodocumentary television programs, along with lurid websites and YouTube videos, demonstrate how to capture supernatural phenomena on camera. A variety of marvelous images from historic and modern Marian apparition events are freely available online (as I discuss in the last chapter of this book.) In particular, images from famous apparition events at Medjugorje, Bayside (New Jersey), and Conyers (Georgia)—where pilgrims also regularly wielded cameras—occupy major territory in cyberspace.[54]

As the anthropologist Paolo Apolito observed in 2005, the Internet has become a premier site for exchange of information within, and about, Catholic visionary culture. Cyberspace hosts virtual pilgrimages and sites of Marian worship.[55] The makers of websites and YouTube videos dedicated to Marian apparitions acknowledge the pedagogical and evangelical value of their work. At Catholictools.com, a web user can download a film called *Marian Apparitions of the 20th Century* which, the site claims, "is a powerful movie on apparitions of Blessed Mother which will provide an excellent teaching opportunity to a youth group or parish group. . . . This video would also make a great addition to any parish or group email list. Or go old school and take notes and then present it to your group."[56] Many websites discuss the special iconography embedded in apparition photographs. The nighttime images produced at Bayside, for instance, speak in a much more complex language of letters and numbers than found in the visual language of the desert photos and require some explication. On still other websites, pilgrims can research equipment best suited for snapping apparitions and learn techniques for handling their cameras. "Dollar for dollar, the Polaroid SX-70 is the best camera on the market for taking miraculous photos of apparitions of the Virgin Mary," proclaims one website devoted to the Conyers apparitions, quoting an *Orange County Register* article from 1986.[57]

Apolito has argued that the use of web-based technologies by visionaries and witnesses has detached them from the solid ground of actual Marian shrines. With visions online, he writes, believers no longer require individual seers like Maria Paula Acuña to mediate with the Virgin on their behalf.[58] Yet pilgrims to Our Lady of the Rock clearly do not believe this, or they would not journey to the desert. Thousands of devotees continue to visit international Marian shrines every day of the year. *Pace* Apolito, information flows both ways between Marian websites and actual apparition sites. Pilgrims copy the methods of web-based slide shows when they display photo collections to friends and relations, explaining their serial images of the desert's skies. They recount personal histories with visual references to vision events, thus educating and inspiring new generations of pilgrims to Our Lady of the Rock.[59] A virtual quest cannot replace a physical journey into the desert, and anyway, the Lady of the Rock does not maintain an official presence on the Internet.

Pilgrim photography offers two kinds of proof for visionary authenticity. First, photos demonstrate that witnesses have personally witnessed and assessed the seer's performance. They saw her fall into a trance or heard her use a strange voice and observed the resulting effects on fellow pilgrims who cried, smelled invisible roses, felt shocks of divine presence, or experienced healing. All these phenomena have been reported at Our Lady of the Rock.

Second, photographs link the latest visions and visionaries to the venerable tradition of Marian apparitions, previously publicized by newspapers, postcards, and printed images. They give evidence that this event resembles earlier, authentic vision events. Even before cameras became available to ordinary citizens, formal portraits of seers and scenes of religious visions, restaged in photographers' studios, had circulated among national and international audiences, revealing exactly what an authentic seer having a genuine vision actually looked like.[60] Visitors to Lourdes, Marpingen, Rome, and other shrines sent home cards featuring pictures of pilgrim parades and enormous crowds at apparition shrines. Holy cards and pamphlets allowed them to relive the experience of pilgrimage and imagine themselves in the place of Bernadette or Lúcia dos Santos. From printed pictures, believers learned to recognize appropriate settings for apparitions, such as grottos, woodland glades, and other deserted places. Before the modern period, drawings, paintings, sculpture, and architecture offered visual models.

In the mid-twentieth century, more witnesses began wielding their own cameras to create visionary proofs. Cameras caught the children of Garabandal (Spain) in synchronized, entranced motion as they gazed at the Virgin periodically between 1961 and 1965 and as they received the Eucharist from angelic hands.[61] When Polaroid brought its inexpensive SX-70 camera to the market in 1972, the perfect medium for evaluation of visionaries and the discernment of apparitions became available to the masses, as anthropologist Dan Wojcek has argued. Henceforth, pilgrims did not even require the intercession of professional reporters, photographers, or film developers in order to generate evidence of visions and apparitions. They could focus their lenses on a visionary of their choosing and produce instant testimony, on site and in the presence of other witnesses, in the form of tamper-proof squares of Polaroid film slithering out of their cameras. The resulting pictures were at once aides-mémoire and contact relics of the Virgin—like the cloths that ancient pilgrims touched to a saint's tomb to sop up a little holiness—through which they might reexperience her presence.

Pilgrim photography reflects both the populism of the post–Vatican II church and an ancient tradition of divine portraiture. Until the invention of photography, Christians relied on artists to reveal the human faces of Jesus and Mary. But after the last apostle had died, no one knew for sure what the Incarnation or his Virgin birth giver had looked like, short of meeting them in dreams or as apparitions, because neither Christ nor his mother left life portraits. Even in those situations, Christians needed visual guidance in order to recognize the Blessed Mother and her divine son among the demons, angels, ghosts, and saints that commonly turned up in day and night dreams. This problem prompted the appearance, around the sixth century if not earlier, of "unpainted" or miraculously created portraits of Jesus and Mary in churches from Rome to Edessa. The Mandylion and the Vera Icon (or Veronica), for instance, were images of Jesus' face believed to be divinely imprinted on cloth by the savior himself. Portraits of the Virgin pointing to the Christ child in her lap (called Hodgetria) were supposedly painted from life by the apostle Luke; they occasionally reproduced themselves, miraculously conveying the true Mary from one canvas to another.[62] The shroud of Turin and the tilma of Juan Diego are also examples of allegedly divine self-portraits. All these simulacra allegedly channeled the authentic image of their subjects for the benefit of believers who lived too late to meet Christ and his mother on earth.

Debates over the legitimacy and authorship of such apparitional objects have always focused on their provenance (who found and owned the items) and the dating of their materials, techniques, and artistry, in order to prove or disprove their human manufacture. Art historians still argue about who painted Juan Diego's tilma, and thousands of pilgrims flocked to Turin to see the shroud when it was lasted exhibited in 2010.[63] However, the religious value of these images—whether painted likeness or contact relic—depends not on the human skill involved in their creation but on the participation of the Virgin. Divine agency guarantees both the accuracy and the efficacy of the images.

In the nineteenth century, photography revived the possibility of glimpsing the authentic face of Mary. As early as the 1840s, professional photographers were experimenting with spirit photos, in which they claimed to capture the forms of departed loved ones lurking in the same frame as mourners. Spiritualists and scientists alike generated theories as to why ghosts, fairies, angels, and other sympathetic manifestations, normally invisible to the human eye, should be caught in the lens of a camera—something to do with electricity, they said, or vibrations and emotional waves, or possibly chemistry. Others suggested that mechanical flaws in cameras or lenses or photographers' tricks produced the eerie images. Most viewers regarded photographs as products of marvelous vision that, like other inventions of the period, improved the natural human capacity to see; as steam locomotion carried people faster than their own legs could, so cameras isolated and seized moments of rapid movement invisible to ordinary eyes. Cameras could see lightning strikes, ghosts materializing, and all four hooves of a horse lifted off the ground in a gallop.[64] Hence, the dancing suns of Fátima appeared on film because camera shutters were quicker and more sharply focused than the human eye.

In addition, cameras caught the full brilliance of the Christian supernatural, which had previously evaded the prose of Gospel writers as well as the paintbrushes of artists. There was the dazzling whiteness, brighter than any bleach could produce, filling photographic spaces with nothing but light; the blankness of photographic prints proved the presence of the divine.[65] The imprecise descriptive vocabulary of witnesses also became more reliable when supported with visual evidence. If the images were abstract or blurry, it was because of the subject's supernatural qualities, which could be only partially represented by man-made machines and lenses. By catching the apparition in motion and preserving it on film, witnesses could get a partial squint at what bona fide visionaries saw. Visionaries no longer had sole responsibility for interpreting what they had seen or felt because witnesses could offer replicas of their perceptions for discussion and debate. Hence, photography offered scientific proof of visionary authenticity. Arguments for the reliability of apparition photographs hinge on the same question of artistic agency used to evaluate earlier archeiropoieta (images made without use of human hands). Pilgrim photographers at Our Lady of the Rock assert that the Blessed Mother colludes with

July 24, 2008

them in manufacturing pictures, graciously permitting them to obtain her likeness and more abstract signs of her presence.[66]

Verbal testimonies and material evidence of the Virgin's presence supplement every visual case for visionary authenticity. At Garbandal, onlookers also treasured pebbles clutched by the children who saw the Virgin Mary; many pilgrims to Medjugorje have brought home rosaries colored gold by the Virgin's presence.[67] Abandoned crutches and brightly painted ex-votos still signify miracles at Marian shrines too. Pilgrims to Our Lady of the Rock use all these methods, although they rely primarily on their cameras for evidence of the Virgin's presence. Their photography *is*, in a sense, the main vision event at Our Lady of the Rock. The apparitions mark a spot in the desert where heaven opens, but Maria Paula's exclusive communications with the Virgin create the conditions for the pilgrims' own discrete encounters with the Mother of God. Only Maria Paula hears and conveys the words and wishes of the Lady of the Rock. The visionary often advises witnesses to aim their cameras upward—"Take it now!" she cries out. But pilgrims do not require her urging or permission. They begin shooting from the moment they arrive at the site and continue snapping while the visionary speaks with Mary and throughout the sermons. They take pictures while Maria Paula lays healing hands on friends and strangers and while she rests in her trailer. Sometimes a cluster of photographers will notice an unusual configuration of light and clouds and turn to capture it, diverting the crowd's attention from Maria Paula's performance in the sanctuary.

Witnesses will gladly demonstrate how to benefit from the sacralized environment at Our Lady of the Rock. They help newcomers gaze in the right direction and set up the best shots possible. Many will lend a camera so that a novice can capture an image for herself. The technique is not as obvious as it first seems, as pilgrims remind each other—you have to keep an eye out for particular qualities of light and distinctive cloud formations. Sometimes Ron will use his microphone to point out a rainbow caused by springtime vapors on the horizon. "That means our Lady is present," he might explain excitedly.[68] Cameras immediately begin clicking. Pilgrims do not hesitate to correct an inept photographer either. "They're looking over *there*," an exasperated teenager told her father at one vision event, gesturing impatiently behind him as he squinted uncertainly at the sun.[69] Although most photographers aim for the sun, there are always some focusing on another region of the sky at the same time. One pilgrim explained in 2009,

> It was funny cause [the apparition] doesn't stay in one place, she'll move, like you'll look and you'll [say] "oh look, there she is," and a lot of people come, and they'll start pointing, and they say they see her, but sometimes they don't, they just think they do, and they're all pointing in the same area. I turn around and I [realize] she's not there, she's over *there*, [so I say] "she moved *that* way"—and then they start laughing.[70]

Discussion of the resulting images goes on at all moments of the vision event. The code of the photos is not always obvious to the uninitiated, despite the increasingly global iconography of Marian apparitions available online.[71] The apparition at Our Lady of the Rock, like all vision events, has its own local dialect of photographic images available only to those who practice and perfect their skills at the monthly vision event. The sun over the shrine never sends a simple message with fixed meanings. In fact, lessons usually begin with learning how to look at the sun and watch it dance. Maria Paula herself will demonstrate, if asked, how to crook thumb and forefinger to frame a proper view, which pilgrims practice with or without cameras or sunglasses to shield their eyes. Although seasoned pilgrims have learned to recognize common symbols in a variety of abstract images, they frequently deliberate about nuances within single images and motifs that recur in their collections of photos.[72] A ball of light typically indicates divine presence. A shining cross signifies Jesus' crucifixion and resurrection. A triangular shape is the veiled Virgin, sometimes holding her holy baby or embracing another figure. A rectangle with rounded top and bottom represents the Gate of Heaven. Red spots are the savior's blood. But less regular blurs of light may symbolize Mary descending through the clouds, rosaries, angels, doves, or the face of Jesus. Sometimes the image has to be rotated and held at the proper angle in order to read its messages.

When multiple symbols appear in a single photo, the grammar of evidence becomes more complicated. What looks like the doorway to heaven can be the Sacred Heart if

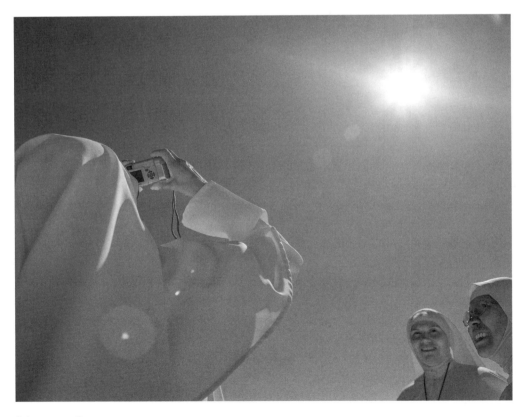

July 24, 2008

April 13, 2008

pierced by a cross. Symbols caught in the same frame as the visionary, fellow witnesses, or structural features of the vision site also change the message of photographs. The photo of a British cancer victim posed on the grotto's rocks, taken by a member of the Marian Movement, was reinterpreted as a prophecy when the man returned a year later, miraculously recovered from terminal illness. The image then functioned as an ex-voto, displayed at the vision site in thanks for his cure, a reminder of his two pilgrimages, and proof of the efficacy of Maria Paula and her mysterious rocks. Skillful photographers purposely create such complex visual and religious statements by combining abstract signs and tangible symbolic objects, such as the large cross that looms behind the stage, in a series of shots. Recently, pilgrims have begun to take pictures of the new grotto, trying to capture dawn's orange reflections on the windows that screen the Lady's statue from the naked gaze of pilgrims. They also catch the statue and its own reflection in a kind of double apparition. These staged images are exclusive to the vision site and to particular moments on the thirteenth.

Still, the photographers never stray too far from a well-defined range of techniques and familiar images that, as most witnesses appreciate, look much alike. Comparison of images with the photos of others and with their own previous shots helps them locate their new pictures in the visual grammar of the Lady of the Rock. Memories of statues in

June 13, 2006

churches and on holy cards also assist them in identifying iconographic references in the sky more precisely. In December of 2010, for instance, one man spent the day capturing image after image of a Virgin-shaped lens flare. Late in the afternoon, he asked his young daughter to remind him what to call the white shape in his pictures. She responded, "The little figure of Guadalupe!"[73]

Pilgrims also examine their fresh shots next to locally famous pictures taken at the shrine many years ago, such as Pat's picture of the Briton, and beside depictions of apparitions from more famous Marian shrines such as Fátima and Medjugorje. Miraculous images from historic shrines reinforce the meaning and value of pilgrims' own pictures, offering supporting evidence that others have done what they now do and that the monthly photography sessions in the Mojave belong to an established Catholic tradition. Pamphlets about earlier apparitions, for sale on vision days at Our Lady of the Rock, offer additional textual support by recounting histories of Saint Bernadette, Lúcia dos Santos, Saint Pio, and other orthodox Catholic visionaries, which are illustrated with photographs or drawings. (However, the so-called popular saints of the borderlands who are dismissed by the Catholic establishment, such as Santa Muerte and el Niño

Perdido, are invisible at the shrine.) Copies of Polaroids taken at other Marian shrines usually reveal a less abstract and more anthropomorphic Virgin. Pilgrims use them as primers for learning to read more difficult images taken at Our Lady of the Rock. Photographs supposedly snapped at famous shrines are popular items for sale at the vision site, even though obviously retouched or otherwise manipulated. For instance, a popular, rainbow-tinged photograph featuring a pale Virgin spreading her cloak over Apparition Hill at Medjugorje is available and sells well. A pilgrim at the vision site once showed me the same image and insisted that the picture had been taken at Our Lady of the Rock.[74] It doesn't matter whether she was mistaken; the association with Medjugorje charged that particular picture with meaning. Photographs snapped by Maria Paula have added value for pilgrims too. Although her work is not artistically superior, it is more authoritative because she can see better and knows what the Lady looks like. Copies of Maria Paula's shots, occasionally for sale at the vision site, are neatly labeled with identifying dates and locations. Some were taken elsewhere, for example, on Maria Paula's balcony and in a car traveling to the vision site.

Most pilgrims are aware of the evidentiary problems posed by easily reproducible photographs. Anyone with a computer and image-altering software can enhance digital images or fabricate the kinds of pictures that, for the previous five decades, have consti-

March 12, 2009

tuted proof of authentic visions and apparitions at sites around the world. Many visitors to Our Lady of the Rock agree with pilgrims elsewhere that Polaroids are best for capturing evidence of divinity, although they also freely use other technologies. When Polaroid announced in 2008 that it would end production of its famous film, only a few pilgrims seemed concerned. Some complained about the rising cost of the dwindling film stock. Although Polaroid tried to revive its classic Instamatic camera in 2010, photographers at Our Lady of the Rock had already resigned themselves to the proof of pixels. It seems that half the crowd is peering at their cell phones and e-mailing images to viewers far away while Maria Paula sermonizes. Although they acknowledge photographic technology's role in facilitating their devotions, it does not matter to pilgrims what kind of equipment they use. If a believer and a nonbeliever deploying the same cameras simultaneously produce identical images of the skies, only one of them will be able to offer evidence of an apparition.

How They Negotiate

For more than a century, academics and journalists have trained themselves to investigate the social, cultural, and political contexts of Marian apparitions and other instances of the supernatural or paranormal, but they rarely solicit sensory evidence for theophany or the witnessing of it. Researchers know how to collect demographic and cultural data about visionaries and witnesses, but most scholars are unfamiliar with the vocabularies used by pilgrims to convey religious experience. Witnesses also have trouble translating what it feels like to watch the sun dance or become suddenly aware of the Virgin's presence. They in turn must rely on Maria Paula's descriptions of her visions and explanations of the Lady's monthly messages and seek her guidance in how to make best use of the Virgin's visitations. Visionary, witnesses, and outsiders at the vision site watch the same events, listen to the same words from the visionary's lips, and occupy the same space at the same ritual moments, but they still find it tricky to share what they each have witnessed.[75]

The stakes are highest for dedicated participants in vision events because their responses to their visionary indicate to themselves and fellow pilgrims the depth of their belief and their degree of intimacy with the Virgin. Some witnesses realize that merely thinking about their experience is a way of interpreting it and reducing it to human terms. One pilgrim spoke of her elation at watching the sun dance and how, at the same time, her "analytical mind" had expressed skepticism about the reality and religious meaning of the event.[76] When a visionary tells what she sees or a follower explains what she or he has witnessed, the experience has already been translated twice. It has become an explanation of religious experience limited to the terms used to describe and authenticate it. As one sociologist has put it, religious experience is interpretation "all the way down."[77]

Witnesses' conversations with Maria Paula and researchers' discussions with pilgrims require everyone to translate the process of looking and feeling into words, gestures, and expressions. Much depends on the willingness and ability of all parties to avoid the restrictive glossaries imposed by their respective aims at the vision site. Christian visions are profoundly personal yet gain religious and social meaning only when shared. On the thirteenth of the month, it is pretty easy for everyone to tell who speaks the language of visions and who struggles with the idiom. Witnesses tend to protect their hard-won epiphanies by speaking elliptically and metaphorically. The questions of reporters, documentarians, and academics rarely correspond to the answers that pilgrims give. Class and ethnic politics clutter the conversation between interviewers and interviewees, along with language difficulties and the presuppositions of intellectual observers, especially the neat categorization of religious experiences as visions, epiphanies, trances, transcendence, psychoses, delusions, or frauds. All these contexts hinder the talk.[78]

Yet everyone at Our Lady of the Rock is curious about what others have seen. Pilgrims have developed protocols for inquiring about what other believers may experience on the thirteenth of the month and on the anniversary of Maria Paula's visions. They learn codes for conveying their private perceptions of a vision event. They form their language from the lowest common denominators shared by witnesses, drawn from historical Marian devotions, pilgrimage traditions, and Catholic liturgies, among other sources. Together, they negotiate and create a collective imaginary exclusive to Our Lady of the Rock.[79] The pilgrims' grammar of witnessing speaks of the holy desert, the Blessed Virgin, seers of earlier generations, and Maria Paula's unique visions. Their verbs are the rituals that they enact each month. Their nouns are the site's physical environment, its iconography, relics, and above all, the photographs that they take, share, and keep. Month by month, pilgrims and visionary continue to build religion at Our Lady of the Rock. They struggle to express this religion as effectively as possible in order advertise their individual spiritual progress and teach neophytes how to look for the Virgin.

Witnesses offer a limited set of discourses about what they have seen and felt. When obvious outsiders ask questions about Maria Paula and the Lady of the Rock, pilgrims switch codes and answer unasked questions. Many volunteer personal proofs of Maria Paula's authenticity, as Alejandro felt compelled to do after Larry's rude departure.[80] This unsolicited evidence establishes witnesses' shared understanding of Maria Paula's visions and argues for the efficacy of rituals at the desert shrine. Some witnesses hone a narrative that they repeat for any and all interviewers. Others try to explain the experience of witnessing or vision with multiple, sometimes contradictory, metaphors. Carolina, the young woman who battled her analytical mind, described her first mariophany variously as a feeling of joy, of spinning, like being an ant at an elephant's foot, a sense of peace, fear, transformation, "something immense, like God's power," awe, and an indescribably lovely rainbow outlined in green. Ultimately, she said she was "touched in a way I can't describe."[81] Still other witnesses employ conversational pauses and silences to hint at their most profound experiences, while keeping those experiences private. "I can't explain it," a pilgrim will often say when trying to describe something she or he saw or felt. "I saw something, I don't know what." They literally lack the words in Spanish or English with which to articulate their experiences.

In the summer of 2008, a middle-aged Mexican American pilgrim named Ray struggled for the right phrase to communicate his vision of Jesus. It was like looking upon "nuclear waste," he finally said, although he seemed to mean cosmic emptiness or maybe the swirl of a galaxy's stars (I visualized cinematic images of deep space and black holes). In similar terms, Adelia has drawn on cinematic science fiction to describe an apparition that looked to her "like E.T." She did not mean that she had met a tiny, wizened alien with glowing fingers but that she had encountered something unearthly.[82] Witnesses' difficulties in selecting appropriate metaphors for interior experiences protect them from being misunderstood. Their stuttering and pauses posit a mystery that they have already parsed but that nonbelievers will never fully comprehend.[83]

Pilgrims to Our Lady of the Rock willingly discuss the necessary skills for successful witnessing. "I sometimes take photos," confessed Javier, who helped build the grotto, but he also cautioned that "you have to believe in them, to believe what you see. There are many different holy things in them and you have to know how to find them. If you don't believe you won't see."[84] As Adelia first put it, you have to look the right way to see an apparition in the sky or in Polaroid photographs. An observer who openly admits the possibility of apparitions signals potential ability to witness. On the anniversary of Maria Paula's first vision, when I asked a middle-aged Spanish-speaking couple what it felt like to touch the Virgin's hem, they stared at me for a long moment and then suggested brusquely that I just try it for myself. Only as I sheepishly thanked them did I notice that the woman was softly weeping after an exalting encounter with the Blessed Mother. If I did not myself reach for Mary's robe, I would clearly not understand any description of the experience. I eventually learned how to choose better moments and ask more appropriate questions, but I have never yet touched the Virgin's hem.

Ray told me a series of entertaining stories that, as I only realized months later, were actually lessons in the pilgrim way of seeing and sharing. On that same torrid twenty-fourth of July, 2008, we waited throughout the afternoon for the Virgin to appear. As the temperature rose, the crowd thinned. Witnesses and outsiders, sweating together, worked a little harder to exchange useful information. People asked me what I was doing at the vision site. I launched questions about meaningful religious episodes in their lives. Ray talked about his own visions of the Virgin and Jesus and how he had learned to interpret them. His first lesson had occurred several years earlier at Our Lady of the Rock, at the moment just before Maria Paula saw the Virgin. Ray had been standing behind the stage while the visionary and monjas circled the sanctuary prior to kneeling for the apparitions' descent. Ray happened to glance southward beyond the crowded sanctuary and glimpsed a bright, low "cloud" rising near the tamale stand. A shining bubble of light whizzed into the arena toward Maria Paula (Ray's description reminded me of the scene in *The Wizard of Oz* when Glinda the Good appeared in the Main Square of

Munchkinland.) When Maria Paula finally noticed the ball of light, she announced that the Virgin had arrived. She frowned at Ray, though, he recalled, as she described the brilliantly white apparition for the crowd. She was annoyed that Ray had seen the Virgin first, without her assistance. He chuckled at the memory as he repeated it but admitted that Maria Paula was the one who recognized the little cloud as the Blessed Mother.

On another day, as Ray drove home with his wife after a day in the desert, he topped a rise in the road to Palmdale. A blazing sunset confronted them through the windshield. Ray was startled when he realized that he was staring directly into the sun without blinking. He tested himself twice, he told me, by looking away from the light, then back, away, then back. It seemed as if a "color negative"—a dark translucent film—had dropped in front of the sun or as if an iridescent teardrop was growing on the sun's surface. Suddenly he beheld Jesus on the fiery horizon. Not trusting his own archive of visual interpretations, Ray consulted his wife. He did not drop a hint by asking, "Do you see anything?" Instead, he asked "What do you see?" She saw Jesus. Ray trusted her because she was a regular churchgoer and knew something about Christ's iconography.

As we awaited the Virgin, Ray also offered more details about that vision of bubbling nuclear or cosmic waste. He had been praying at home in his bedroom when it happened, kneeling by the bed with his eyes closed. A missal lay open before him. Behind his eyelids he observed a tiny, curly-haired child. The child's image rippled so that the boy was blurry—this was the scene he had described as waste. He had wondered to himself, who is it? Then he had realized that the adult Jesus—whom he had previously met on the highway—was standing behind the child. Ray still puzzled over the child's identity, though. Later that evening, after he finished his prayers, he had sought his wife's opinion once again. She led him back into the bedroom and flipped the missal open to an illustration of the Infant of Prague (Ray pronounced it carefully, "Prrr-ayg," to underline his unfamiliarity with the icon). He laughed at himself in retrospect as he confessed that a statue of the very same child stood on the home altar atop his wife's bureau. The boy had been there all along, but Ray had never noticed before.

Ray's narrative revealed how he had gradually built confidence and learned rudimentary iconography through a series of visions, which readied him to risk discernment on his own. He had another story about that too. He often attends the parish church of Saint Genevieve's somewhere in the San Gabriel Valley, he told me. A Korean woman in his congregation seems to be meeting apparitions there on a regular basis; he was not sure about the particulars since she cannot speak Spanish or English and he does not know Korean. Anyway, Ray said, he learned from fellow congregants that the Virgin tells the Korean woman who needs praying for. One Sunday she motioned to him after Mass and indicated that he should kneel before the altar on which the Eucharist (communion wafer) was displayed. Ray was a little confused when she left him alone to pray. Suddenly, though, he saw Jesus yet again. This time the savior was a fine-featured man dressed in a white robe with a hood that covered his hair. He did not acknowledge Ray but stretched out his arms, palms up, and gazed calmly over Ray's head at the empty church. Later, Ray drove down to Cotter's warehouse of religious goods in L.A, seeking an exact copy of that unusual manifestation of Christ. Ray implied that the apparition was unique, especially the hidden hair, because Christ had never appeared in that particular way to anyone else. No statue existed to set the visual terms of Ray's apparition this time. Too bad that Jesus had not spoken or even glanced at him, Ray added.

Ray abruptly finished his discourse by calling his young granddaughter over and introducing her. He patted her head and admitted ruefully that the girl loved her *abuela* more than anyone else in the world. Ray's wife was suffering from cancer and was too weak to join the conversation. He left me to ponder his four-part lesson about looking the right way. His stories not only recounted his personal journey toward faith in apparitions but also betrayed the resources that he had used to make sense of what he saw—his wife's expertise, a prayer book, traditional Catholic iconography—and the skills of discernment that he had gradually developed—thoughtful observation, prayer and meditation, research in iconography, and the methodical comparison of images and vision experiences. What is more, Ray's stories showed how skeptical observers and reporters also played a part in his discernment of his own and Maria Paula's visions. He used his conversations with me to structure his personal history of revelation. Similarly, Alejandro relied on Larry, me, and various news reporters to hear and help shape his testimony on Maria Paula's behalf. Just as Maria Paula's visions require witnesses, so witnesses require audiences in order to publicize the vision event and their part in it.

Ray's personal history also subtly revealed his evaluation of Maria Paula and the evolution of his relationship with the visionary. Ray initially depended on her to locate and identify apparitions of the Virgin. He had accompanied his wife to Our Lady of the Rock the first time but returned after learning how to look for himself. If Maria Paula did not know how to express persuasively what she sees in the desert, witnesses such as Ray would not attend her on the thirteenth of each month. If she had not learned how to present herself as a recognizable Marian visionary, there would be no apparitions, no shrine, and no opportunity for Ray to look the right way. Like Ray, Maria Paula had also trained herself to see and to express her visions in terms accessible to witnesses. She learned from the same resources as Ray how to mimic historic visionaries, how to dress and behave, and how to speak to and about the Virgin. When challenged by eviction from Lopez Canyon and dismissed by high-ranking Catholic clergy, she had responded with the typical visionary's silence, disappearing behind her spotless veil. Ever since, she has worked to spread the Virgin's news to everyone, as she regularly reminds the crowd. She hopes everyone learns to see the Blessed Mother, even unbelievers such as news reporters and professors.

Pilgrims and even a few reporters appreciate her efforts. One television news correspondent faced his camera in 2009 and intoned, "This desert is now [Maria Paula's] place of union with thousands, and her roof will be the house of the next person who is ill and who seeks relief, and the next terminally ill person who seeks the light of heaven when she or he goes to sleep forever. Never comparing herself to a saint . . . she categorizes herself as a messenger of faith."[85] Pilgrims demonstrate thanks for cures, blessings, and lessons in looking by trekking to this shrine in the middle of nowhere. They offer donations toward the grotto's beautification and sustenance of the monjas. They purchase roses blessed by Maria Paula and buy raffle tickets. They take home bottles of water made holy by the Virgin's presence at Our Lady of the Rock.

The money allows Maria Paula and her sisters to devote their days to prayer and ministry. Rumor has it that the visionary has made several trips to Mexico and the Philippines on the Marian Movement's dollar. Pilgrims do not grumble about the cash. If the visionary seems to exploit their need for desert religion, they also take advantage of Maria Paula in order to educate themselves and create their own religion in this sacred place. They respect what Maria Paula teaches them through her reports of Mary's messages, but they also come to watch for private messages.

If all her witnesses are as adept as Ray, and if donations continue to flow to the Marian Movement, Maria Paula ironically risks losing what she has won by her service to the Virgin and the pilgrims. In the winter of 2009 the collaborative relationship between the visionary and her witnesses was threatened when the grotto formally opened for business. As bone-chilling winds blasted pilgrims on the thirteenth of December, members of the Marian Movement made ready to welcome the Our Lady of the Rock to her new home. They were not sure where to park her ride, a jacked-up Ford pickup truck, in order to unload the statue. They repeatedly shooed clusters of pilgrims out of the way. The statue of Nuestra Señora de la Roca was heavy and almost too big to fit through the shrine's doorway. It took a while to boost her onto a temporary pedestal covered in aluminum foil, which took up most of the little room's floor space.

Meanwhile, everyone waiting outside was freezing. The site's only shelter belongs to the Lady of the Rock. Maria Paula hardly appeared in the sanctuary that day. She may have been ailing. Pilgrims could not recall whether she even had a vision, distracted as they were by the statue's installation. No one shot pictures of the sky, but some witnesses took photos of the shrine, which at that point still lacked a functioning fountain, a proper approach, or shrubbery. In the coming months, as the place gained more trimmings, visionary and witnesses repeatedly rearranged the vision event to fit the new locus of worship.

I had wondered what would happen when the Virgin went inside. The trinity of sacred desert, Virgin Mary, and visionary had brought thousands of pilgrims to this holy place, but if the Virgin remained under a roof, would the visionary still be able to see her every month? Unless the Lady emerged and spoke with Maria Paula, the visionary would have to alter or give up her public performances. This is not to say that pilgrims believe that the statue actually takes to the air and talks. However, it represents the invisible Virgin whom Maria Paula sees and remains prominent in all the shrine's liturgies. After December of 2008, pilgrims were initially uncertain about how to behave at the vision site. They did not know what to photograph or whether they should even take pictures at all. That spring, pilgrims seemed to separate into two groups: those who resolutely continued

December 13, 2009

snapping the skies and those who knelt around the shrine.[86] Like Ray, both groups had learned from Maria Paula, from each other, and from their diverse personal experiences how to interact with the invisible powers of heaven.

At one tense point, Maria Paula announced that copies of photographs taken at past vision events were no longer to be sold on the thirteenth. Pat, who ran the Movement's information table, reported that the monjas had confiscated all reproductions of Maria Paula's own shots. Pat had heard that the church disapproved of pilgrim photography at purported apparition sites (it was unclear whether this meant local bishops or the Vatican.) Perhaps Maria Paula was sensitive to doctrinal shifts, but she had more immediate reasons for hiding all the evidence. She was claiming the Lady of the Rock and the shrine for herself at a moment when she feared losing leadership of the vision event. In that spring of 2009, Maria Paula had become increasingly annoyed by the pilgrims' focus on the grotto and its simulacrum of Mary instead of attending to her reports of the Virgin. When pilgrims scanned the skies and took photographs, it confirmed both their confidence in her and their inability to see what she saw. The visionary threatened to take the statue home with her to the house she shared with Sister Thelma, the address of which was unknown even to the most diligent reporters. After all, the statue represented the apparition that she alone had seen, month after month, first in Lopez Canyon and

July 23, 2011

then in the Mojave. The Lady of the Rock did not reveal herself to anyone but Maria Paula—or so the visionary supposed anyway. The Mother of God had directed Maria Paula and no one else to this desert and had commanded her alone to lead the army of believers.

Apparently, negotiations between Maria Paula and the witnesses went the visionary's way. Pilgrims took this new lesson to heart, for by April of 2010 they were once again gazing hopefully at the sun and clicking away on their digital cameras. When a student interviewer asked witnesses, "¿Que significa Maria Paula para usted?" ("What does Maria Paula mean to you?"), they responded that the visionary had superior access to the Virgin. "[Maria Paula] comes here and talks to the Mother, and then she tells us what the Mother would have us do. She delivers the message," one explained. Another answered, "Maria Paula is the door to the truth—*la puerta*. She provides us with guidance." Others reported:

> "[She] gives us the truth and a way to communicate with the Mother."
> "[Maria Paula] connects us to the Mother. Mother gives us protection."
> "Maria Paula is like our *hermana*. She is our *hermana* to the Mother. She gives us the truth, a truth by which to live."[87]

December 13, 2007

So long as Maria Paula lives and reports visions of the Virgin, then, her witnesses will keep watching her. Pilgrims have decided that Maria Paula can teach them how to interpret apparitions or possibly even have visions of their own. Watching a woman who sees the mother of Jesus is as religiously beneficial as kneeling in a church to watch an ordained priest transform bread and wine into Christ's body and blood. Maria Paula's interpretation of events at Our Lady of the Rock has become the official history of the apparitions and the shrine.

However, that history is not yet complete. When the student interviewer asked pilgrims whether someone would eventually succeed Maria Paula as the visionary leader at the desert shrine, one follower replied:

I do not know if there will be another person who is going to . . . do the same things as Maria Paula does. . . . We do not know if there will be another person selected by God . . . We know that Maria Paula—that that is the gift that God has given her, to be able to see the Virgin and to speak with her—I think it is not going to end, simply, if there is no one else after Maria Paula. We are going to continue believing in the Virgin until the day we die.[88]

From Witness to Visionary

At the end of the vision event, usually around three or four o'clock on any thirteenth of the month, pilgrims would always fold their lawn chairs, close their umbrellas, and repack their coolers. They would gather their children and other possessions and climb into their cars for the drive home. They had spent another day in the desert with Maria Paula and the Virgin. They had processed, prayed, and stared at the sun. They watched each other as Maria Paula explained what the Virgin wanted this time. They took pictures. They socialized. They learned a little more about managing the intersection of visual and spiritual realities. Some witnesses confessed to feeling the loving presence of the Virgin Mary, mother of Christ. Month after month, pilgrims made religion together once a month at Our Lady of the Rock. They continue to do so.

Pilgrims' baggage is always heavier on the return trip from the desert, despite the water bottles and other provisions that they tote and consume at the grotto. They leave the shrine burdened with another day's sights and sounds, which they will mull over and then add to their accounts of what they do here each month. They carry home new photographic evidence for the apparitions. Those who chat with Maria Paula or her secretary, Sister Thelma, may take with them advice about urgent problems or the visionary's promise to pray on their behalf. Several pilgrims depart with appointments for private rosary sessions later on. Some take roses or jugs of water blessed by Maria Paula, which will become relics as well as tonics. Others depart with new rosaries or pamphlets purchased from the Marian Movement or wooden bracelets imprinted with images of the many different Virgins. Their wallets are a bit lighter as a result of this investment in religion.

Most pilgrims regard their journey into the desert as a recurring opportunity to practice self-improvement in the presence of the Virgin. Three of them—called here Juan,

, and Carolina—agreed to lengthy interviews in which they explained their motives joining the vision event. They roughly represent the range of believers at Our Lady of the Rock. They come from different countries, classes, generations, and educational backgrounds. Juan Rubio's story of migrant labor and miraculous escapes began in early twentieth-century Mexico. Adelia is an educated, middle-class refugee from Nicaragua who survived a perilous journey to the United States and eventually found a home in California City. The third of these visionary pilgrims, a recent college graduate named Carolina, is still trying to understand her past, as well as her motives for attending Our Lady of the Rock. She has found comfort in the desert and hopes that Maria Paula can guide her to a happier future.

For Juan, Adelia, and Carolina, the grotto became a religious classroom. Maria Paula offered them a model for visionary practice. The community of pilgrims helped them distinguish their visions from ordinary witnessing. Eventually, each of the three learned that they no longer needed the desert or Maria Paula in order to meet the Virgin. Each uncovered a divine plan in his or her life's adventures, revealed via wonders of escalating profundity, which they only recently began to see. With persistence, vigilance, and tuition by the Ladies of the Rock—the Virgin Mary and Maria Paula Acuña—these three witnesses learned how to become bona fide Christian visionaries, although none of them would presume that title. All pilgrims to Our Lady of the Rock take home memories of exceptional religion in the desert, but only a chosen few leave the Mojave able to see as clearly as Maria Paula.

Just as Bernadette's visions at Lourdes inspired other young French girls to see the Virgin, and the Gospa of Medjugorje provoked visions around the world, the Lady of the Rock and Maria Paula Acuña have prepared other Christians for mariophanies and other revelations. Witnesses' mimicry adds another link to what a French sociologist has called the "chain of memory and devotion."[1] The reproduction of visionaries has proved to be an extremely effective means of publicizing Marian apparitions and of authenticating seers and shrines. Maria Paula has led her dedicated witnesses into a closer relationship with the Mother of Christ by creating a ritual meeting place and teaching them how to discern genuine signs of the Virgin's presence. Maria Paula recognizes that her best recruits might challenge her authority, which is based on her exclusive relationship with the Lady of the Rock. In April of 2008, one of the crowd suddenly announced that God had spoken to her directly. "I come from God!" the other seer shouted. "So do I," snapped Maria Paula and then ordered the woman to pray the rosary and keep quiet.[2]

It is possible that one or two of the privileged few at Our Lady of the Rock could establish themselves elsewhere as the next Maria Paula. Like her, they may successfully link their visions to the historical chain of Christian revelations that began two thousand years ago, when Jesus and his mother were reportedly still alive. Or, despite pilgrims' loyalty to Maria Paula, one of her protégés could replace her as the most famous Marian visionary of the twenty-first-century Mojave.

Juan's Journey

Juan Rubio is one of the oldest witnesses at Our Lady of the Rock. Juan was in his nineties when we spoke with him in 2008. He was living by himself in a townhouse in Hemet, California, a mid-sized city (seventy-two thousand) whose population is one-third Latino/a. Hemet is about 150 miles southeast of California City, closer to Palm Springs than to Los Angeles. Juan's small home was crammed with memorabilia from a long life begun in Mexico, spent picking fruit in pre-casino Las Vegas, sleeping in migrant laborers' camps in Montana and Colorado, and later settling with his family in California. His wife died some time ago, after which he moved into an unassuming gated community.

Every horizontal space in Juan's home was covered with relics, not all of them religious. Assorted old-fashioned figurines adorned shelves and tables, along with tiny decorated dishes, bottles preserved from special occasions, and sundry mementos of various other kinds. He had a whimsical fondness for elephants. Tiny pachyderms of porcelain, stone, glass, and wood were poised to lumber around the room. Juan said that his daughter brings him another elephant every time she visits. On the walls hung photographs—not shots of animals or apparitions but formal portraits of men in stiff three-piece suits and ladies in dark dresses, with hair flawlessly piled atop their heads. Each image had been carefully hand-tinted so that subjects' cheeks and lips blushed. Juan took those photographs many decades ago when he owned a studio in Mexico. The portraits competed for wall space with framed newspaper articles, images of Mary and saints, and several broken clocks. In his bedroom Juan kept a small shrine dedicated to the Virgin. Behind his townhouse, next to the communal carport, was a patch of ground that Juan had claimed for a garden of flowers and vegetables. He often sat there and took photographs of the Virgin among the plants, he said.

We asked Juan how he came to Our Lady of the Rock. He was initially skeptical about visions and apparitions, he said. One day, about fifteen years before, he had watched an evening news report about Maria Paula Acuña. "When I seen the television, I say, Where is that? They say the place; I start to see her on television and then I go over there," he recalled. "I had to go see it to be sure that's true." He started taking pictures. With persistence, he found himself able—like a blind man healed by Jesus—to see the signs of God, the Virgin, and angelic emissaries. He learned to find personal messages in his photographs, which he explicated in an interview as he pointed to one photo after another from his substantial collection: "For me, yeah. For me it's Jesus but I don't know for another person. . . . To me that's Jesus and—before, I see Jesus in the little rocks in this one." He had critics. "Everybody say, ah, you're cuckoo."[3] But Juan knew better. Before long, fellow witnesses were asking him how to capture the Virgin Mary with a camera.

Then Juan told another, truer story about how he had learned to look the right way, beginning ninety years earlier in a small unnamed Mexican town. He told his tale with style and wit, switching easily between comic dialogue, dramatic moments of great danger, and scenes of deep spiritual meaning. He often shrugged as he segued from one bit to the next, as if ideas occurred randomly to him, but Juan had clearly recounted his history before. Obvious themes and motifs flowed through his stories. He talked a lot about traveling—riding in trucks, on buses, on a horse. He shaped his autobiography as a voyage from childhood to manhood, thence to old age, punctuated by heavenly interventions. When he began a response to a specific question, he sometimes paused to supply background so that we could properly appreciate the point he was about to make. Like a Bible scholar using Old Testament prophecies to advertise the Christian Messiah, Juan used events from early in his life to explicate events later in his life.

As a child, he was a regular churchgoer who first learned about Christ and the Virgin at weekly Mass. His town held an annual fiesta in honor of the Savior, to whom the local church was dedicated (as many are in Mexican towns). In this church, Juan had his first extraordinary sighting, although he did not appreciate it at the time. "I see the vision, I like it, but I know nothing," he explained. Not long after, he fell from a tree onto some river rocks. Residents from farms nearby found him badly mangled. A bone had punctured one of his internal organs. Someone went to town for help while the rest gathered around him on the riverbank, praying he would last long enough to be rescued. Juan recalled the arrival of a horse and rider and being hoisted onto the horse's back. He awoke later to see unfamiliar faces hovering over him. As a pharmacist tried to put him back together (they had no doctor in town), Juan prayed to another face—the one he had seen in church. His panicked mother made a vow to Jesus in exchange for Juan's survival. She promised to donate "a little face, silver or gold face" to the church. Juan laughed as he told the story and pointed to a framed newspaper article about his miraculous recovery that hung on his living room wall. "The picture's right there. . . . This is from our town. It says: remember." He added, "That place was full of *milagros*," meaning the tiny metal limbs, organs, and faces that pilgrims leave at the shrine in thanks for divine interventions, as his mother did.

Juan would not discuss his departure from Mexico, except to say that he left a career in professional photography because his eyesight went bad early in life. He picked up his story around 1950 when he traveled north with his uncles to find work in Las Vegas. Juan recalled the long bus ride over the mountains, past pine forests, and through tunnels. "Everything was beautiful," he reminisced. "I can get a job, yes—'we need people.' But I tried to rent a room—no! not in the hotels, no way to get it." Local employers were happy to offer low-paid work but would not allow Mexicans to stay in the hotels they helped build. For the next fifteen years, Juan slept with other migrant workers in tents and dormitories as he worked his way farther north. He chuckled when recollecting the irony of his own racial assumptions in those days. When he had jumped off the bus in Idaho, none of the local Anglos spoke Spanish, so he was delighted to spot some men with brown skin like his. Juan rushed over to greet them and asked where to find work. "Ay, Señor, donde está—?" he began. They turned out to be Native Americans who could not speak a word of Spanish.

Juan kept asking around until "a guy" offered him six months' work and a lift, then promptly hauled him off to jail in Walla Walla on a charge of illegal immigration. Juan spent six months in a cell listening to the nightly beating of other prisoners ("Waaaaaa! Waaaaa!") Like them, he lacked the money to pay bail and buy a bus ticket home. After his six months' sentence was over, he was freed and put on a truck back to Mexico. "What happened to me?" Juan pondered impassively as he reconsidered his story. He shrugged again and claimed, "I forget."

As if the years of field work and constant threats of deportation were not enough trouble, Juan survived two subsequent moments of peril. Some years later when he was living in the San Bernardino Valley, Juan checked into the hospital for minor surgery. He recalled waking up once more to find concerned faces peering down at him and voices discussing his condition, as if he could not see or hear. "In San Bernardino they opened my stomach," he explained. "They say I have five complications." He remembered being afraid when doctors and nurses touched him, because it was painful—they were "squishing" him. He realized that he was watching his own body lying on the operating table. "Oh, oh, what happened?" he had asked himself as he realized that the doctors were uncertain about what to do next. He too felt indecisive, wondering vaguely about whether to return to his body. He recovered. He did not dwell on the incident until years later, when he came across a television program about near-death experiences. "I see in the TV, the people tell themselves they come back. Aaah! That happened to me!" Juan believed his return to life was the second miracle of his life.

The third miracle, though, was of a different kind. By this time he was married. He arrived back in the Los Angeles area after working elsewhere, well aware that immigration authorities were on his trail. They had visited his house in San Bernardino and questioned his wife. Juan stayed away from the house, but the agents eventually caught up with him. Juan had little to say about his wife as rehearsed this part of the tale. He had told the INS that he was a "free" man and that he had abandoned his family to work far away from California. Immigration officers accused him of lying and insisted that he sign a confession to entering the United States illegally. Juan took on a carefree air as he performed this part of the narrative with the usual shrug, and he repeated what he had told the immigration men: "OK, bring me those papers and I sign it. I say, OK, send me to Mexico."

Instead, however, immigration officers sent him to jail again to await trial. Juan recounted a dramatic courtroom scene involving a lawyer who charged too much, a judge who turned mysteriously lenient, and a green card that finally granted Juan the right to remain in the States legally for as long as he wished. "That was a miracle," he declared. "I never pay attention, never," he admitted, but "now I believe." Juan had always trusted his quick wits and strong body to get him out of difficulties, but after three miracles and half a century of picaresque journeying, he finally grasped that the Blessed Mother and her son had been protecting him all along. He had been following a well-marked path through his life since the moment he first saw that celestial face in his parents' church.

In 2008, suffering prostate cancer and nearing the end of his journey, Juan saw heaven-sent signs everywhere. Over the previous fifteen years, his photographer's eye had learned to discern the Virgin's revelations in the mysterious blurs and flashes produced by his cameras. After personally investigating the Lady of the Rock and several other apparitions reported on TV, he had become an adept who trained others in handling a camera and explained how to interpret numinous images. He pulled out several albums, each packed with simple shots of the vision site, along with pictures taken in his garden, in front of his house, and among his rosebushes and trees. He had made many self-portraits too. "Look here, look here," he said, pointing to an image of the sanctuary at Our Lady of the Rock, "look there, over there. You see her?" His finger darted from image to image, finding a triangle of light in a water jug, a flash between shrubs, and sparkles in the leaves and on his own shirt collar. A close-up of his profile revealed Our Lady in his ear. One picture revealed three little Ladies floating around him. Every day, for years, Juan had been shooting dozens and dozens of photographs of the Virgin Mary. Sometimes, he told us, she paused only briefly; at other times, she perched on a twig or a wall for hours. Mary was a constant visual presence in Juan's life. Our Lady of the Rock was but one of the many Marys whose formal icons decorated his house.

October 12, 2011

Juan's autobiography actually consists of parallel lessons in learning to look the right way at the Virgin and her disguised signs. He rearranged the events of his long life into four chapters, three of them marked by miraculous rescues and the fourth by his new ability to envision the cause of his salvation. His picaresque journey from Mexico to Hemet was also a passage from innocence to enlightenment through a series of personal trials. At the same time, his story relates a continuing education in religious vision, which transformed him from ignorant observer to witness and from witness to bona fide visionary. We asked Juan whether he had shown his photos to Maria Paula or discussed his nonstop sightings of the Virgin with her. Juan chuckled when he replied, No, it would make Señora Acuña angry to know that he could see the Virgin too. Unlike Ray, who had accidentally confessed his sighting of the Lady as a whizzing ball of light, Juan kept quiet about his abilities. Like both Maria Paula and Ray, though, he was teaching others how to see. He, too, required witnesses who might discern and thus substantiate his visions. That is why Juan gave full approval for us to use his story in this book. He wants others to discover how to see the Lady in a leaf, a cloud, or an earlobe.

May 22, 2013

The Journey of Adelia

Adelia faithfully attended weekly Mass in Nicaragua, where she was born and lived until the early 1980s, but she never had a vision until she crossed the border between Mexico and southern California. Her husband had been a bank official in the late 1970s, when opponents of the dictator Anastasio Somoza Debayle overthrew the government in 1979. Adelia's family was not sympathetic to the Sandinistas (la Frente Sandinista de Liberación Nacional), who gained control of the country during the following years. At some point, Adelia's husband went to jail. She was living in the northern town of Somoto near the Honduran border by then, where she supported her two young sons by running a coffee shop. She spent a lot of time, though, scurrying from one government office to another, trying to persuade someone to free her husband. Thanks to a police officer who patronized her shop, Adelia was eventually able to liberate her husband and, with support from relatives, get him out of the country. He took their older son with him, while Adelia remained behind with the toddler. She saved money, applied for a passport and visa, and kept a low profile as she waited for a chance to follow.

Then came the "milagro in Mexico," Adelia told us, sitting in her tidy kitchen in California City in 2009. "Oh my God, I never figured out what happened to me; if I figured [it] out, believe me, I don't go." She got tired of waiting for a visa, so she left Nicaragua with her younger son and her passport, making her way to the Mexican border with Guatemala. She avoided the queue of non-Mexicans waiting to have their papers inspected and instead grabbed her son's hand and joined the Mexican nationals in another line. She told him to keep quiet, lest his accent betray them, and marched past the guards to Mexico. They eventually reached Tijuana, where Adelia telephoned her husband and arranged to send the boy northward with a female "coyote" who specialized in transporting children over the border.

Adelia was supposed to travel with another family and a different coyote to Los Angeles. She followed instructions, taking a taxi to a rendezvous point and waiting nervously as the coyote appeared, but the other family never arrived at the appointed meeting place. Adelia decided to travel alone with the irritable, desperate-looking young man who smelled of alcohol. They walked a long way in darkness. They had to clamber over a tall wire fence where Adelia almost sacrificed a shoe to Mexico—the coyote was annoyed when he had to go back for it. They sloshed through an arroyo, holding their clothes over their heads. Fortunately, when the coyote had ordered Adelia to strip, she had already hidden her cash in her underwear. The two dashed across a large paved space like an abandoned runway; Adelia's heels tapped noisily on the cement, which further angered her companion. Somehow, they ended up in a backyard in Imperial Beach, California.

With no clue about where she was, Adelia fended off the coyote's constant demands for more money. She asked him why they were hiding and where they would spend the night. He peered over a fence and found a mattress in the next yard—they would share it, he told her. Adelia watched him hop the fence and then plunged in the other direction. She had to telephone her husband to be picked up, but she had no idea how to use American pay phones. She had only "emergency English," as she called it. She wandered through the dark suburban streets, looking through windows where families sat contentedly watching television, and wondered what to do next.

Then, Adelia recalled, "I saw a big huge cross, and I said, oh that is one church, OK in the morning I go to the church and I talk to the priest and he has to help me." She sheltered in a doghouse until first light. When she emerged at dawn, though, she could not see the cross or find the church. She knocked on a random door to ask for directions but had trouble explaining her dilemma in English. The man who answered the door sent her to the nearest 7-Eleven shop, where there was a public telephone.

As Adelia recounted her harrowing adventures, she kept huddling and shivering at the memories. She still cannot explain how she managed to find her way on that dark night of the soul. She had no idea what a 7-Eleven was. She did not know what the cars of the immigration patrol looked like, which is why she entered the store to find two officers taking their break inside. And she still cannot understand why they paid no attention as she bought coffee and managed to use the public telephone to call her husband. He was at work; it was hours until she could call him again, so she sat on a bench outside the store and realized, "You know what? I need help."

At that moment, Adelia spotted a young couple on a motorcycle. She waved them down and spun a story in Spanglish about being dumped by a friend in Imperial Beach and needing to get home to L.A. The young man—an "angel," she called him—spoke no Spanish, but he took her home to his mother and explained, "Mom, a poor lady." Adelia interrupted herself at this point in the story to demand rhetorically, "Ask me, how I understand the whole conversation. I don't know." Her angel offered to take her on his motorcycle to Los Angeles, refusing her offers of compensation until Adelia finally forced a $100 bill on him to pay for gasoline. He paid for gas and returned every penny of the change. When they encountered a police roadblock, he chatted amiably with police until they were allowed to drive on. He safely delivered her to her husband and older son in Alhambra. Adelia stayed in touch with her hero and his mother for four or five years, she said. They exchanged small gifts and cards at Christmastime. "This was my history when I came here—and my son didn't show up," Adelia announced, referring to her younger child and thus finishing the first part of her life story with a cliffhanger.

Adelia was a patient interview subject, alternating her attention between her questioners, our video camera, and interior visions of her past. She grimaced as she explained how she had finally found her four-year-old, thanks to an extended network of friends, allies, and coyotes that spread from Somoto to South L.A. Adelia had been told that a contact would alert the family once the child made it safely out of Mexico. When the call came, Adelia's friends went to fetch the boy and found him bawling on a couch in a house where several men lay motionless on the floor. Her son, who is now in his late twenties, cannot remember the details, Adelia says, although in the early years of their new life he used beg to return to Nicaragua. He wanted to live in the grand house they had occupied in Somoto rather than the small place they rented in Los Angeles. He could not grasp that the old house had burned to the ground in the civil war. He had no recollection of wartime in Nicaragua.

As Adelia rehearsed her history, she occasionally gestured or laughed in disbelief at her own past. She shivered dramatically again and again. Her hands shook and her eyes teared. As she finished the tale of emigration, she gazed directly into the camera. She had later tried repeatedly to find the church in Imperial Beach, she said, along with the giant white cross that had revived hope during that terrible first night in America. "OK, where is the church?" she asked the camera. "No church—I asked. Where is the cross?" She never found it again. What had saved her that night if not the white cross? "It was my hope," she declared. "God loved me. Now I say it was my hope." It was also her first visionary experience. It changed her life; she realized that she needed very little to be happy. Clothes, jewelry, perfume, and all the other trappings of her comfortable past meant nothing to her now. "This is a milagro. That is God. My hope, my vision is for me today, how many years, continually asking myself, What is *that*? . . . Who I am for *that*? . . . Something happens when you have faith. That is my experience, my religion." As in Juan's case, her faith enabled her to travel on. Since then, when she feels sick, alone, or depressed—when her sons forget to telephone her—she reflects on her miraculous rescue and feels comforted by God's love.

Just as the Virgin had consoled Maria Paula Acuña during her daughter's illness and as the Virgin's son had thrice rescued Juan, miracles arrived in Adelia's life when she most needed them—not out of the blue, although God's plans remained mysterious to her, but because she was strong enough to seek help. Milagros were perfectly timed, even though they seemed to occur at the whim of negligent immigration officials or in night-time hallucinations. Adelia emphasized both her cunning determination—as when she defied border officers in Mexico and resisted the coyote's demands for money—and her hapless innocence—as when she lost a shoe in the flight to California, stumbled across the border patrol in the 7-Eleven, and guessed the meaning of English conversations. The episode of the white cross summed up both traits.

Adelia immediately grasped the significance of the symbol that shone in the night but only later recognized it as divine intervention. Her vision built on stories and images of other Christians in distress long, long ago. Crosses in the sky infiltrated Christian writing in late antiquity, when Emperor Constantine supposedly spotted one (a *chi-rho*) over the battlefield at Milvian Bridge. The same sign has guided many a convert and pilgrim along a lonely highway or barren desert and still pervades popular religious illustrations, greeting cards, and religious billboards. The glowing white cross is also a common feature in Polaroid photographs of visionary witnesses at Our Lady of the Rock, Conyers, Bayside, and elsewhere. Like Constantine, Adelia had made a vow when she spotted the heavenly sign; whereas the emperor had promised to convert to Christianity if his troops won the day, Adelia resolved to quit hiding and take charge of her own journey. The cross prefigured her later visions and signified her expanding faith. She was telling a parable for other life travelers who face trying times. Her personal metaphor—the illegal crossing of national borders—is especially appropriate for Christians of the twenty-first-century American Southwest.

The cross of hope prepared Adelia for her new life too. After she had rejoined her family, she went to work as a housecleaner; it is a career path dismally common among Spanish-speaking newcomers to Los Angeles, regardless of their education or skills. She developed chronic and debilitating back pain, however. She sought out a famous curandera at a botanica in East L.A., rising at 3:00 a.m. in order to get a place in line for that day's clinic. She had to lie on the floor in the waiting room because the pain of sitting was unbearable. The curandera could not help her, though. Meanwhile, a doctor friend urged Adelia to visit a woman who reputedly cured all sorts of ills and who also saw the Virgin Mary on the thirteenth of each month. At the time, Adelia thought her friend was crazy. But the pain finally drove her to Our Lady of the Rock, where she met Maria Paula Acuña. The visionary prayed and laid hands on Adelia's shoulder. The pain on one side of Adelia's back disappeared. After a second visit with Maria Paula, the other side was healed too. Yet Adelia did not grant all the credit to Maria Paula. "I think we have to prepare before," she reflected during the interview. "You have to open the door for the healing. I open, I say, 'forgive my sins, I will be better' . . . not physical, in the spirit. And, 'give me my healing, I need it,' . . . and I said 'thank you.'"

Adelia had been unable to walk until she met Maria Paula. In 2009, when we spoke, she was free of back trouble, although she had some pain in her hands and suffered chronic bronchitis. She had moved to California City shortly after meeting Maria Paula in order to be near the vision site. She lives alone, although her grown-up sons and her husband visit her. Adelia works part-time for an elders' social center and spends much of her free time in her garden. She is a thoughtful observer of the desert landscape. She keeps her camera handy to take pictures of whatever catches her eye—a lovely bird, her roses, the sunset. She was telling us about her garden and its animal visitors when she suddenly straightened in her chair and exclaimed, "Oh, I forgot, sorry, my mind!— another vision I have here was the beautiful Virgin de la Roca. Up there." She pointed to her roof. "Up there, five years ago exactly."

In 2004 Adelia had been cleaning her backyard on a windy, bright day when she noticed some extraordinary clouds. One was very bright, another very dark. In their midst, Adelia saw angels. She had shouted involuntarily, "Hey, somebody important up there!" but was glad that no neighbors were around to hear her. Yet a voice ordered her to look upward, and she felt as if someone was tipping her face up. "Ooooh," she half-moaned as she recounted the moment, "I see, my God, that was beautiful!" When we asked Adelia to describe more precisely what she saw that morning, she sighed and considered. "A lady, well, exactly de la Roca. Different to the Fátima, different to Lourdes," she responded. La Señora de la Roca had worn a white dress and veil and had gazed down on Adelia from a white cloud. The Lady was "big, like big, like a regular lady . . . you [could] see it, you don't need glasses, you don't need camera, you don't need nothing."

The Virgin was not smiling yet was not angry as she gazed directly into Adelia's eyes. Adelia recalled having goose bumps and joyfully weeping as she thought, "To me! You visit to *me*! Thank you!" Adelia asked the Virgin why she had brought her to California City. "I didn't get the answer yet," Adelia admitted. "For what reason she brings me in this town. What I had to do in this town. Something I had to do in this town. I don't know what."

At some point in the morning, as the Virgin continued to hover, Adelia remembered that she had left her camera by the bedside. She would have no visual proof of the apparition. Nonetheless, she continued praying on her knees beneath the floating Lady, pleading for every friend, relative, and worthy cause she could think of. Later, Adelia realized that the lady in the sky exactly resembled a statue of the Virgin that she had purchased in Los Angeles three years previously, which provided some kind of evidence at least. Adelia told her family what had happened. They know, she says, that she never lies, but they thought the apparition was an illusion, like the white cross. Still, her only friend in town, not a Catholic, had been excited and told her, "Adelia, oh, you're lucky!"

Adelia had not, however, told Maria Paula Acuña about the visitation. She made a face at the camera when she confessed this secret. "[Maria Paula] said, like two months ago, 'Nobody can see the Virgin Mary. Not everybody is ready to see the Virgin Mary.'" Maria Paula had advised witnesses that their souls were not ready for visions because of their many sins. Adelia had silently disagreed. She never showed her photographs to Maria Paula either because she had seen Maria Paula dismiss the photos of other pilgrims—the images did not reveal the same Virgin that Maria Paula knew so well. Adelia speculated about why the visionary encouraged photographs if she disdained them. Adelia thought Maria Paula was thinking scripturally. "Because other people, like Saint Thomas [the apostle], had to see it for belief. Probably." Witnesses required tangible proofs of divine presence, which they could study in order to realize what they themselves could not see.

When Adelia went to her first vision event in 2004, she had used her husband's camera to take pictures of the sky, as everyone else did. She left the film at a local Costco to be developed. Her husband was more eager than she to view the results. He nagged her to retrieve the photos. On March 12, Adelia's sister-in-law came to visit. She had been to the famous shrine of the apparition of Cuapa in Nicaragua. Her brother—Adelia's husband—was eager to show off his wife's pictures, despite his doubts about her visions. He ran out to get them. Adelia was cooking when he returned with the packet of prints, calling, "Hey, hey, look, look—Look what is here!" Adelia shrugged as she recalled the scene. "He was excited, he saw [it] first. He said, look at what you got!" Adelia's heart was open to all sorts of possibilities, but she had not been anticipating anything special in the images—or, if she was, that expectation had diminished by the time of her interview in light of later visionary experiences. "In my case," she told us, "that picture I took when I came [to Our Lady of the Rock], I don't believe it. But I saw that angel [in the garden]." Adelia had come to consider herself a different kind of seer than most pilgrims to Our Lady of the Rock. She regarded photography as a superficial technique for visionary work. "You don't need to open your heart [to] take a picture," she warned. "You don't need the camera for seeing that. You don't need it."

Still, Adelia has taken hundreds of photographs at Our Lady of the Rock, as well as around her home and on visits to shrines elsewhere. As she pulled out scrapbooks and boxes of her best shots, she reminisced about a week-long visit to Somoto, where she had lived for almost five years. Among the friends and family she left behind was Francisco Tercero, known more widely as Panchito. Panchito is a famous *vidente* who has been seeing the Virgin at Cacaulí, just outside Somoto, since 1989 when he was twelve years old. That was right around the time that Adelia left Nicaragua.[4] No one had believed him at first, Adelia told us. When the boy tried to describe the bright light and beautiful lady who had appeared to him, the new priest in town had humiliated Panchito in front of an entire congregation. He was a *communista*, Adelia said, sent by the government (presumably as part of the Sandinista literacy campaign of the 1980s). However, Adelia had urged a more conservative priest to work with the boy.

Panchito had confided in Adelia about the beautiful lady who appeared on the eighth of every month. The Virgin's choice of dates refers to her most important feast day in Nicaragua, the celebration of la Purísima, the Immaculate Conception of Mary, on December 8. It has been a major holiday in Nicaragua since the mid-nineteenth century when the Immaculate Conception became official church doctrine, partly in response to the popularity of Marian visionaries such as Bernadette Soubirous. Panchito told Adelia that the Lady appeared to be about fourteen years old and that "nobody can paint, nobody can describe how beautiful she is." She had appeared just two or three feet away from him. Her hair was medium brown, not blond, but so beautiful; her eyes were the clearest brown too. Adelia noted that another well-known Nicaraguan visionary named Bernardo Martínez, who saw the Virgin at Cuapa beginning in 1980, described her the same way.[5]

Rather than suspecting Panchito of imitating Martínez's vision, Adelia understood the identical descriptions of two different apparitions as proof that both were genuine. She also considered Panchito's visions in relation to those of Maria Paula Acuña. When Adelia had visited Somoto a few years previously, she had spent a day talking to the now adult vidente about apparitions and miracles. She happened to mention a medicinal plant that Maria Paula had recommended for back pain. Panchito revealed that the Virgin had told him about the very same plant but that he had not understood the Blessed Mother's purpose at the time. This apparent coincidence further strengthened Panchito's credibility, as well as that of Maria Paula, in Adelia's eyes. Panchito had no other motives for discussing that particular plant, according to Adelia, because he is an "innocent" like "the white, clear fish you can see through." This time she was the tutor, and the visionary Panchito was a student in the art of discernment.

However, Panchito tutored Adelia in a more nuanced reading of her photographs of apparitions, turning them this way and that in order to display hidden messages. She showed us a pair of photos snapped in Nicaragua, abstract images of swirling lights that, according to Panchito, meant that "God is so no-limited, unlimited . . . that is the fire." He explained the mechanics of apparitions on the basis of the Virgin's own words to him—something about how the Mother of God crossed long distances from heaven to earth in order to reach her devotees. "Like E.T.," Adelia told us. She admired Panchito for living ascetically in a tiny shack with a dirt floor and a hammock that served as both bed and sofa. Panchito's unworldliness reinforced his visionary credibility. When Adelia spoke of Maria Paula's financial situation and the Movement's purchase of property in the Mojave, she was more critical.

Panchito's words came back to Adelia when she reexamined her reasons for moving to California City and becoming a regular visitor to Our Lady of the Rock. Although she did not admit it until halfway through our interview, Adelia had discerned Maria Paula's spirits early in their relationship. When she heard Maria Paula's description of La Señora de la Roca, she wondered "about the eyes, did she see the eyes of the Virgin Mary, you're supposed to see the eyes, the color, the face." Having also experienced the gaze of the Virgin, Adelia believed it crucial to authentic vision. She knew why the Virgin arrived in the Mojave on the thirteenth of the month—Maria Paula also knows all about Fátima, she says. Still, when Adelia came to the desert shrine for the very first time, she felt genuine peace descend upon her. She had cried with relief. "If that's what you feel when you die, I'm ready to go," she told us. It felt like another place to her, like home, like Nicaragua.

Although Adelia still frequently attends the vision event and remains friendly with Maria Paula and the monjas, she keeps her distance. She disapproves of Maria Paula's encouragement of miraculous Polaroids. While she agrees with the Maria Paula that most witnesses are not ready to see for themselves, Adelia does not judge other pilgrims as sinners. Perhaps they are not sufficiently open to personal visions, she suggested in the interview. The labor of faith, exercised by free will, is far more crucial to Adelia's personal history than photographs of the sky, no matter what they capture. She told us about an Italian priest whom she had met in Los Angeles, who has been credited with miraculous healing. When Adelia showed him one of her photos of the Lady of the Rock, he declared that he did not need pictures to see. He had gone to watch the Virgin cry—probably in Sacramento, where a statue of the Virgin was reported to weep in 2009—but was not moved.[6]

Adelia also spoke wryly about Maria Paula's contests with local clergy. Panchito had problems with just one priest, who was, after all, a godless Sandinista—a Judas compared with the more traditional priest of Somoto, who supported his visions. Maria Paula often speaks negatively of priests, Adelia said. Roman Catholic priests never want to remain with Maria Paula, she added. The visionary and monjas quit attending Mass in California City because the former pastor forbade them from singing in the choir. Adelia laughed when she recalled their off-key voices. Maria Paula made excuses for poor attendance at Mass. "Adelia, the problem is I can't go to the church because I am busy," the visionary told her. She added that Maria Paula is often too unwell to attend church and the monjas have had problems of their own. "One Philippine, her mother is sick; the other one, something happened to the mama," Adelia reported, ticking off sisters on her fingers.

Adelia recalled the fake priests who appeared at Our Lady of the Rock. They said they had come to bless the foundations of the grotto some years back. Adelia has pictures to prove it. Maria Paula was initially taken in, but Adelia suspected them from the start. For one thing, their leader wore a big gold chain with an expensive cross hanging from it. His attendants were arrogant, "like [they] didn't want to touch anyone," she recalled. They refused to pray for witnesses. Adelia did some research online and found that the priests belonged to the Apostolic Catholic Church. She consulted Father Charlie, their pastor at Our Lady of Lourdes, who had explained that the major difference between that group and proper Catholics was the pope; only Roman Catholics are the true church because they have a pope. Father Charlie had come to visit Adelia at her request, to bless her house with holy water. He had admitted his own reservations about Maria Paula at the time. He believed that Maria Paula saw the Virgin, but he could not visit the vision site regularly because "the *obispo*, the bishop don't accept it. . . . If I go there, I have a lot of problems," he had confessed.

Ultimately Adelia decided that it did not matter whether priests believed in the pope or in Maria Paula, so long as they all honored the same God. Maria Paula had ordered Adelia not to visit the church of the false priests or attend their services. As Adelia pointed out, Maria Paula did not see the need for churches or priests of any kind. The visionary is suspicious of clergymen, and they doubt her. Maria Paula also rejected major points of modern Roman Catholic doctrine and practice. Despite recent Catholic reforms that permit women deacons, the visionary told Adelia, "You don't have to receive the Holy Communion when [a] woman gives it to you." Adelia witnessed an argument between the visionary and a pilgrim who was a deacon in her own congregation, where she helped to distribute the Eucharist during Mass. The deacon "probably never showed up again" at Our Lady of the Rock, Adelia concluded. Adelia did not reveal her own opinion about women distributing the Eucharist.

Since the Second Vatican Council, arguments about Communion liturgies have become flashpoints for a continuing debate between conservative and mainstream Catholics around the world. The followers of Marian visionaries tend to favor more traditional liturgies, such as the prohibition against laypeople's touching the Communion Host, in disobedience to the Vatican, bishops, and ordained priests. Maria Paula has several times reported the Virgin's plea never to accept the Eucharist by hand, which became common practice after Pope Paul VI permitted it in 1969.[7] The argument is not about ritual per se or about the worthiness of ordinary Christians to touch the wafer that becomes the body of Christ through a miracle of transubstantiation but about the role of ordained priests who act in place of Jesus during the Eucharistic sacrifice.[8] Maria Paula sees no irony in her support of clerical privilege; she has suggested that her visionary status renders priestly sacraments unnecessary for her. Once, Adelia told us, when the visionary was unable to attend Mass, Maria Paula had asked a monja to stay home with her. When the monja objected, "Madre, madre, I want to go to church!" Maria Paula announced that she would miraculously receive Holy Communion on behalf of her sister, right there at home. Adelia had apparently not heard the rumors that Maria Paula receives the Communion wafer from an angel.[9]

Adelia still cannot fathom why she ended up in California City or why she continues to visit Our Lady of the Rock despite her doubts. She acknowledges the visionary's healing ability, but she has seen Maria Paula and the monjas outside the desert sanctuary. Once she spotted them at the local shopping mall wearing street clothes rather than their stiff white habits, laughing, chatting, and shopping. Adelia has chauffeured them. Once she drove out to Maria Paula's house when the monjas had locked themselves out. Adelia gossips with the monjas at the vision site and speaks regularly to Maria Paula. She says that other witnesses are more gullible, though, about Maria Paula's claims because they are uneducated. "You and Matt," she told us in 2009, "you went to school, you know different." She thus positioned herself as an objective and sharp-sighted observer of the visionary, whereas less expert witnesses lacked the ability to see so clearly. "They believe in all sorts of visions," Adelia declared. Other pilgrims need a powerful prophet who looks and behaves a certain way, which apparently does not include visiting the shopping mall. "They don't want Maria Paula to get remarried, to have a husband. She has to look a certain way," Adelia pointed out.

According to her own life story, Adelia has learned better. She left a privileged life in Nicaragua and landed almost penniless in California. She has endured severe physical and emotional pain. However, with the help of the Virgin and a network of other believers, visionaries, and witnesses—including her husband, her neighbors, Panchito and Maria Paula, the sister-in-law who visited Cuapa, the monjas, Father Charlie, and the neighbor who congratulated her on seeing the Virgin—Adelia has progressed from needy pilgrim to confident visionary. Her direct encounter with the Lady of the Rock helped her assess Maria Paula's routines and pronouncements and, as a result, to make sense of her own visionary experiences. Adelia's neighbor Denise believed that the Holy Spirit informed Maria Paula but admitted to Adelia that she could not believe in Maria Paula. "I don't either," Adelia responded.

Carolina's Progress

Visionaries must imitate visionaries in order to be recognized and sanctioned. Witnesses require their mystics and prophets to appear and behave according to both historically informed and locally negotiated standards. Believers learn how to see for themselves by doing what visionaries do, repeating what they say, and looking like them. Although many witnesses claim to experience contact with the supernatural as a result of watching another visionary, few have both the skills and the opportunity to share a well-crafted narrative of their life's pilgrimage, as Juan and Adelia did in interviews. Carolina, another pilgrim to Our Lady of the Rock, is a young single mother who still wonders what to make of her flashbacks, visions, and the singular day that divine love blazed over her like a fallen sun.

Carolina's interviewer, Jake the budding filmmaker, had a different approach to pilgrims than Matt and I. Together with his cameraman and sometime interpreter, George, he met Carolina at the vision event in 2010 and subsequently visited her home several times in order to record conversations about her experiences. The two men also accompanied Carolina and her young son to the vision event at Our Lady of the Rock in February of 2011, where they filmed her conversations with Maria Paula Acuña as well as her reactions to the vision event. Carolina tried to recount her life story as a narrative structured around her increasingly meaningful visionary experiences. She was more forthright than Juan and Adelia about reinterpreting past events in light of her newly expanded view of the world around her, but unlike more seasoned pilgrims, she has not yet learned how to construe her life.

Carolina was not prepared for the Lady of the Rock. She claims that she was blatantly skeptical. She is a college-educated publicist who was considering law school when she met Maria Paula, whom she asked for help in choosing a career. Maria Paula had responded with "three key things" revealed by the Virgin. Whereas Juan presented his life as picaresque and Adelia punctuated her story with outbursts of memory, Carolina rehearsed her life as an outline for continuing study. While Jake interviewed her, she continuously debated with herself, using the same *sic-et-non* technique that medieval theologians employed to analyze difficult doctrinal problems. She would begin each segment of her story by gently, humorously criticizing gullible believers, then offer evidence of her own irrational responses to apparitions and the visionary, and would finish by trying to reconcile her conflicting impulses as faithful witness and rational observer. For instance, Carolina described witnesses at the Lady of the Rock who stared dumbly at the sky. "What are we supposed to be seeing?" she had asked herself on her first visit to the grotto. She had noticed that some pilgrims paid no attention to Maria Paula's summary of the Virgin's message. "Some people aren't listening, they're just taking pictures," Carolina had thought. She had reminded herself, "I believe without seeing." She had tried to think up provocative questions for Maria Paula, such as, "Will the Dalai Lama go to heaven?"

Carolina was born in Venezuela but grew up in Sweden, then Texas, and finally California. Her parents divorced when she was very young. Her mother then married a Swede, who moved his wife and her young children to his homeland. In her new bedroom, Carolina would pray every night for God to rescue her from the frozen North and take her back to Venezuela. She grew teary-eyed in the interview as she recounted her childish pleas. She used to envision a man listening to her prayers. The memory had surfaced only years later when she began to attend the vision event at Our Lady of the Rock; she had realized that the man was Christ. Yet she had repressed the scene for many years because the subject of Venezuela and her father had been taboo with her mother and stepfather. "That's how come I know that prayers are heard, because [the scene] got played back to me," she told Jake. The listening Christ had been her "vision, so to speak," she added. Yet at the time, all she knew was that no one was coming to rescue her from Scandinavia and return her to her beloved father and abuela.

The family moved to the United States when Carolina was a young teen. In a Texas high school, still struggling with English, she joined a Bible study group. She had no idea that the group was Protestant. She did not know what Protestantism was. The other girls had asked her why she worshipped statues. Carolina began asking herself the same thing and began to doubt the efficacy of prayer before images of the Virgin, saints, and Jesus. Carolina's family moved to California and she went to college but lost her student status and residency permit at graduation. Neither Venezuela nor Sweden was a desirable alternative to life in America.

Meanwhile, a friend of the family told her parents about a place in California City where the Blessed Mother appeared regularly. Carolina had heard similar claims about Medjugorje, "places in France," and Fátima. Her parents decided to attend the vision event but got lost en route, as many newcomers do. By coincidence, they stopped to ask directions at Maria Paula's house on the edge of town. They found the vision event and participated enthusiastically but did not see the Virgin or anything else remarkable. Still, they were eager to return the next month with their children. They began a campaign of friendly persuasion at the dinner table to which Carolina, her brother Jose, and her sister finally succumbed, but not before Carolina made her opinions clear. She told them, "If I could talk to someone who talked to the Virgin Mary, I'd have some major questions." Besides the fate of the Dalai Lama, she wanted to interrogate the visionary about the validity of Buddhism, events in her friends' lives—why was one of them hooked on meth?—what to do with her own life, why God permitted wars, and the secret of life. It was a long and impudent list.

Off they went to the desert on the next thirteenth. "You drive forever into the desert and about five hundred tumbleweeds later, you're there," Carolina said. She spent that first visit observing her parents among the crowd of "all kinds" of people: Hispanic, white, women wearing Chanel sunglasses, people with Polaroid cameras, everyone doing different things while Maria Paula saw the Virgin and then explained what the Lady had said. When the visionary repeated Mary's words, she spoke in the "sweetest voice," thanking pilgrims for coming to the shrine. However, Maria Paula had taken a melancholy tone as she pleaded with the crowd to follow Christ, remember to pray, to fast, and stay close to Jesus' heart. The world is painful, the Virgin had said through her interlocutor, but she would always be present among her children and would never leave them. Throughout the vision and sermon, Carolina kept an eye on the sky but saw nothing extraordinary. Some people pointed out crosses in the clouds. Carolina spotted a sunbeam but knew it was just "light refracting from a cloud."

Then she got the chance to meet Maria Paula. Jose went off to find water for the family and accidentally joined the wrong queue. He thought he was waiting for a turn at the faucet but ended up in line to speak with the visionary. When Carolina searched for her tardy brother, he suggested that she stay in line with him. Why not ask Maria Paula her questions? Carolina took the dare, although her doubts increased as she moved through the line. She heard others voicing far more desperate and personal questions about cancer or family problems. When she reached the sanctuary fence where Maria Paula and Thelma, notebook in hand, waited for her, Carolina found herself asking the visionary to ask God what she ought to do with her life. What was her true vocation? Should she go to law school? Maria Paula told her that "God allows [the Virgin] to come" to her and "knows what's in people's hearts." She would get back to Carolina, she added. Carolina left her name and telephone number, thinking "This is like 1–800-CALL GOD." It sounded too good to be true.

Carolina has an engaging screen presence and a dimpled smile. She speaks vivaciously with extravagant gestures, often laughing. In the video, she joked about herself and her brother, describing how their main goal during their first trip to the desert was to leave as quickly as possible and get back to L.A. in time to go dancing. However, a week after the vision event, she received a call from a member of the Marian Movement. At Maria Paula's request, Rolando offered to organize a cenacle on Carolina's behalf to help her solve her career problems. He suggested that she invite as many people as she could, especially other believers in need of healing. Jose thought the cenacle would be like a party with food and drink but also prayers and sick people. Carolina's mother was reluctant to get involved, though, so Carolina called the Marian Movement to cancel the cenacle. Maria Paula answered the phone herself and claimed to remember Carolina among the hundreds she had met on the previous thirteenth. "The girl with dimples," she said.

To ease Carolina's anxiety, Maria Paula described a typical cenacle. An assorted group of believers would gather in someone's living room, kneeling and praying the rosary. Maria Paula would move among them, touching each one, sometimes questioning him or answering queries. At the last cenacle she had conducted, Maria Paula told Carolina, a man knelt in the back of the room, crying. Maria Paula alone saw the light of the Holy Spirit shining down upon him. She envisioned the man's brother wrapped in a shroud. The Holy Spirit ordered Maria Paula to tell the man that his brother was fine. The Holy Spirit soothed that man's soul, Maria Paula told Carolina. The Holy Spirit was "very direct," the visionary said, "and the words come like a punch." The Spirit did not communicate directly with the mournful man, though, because anger and doubt had clouded his mind. Maria Paula had laid hands on the man's shoulders and prayed, "Lord help this one to remember that all of his loved ones are in your hands." The Virgin had been at the cenacle too. She and the Spirit hovered over a woman who appeared devout but whose heart the Spirit revealed to be "black and hard," full of "hatred and resentment from a divorce." The supernatural duo was unable to help the divorcee because she would not open herself to healing and love.

Despite Carolina's fascination with this scene, obvious in the minute details that she recalled in the interview, she had only agreed to go through with the cenacle when the visionary spoke directly to her own problems. The rest of that telephone conversation had been a dialogue between Maria Paula and Carolina's skeptical, wisecracking persona. The visionary told Carolina that she had a joyful spirit but felt a void in her life. Carolina wondered whether Maria Paul was like television psychics who can identify a certain demographic with predictable problems as potential clients. The visionary had then told her, "You know you need to forgive your father." Carolina was stunned. She remains certain that no one had revealed her personal past to Maria Paula before that day. Then the visionary asked her, "Do you mind if I pray over you?" At that moment, memories of her father and her bedroom in Venezuela washed over Carolina.

Surprisingly, she had little to tell about the cenacle that followed. However, she described subsequent visits to Our Lady of the Rock during the following months. She joined the crowd on July 24 for the annual hem touching too. Maria Paula stood in the middle of the sanctuary as usual, while Carolina hovered on the outskirts feeling hesitant yet joyful. The cenacle had shown her that Maria Paula might help her. At one point during events on the twenty-fourth, Maria Paula summoned Carolina into the sanctuary. Carolina was reluctant but also eager for a sign from the Virgin. She joined the visionary and monjas in front of the other pilgrims. Everyone was watching. She analyzed her own reactions even as her legs began shaking and her mind began to spin. Carolina realized that she was looking directly into the sun without feeling pain. She wondered whether other witnesses could do the same. She felt that she should tell them to try it.

Then Carolina experienced an overwhelming sense of God's majesty. She realized that she was alive only because God willed it. She felt utter awe as a voice commanded, "Carolina, speak." She felt that she must articulate her extraordinary sensations for the benefit of others, but the voice repeated its orders twice more before Carolina began to speak. She named every family member and friend she could remember, requesting prayers for each, while the sun began spinning faster and faster. Suddenly it whirled directly at her. She was terrified that the flames would consume her, yet at the same time she felt that if she could hold out for another second—just one more second—she would witness some marvelous "transformation." Then she fell to the ground. She noticed on the way down that none of the monjas were trying to dodge the sun.

That spectacle, Carolina explained in the interview, was a tiny hint of God's immense power. Maria Paula continued to converse with the Virgin Mary as Carolina lay on the ground. Carolina watched a rainbow spread above her—she cannot describe it, she said on the video. People patted her to make sure she was okay. "I had been touched in a way I can't describe, and then it was over," she concluded. Others asked her, "What did you see? Did you see her?" She still has no answer to that one. Nor had she decided about law school as of 2011. But she had begun attending the vision event regularly along with her parents. She now has a small son. She is one of many young mothers who struggle to shove a stroller over the uneven landscape of the Mojave as they process from Lincoln Boulevard to the sanctuary. She is also one of the intimate few who linger to chat with Maria Paula long after the others have packed up their tents and left the desert. Perhaps

Maria Paula has offered Carolina the career advice that she originally sought—although if the visionary expressed her opinion of working mothers, she probably told Carolina not to bother with law school. In 2010, Maria Paula admonished her followers, Carolina included, "Do not go around saying, 'Go, lazy wife, you should also search for work.' No, that, no. The mother stays at home with the children. That is the old-fashioned life. That is the right life."[10]

One of Jake's videos from that day in 2011 captured Carolina head-to-head with Maria Paula as they strolled out of the sanctuary together. The women did not reveal their private exchange to the men who watched and filmed them. Carolina has since lost interest in baring her soul to the student interviewer and his cameraman. George had begun to tease the two young people about budding romance. Carolina was already dismayed because she had found out that Jake is not a practicing Catholic. Jake left the desert to complete a senior honors project in religion, a short film entitled "Awe: The Spirituality of Science." After graduation, he visited the Dalai Lama and rode a motorcycle the entire length of India. Now he is pursuing a career in the film industry.

The One and the Many

Juan, Adelia, and Carolina are just three of the pilgrims to Our Lady of the Rock who have learned to see for themselves. Ray, too, has seen enough to offer lessons in looking to other eager listeners. Other pilgrims have enthused about their uncanny experiences to fellow witnesses, television crews, and interviewers, although not to Maria Paula. They have smelled roses where none grew. They have witnessed rains of light. They have felt a suffusion of divine love while they watched the sun dance. They have seen clouds take the shape of the Mother of God and have photographs to prove it. A few witnesses have reported phenomena far weirder, even in context of collective mariophany. In November of 2010, for instance, a woman in the crowd exclaimed, "I see her, I see her!" and then collapsed in the dirt shrieking, "Get it off my face! I can't breathe!" Some in the crowd speculated about demonic attack. Maria Paula dabbed the woman's face with consecrated oil to silence her.[11]

Maria Paula is still the only one who meets the Lady of the Rock at the grotto. The Virgin has never visited the desert shrine without the visionary—at least, no one else has publicly admitted to seeing a brightly shining Lady there. On days when either the Virgin or the visionary is delayed, everyone else waits. Pilgrims hopefully take pictures and mumble their rosaries but they do not feel the Lady's presence. On some vision days, Señora Acuña and the Lady of the Rock remained hidden for hours until the sun escaped its veil of clouds. "No veo nada," Maria Paula kept repeating on one vision day in 2009 until the early afternoon, when she knelt slowly in the dust to begin her dialogue with the Mother of God.[12] On other days, when Maria Paula was especially ill, the Virgin bided her time until the visionary was strong enough to begin the liturgy. At the twentieth anniversary celebration in 2010, the desert was finally beginning to cool a bit as evening arrived without a sign of Mary. Many pilgrims gave up and left for home. Adelia asked one of the monjas why the Virgin had not appeared. "Sometimes she doesn't come," the frowning sister answered. "They don't know if she will come," Adelia echoed. Yet everyone smiled a little later when Maria Paula finally gave a shout of welcome and the rituals began.

Pilgrims call her Madre Maria Paula because she cares for them with all the guilt-inducing love of a good mama and because this is the highest title that Catholic institutions will bestow upon religious women. Maria Paula wields as much authority as any abbess or abuela. Ray and Juan Rubio chuckle like bad boys when they tell their secrets behind Maria Paula's back. Adelia and Carolina seem more ambivalent about Madre Maria Paula's control of the visionary role. Yet none of these other seers have openly contested her authority or posed themselves as alternative leaders at Our Lady of the Rock. The crowd has watched silently when misguided pilgrims have performed their own epiphanies at the grotto and consequently drawn the wrath of Maria Paula.

The success of the vision event in the Mojave depends on a tricky combination of secrecy and advertisement. Maria Paula encourages her witnesses to examine the skies and tell what they see there, so long as it is not the beautiful, brilliantly shining Virgen de la Roca who has appeared to her for twenty years. Savvy witnesses learn how to exploit the sacral resources that Maria Paula makes available in the desert, but they do not expose their visionary progress to Maria Paula's discernment. Serious competition among seers would undermine the collaboration of visionary and witnesses. Everyone has a part in making this desert religion, but only one can play the visionary. The job of pilgrims is to attend, scrutinize, discern, witness, and commemorate. A few extraordinary pilgrims have also learned, by the grace of the Virgin and the model of Maria Paula, how to be visionaries, but they must seek their own wilderness and witnesses with whom to share their revelations.

Discernment at a Distance

Religious visions pervade the Internet, but information about la Virgen de la Roca and Maria Paula Acuña is hard to find. Professional reporters and videographers have helped spread the Lady's messages beyond the Mojave through the media of print and television, but only scantily and sporadically. The two *Los Angeles Times* articles of 1997 and 2008 have been republished on Marian-themed websites and discussion boards. Two television news reports from 2008 are available on YouTube, along with a bootleg video of Maria Paula's 2006 appearance on the now defunct *El Show de Cristina*. A couple of short documentaries floating around cyberspace mention Our Lady of the Rock. You have to know where to look, though. This particular Virgin is just as hard to see on the World Wide Web as she is in the desert.

Maria Paula does not have a website, nor does the Marian Movement of Southern California maintain an official Internet presence. The visionary and her followers are either unable or unwilling to join the global conversation about Marian apparitions and religious visions, so Our Lady of the Rock remains obscure to the mainstream of tuned-in, wired-up discerners of spirits. Internet viewers who stumble across references to the vision event frequently plead for more information. "Why is it so hard to find / no one gives directions?" asked one plaintive reader of the republished *Times* articles.[1] A fan of the *Cristina Show* begged on Univision's comment page, "Can someone PLEASE tell me EXACTLY where the Lady of the Rocks is? When you get to Mojave, which way do I go? Does someone know the exact location in Mojave, California, where the Virgin is? PLEASE answer me ASAP (as quickly as possible.)"[2]

Other visionaries, vision events, and apparitions are much better advertised and thus easier to investigate from afar. Several websites dedicated to the 1980 apparition at Cuapa, for example, feature lengthy descriptions of the visionary Panchito, a history of the apparition, precise directions to the vision locale, and schedules for anniversary observances.[3] However, American apparitions claim an outsized proportion of websites dedicated to ongoing and historical apparitions, most likely because more Americans have access to the latest technologies of witness and publication. The visions at Conyers, Bayside, Phoenix, and Scottsdale, along with the episcopally approved apparitions at Green Bay, are among the most visible.[4] New websites advertising previously unknown apparitions pop up all the time, often posted by local news stations, devotees, or amateur videographers. Still, the Internet also offers a platform for updates on continuing apparitions. For example, messages from Giana Talone-Sullivan, the Medjugorje-influenced visionary who began her career at Scottsdale and is now located at Emmitsburg, Maryland, are frequently published for all to read, despite the denunciation by Cardinal Keeler of Baltimore more than ten years ago. "Make No Mistake," the Emmitsburg website assures its viewers, "You have not reached this site by accident. You have been chosen to learn about the prophecies of Our Lady of Emmitsburg for a special reason."

Virtual and live witnessing operate on similar principles. Viewers assess the evidence for apparitions delivered by a website using the same criteria and methods that pilgrims deploy at a vision site and that a bishop uses to assess a potential prophet: Does she look and behave properly? Does she inspire trust? Does she say the right things? Of course, long-distance audiences miss the spontaneous, multisensory experience of a living event. The blinding light of the sun, the charisma of the visionary, and the emotional momentum of the crowd are unavailable to them. What is more, they cannot participate in the immediate negotiation of pilgrims and visionary. By the time they see the evidence for supernatural phenomena, it has already been examined and edited many times. The spirits have been discerned by those closer to the visionary and the event.

At the same time, the pressure to see what others can see is less intense when one is sitting solo before a computer screen. As reporters once did, stay-at-home witnesses choose whether or not to spread the news. If web users post comments on a site dedicated to apparitions or join a discussion list dedicated to religious visions, their contributions add to an already immense archive of visionary history. A long-distance witness also has more ready resources for discernment than those in the desert, who must rely on their memories of catechisms and statues to recognize legitimate visions and visionaries. Pilgrims who travel through cyberspace require training in complex iconographies to navigate the expanding available evidence for visions. They learn a slightly different idiom of discernment than eyewitnesses.

In fact, visionaries and apparitions have always depended on these two distinct communities of witnesses. A group of local believers who share the same visual environment and speak the same cultural dialect as the seer initially discerns the visionary's spirits and spreads word of an apparition. The historical importance of a vision event hinges, however, on whether someone conveys reports of the visions to a larger public. Both the New Testament and the many noncanonical Gospels still in existence today prove that it is has never been easy to break into visionary history. In the last few centuries, not only journalists but also publishers and civic and religious authorities had the power to approve or quash a locally popular vision event. Nowadays, a much larger audience of Internet users may publish reports and images of vision events to the world—or not. Marian apparitions spread more quickly and democratically with every cheap laptop and smart phone sold.[5]

At the same time, skeptics and outright unbelievers have joined the global discussion of apparitions too. Every web page chronicling Our Lady's latest appearance brings believers and their opponents together to consider the ancient problem of visionary credibility. Web-based discussions of apparitions unite people from the entire spectrum of religious belief, and from opposite ends of the earth, in the constant refinement of visionary models and techniques for discernment. To earn a place in history, visionaries and their Virgins now must first achieve collaboration with local witnesses and then undergo trial before this global court of inquisitors.

Maria Paula Acuña and the Marian Movement of Southern California have tried to avoid the whole project of discernment at a distance. They have escaped publicity and the scorn of unbelievers but at the cost of their proclaimed mission to form a worldwide following for the Lady of the Rock. Comparison with other Christian visionaries and their supporters reveals what is at stake. Some religious seers have won far-reaching fame and earned thousands of fans by taking advantage of new communications technologies and learning the digital lingua franca of Marian apparitions. Millions of supporters have flocked to multiple websites dedicated to the visions at Medjugorje; they send electronic donations, fight for Vatican approval of the visions, and presumably draw inspiration from stories and pictures of the six seers. Other contemporary visionaries, such as the Irishman Joe Coleman, have been effectively silenced by critical assessments spread on the Internet. Coleman began seeing the Virgin at various historic apparition sites in Ireland in 2007, but after his appearances on national television and radio, both official news media and private blogs turned against Joe. When he responded angrily to critics, his prophetic career effectively ended.[6] Joe Coleman should have kept one retrospective eye on Christian visionary tradition and the other on the ever-evolving tools of local and global discernment. It is clear that the immediate future of visionary history depends upon the ability of seers and their witnesses to exploit the latest technologies of looking and showing.

Moving Pictures

Still, a determined pilgrim can find a little information about Our Lady of the Rock online. In addition to archived newspaper and television news reports, several independent documentaries featuring the vision event in the Mojave are lurking on the World Wide Web. In 2007 *This American Life*, a short-lived television show, showed a report on quixotic religion in the western American deserts in which Our Lady of the Rock earned a few minutes of fame. The episode focuses on picture-taking pilgrims. "Once a month they come to the Mojave Desert and aim their cameras at the sun," intones the voice of Ira Glass, the show's host, in the opening sequence. "All the nice churches we built for God everywhere, and he and his messengers choose to reveal themselves out here, in exactly the place you'd want a roof over your head." Glass asks, "If God is everywhere . . . why do you need a picture?" One shot reveals Juan Rubio, our photographer friend, explaining a Polaroid picture for other pilgrims. Glass concludes that the point of the vision event "is to see Him [God] and feel something as a result," and that "blurry light" and "vast open spaces" are probably the best way to represent divinity. Maria Paula plays a nonspeaking role in a single scene. No one mentions the Virgin Mary.[7]

A documentary from 2006, *Desert Dreamers* by Frank Suffert, takes a similarly facile approach, treating the vision event as one example of re-enchantment played out at an exotic locale. The filmmaker claims that his work is "a portrait of the Mojave Desert's eccentric inhabitants who find happiness in following their dreams."[8] The film examines six different Dreamers who have sought refuge and blossomed oddly in the cruel desert: a Bottle-Tree Sculptor, Burlesque Dancer, Mountain Painter, UFO Site Caretaker, Doll Village Founder, and the Miracle Maker. About a quarter of the way into the film, Maria Paula appears facing the camera in full convent regalia to explain what the Mojave means to her: "The desert means to me it's a very wonderful place," she says, "where Jesus Christ walked in for fourteen years . . . for fourteen days . . . " She turns to Sister Thelma, who lurks in the background with two other monjas. "Forty?" she asks, "forty days!?" Thelma confirms it. "Maria Paula Acuña, Miracle Maker," flashes a title, before the camera shifts to the visionary hauling a large wooden cross, weighted by a concrete base, along Lincoln Boulevard while pilgrims sing hymns.

At least Suffert asked Maria Paula what she experienced every month. "I see the sky," she responds on camera. "I feel in my heart it's working. . . . I see a very thin white cloud. And then it's coming more and more close to me. I smell roses, I feel the fresh air, I hear the voice of the Blessed Mother. It's in front of me." Maria Paula's face fades out to be replaced by a three-quarter profile of the statue of the Lady of the Rock with a Polaroid-style sunburst crowning her head. Pilgrims pray in Spanish and describe their photographs, although the filmmaker interviewed only English-speaking witnesses. Maria Paula speaks English in the film, but other scenes have English subtitles.

Local news broadcasts about Our Lady of the Rock, like newspaper accounts, also focus on the pilgrims and the desert environment rather than the visionary or the Virgin. Although these reports identify the vision event as Catholic, they resist analysis of the witnesses' practices and beliefs. Maria Paula's dedication to the rosary, her homilies on the importance of the nuclear family, and her call for repentance are largely lost on reporters. The most sympathetic investigation of the vision event and its participants was a two-part news feature by Julio César Ortiz for the Univision network (Los Angeles Channel 34) in 2008. Ortiz is well known in television journalism circles in Mexico and the American Southwest for his award-winning stories about the plight of illegal immigrants to the United States and for his thoughtful examinations of borderlands culture.[9] In his reports,

Ortiz represents the pilgrims as desperate refugees with nowhere to go but the desert. The Lady of the Rock, like the Lady of Guadalupe, offers maternal care to her dispossessed children from Mexico. When the apparition occurs, Ortiz explains in his video, "the sweat, the anxiety and the fatigue evaporate like a drop of water on the sand . . . and the sick, the old, and young have converted into one single pair of eyes, one heart and soul under the feet of the Virgin." The reporter, a self-described "good Catholic," confesses in conclusion that he tried to take meaningful photos in the desert. Although "the pictures only showed the reflections of solar rays," he "discovered that faith continues there."[10]

The conventions of television and documentary journalism hampered Ortiz and other professional videographers. Neither filmmakers nor audiences have seemed able to capture Maria Paula's volatile character or the dense simultaneity of spiritual motives and activities on the thirteenth of each month. By comparison, several short videos created specifically for Internet audiences have emphasized the unfathomable mystery of the desert pilgrimage. Yet these interpretations also stereotype the visionary and also fail to recognize the collective work of discernment that sustains the vision event at Our Lady of the Rock. "Visions of Mary," a 2008 series of two brief videos, is a product of Paranormal TV, a web-based network that has also created such shows as "Voices from Beyond" and "Haunted Hillbillies."[11] The "Visions" series focuses on Acuña's putative healing powers rather than her Marian messages or pilgrims' devotions. Each of the two episodes (3.5 and 5.5 minutes, respectively) intersperses deep-voiced, omniscient narration with interviews of witnesses, some dubbed in English. The occasional cut to a Marian icon is shorthand for the pilgrims' orthodox adoration of the Virgin. Maria Paula is a silent secondary character in dramatic scenes of healing by the priest, Juan Santillan, inside his church. The two episodes reduce the complex aims of pilgrims as well as the visionary's fraught relationships with the clergy. In the second episode, as I mentioned previously, Santillan wears a condescending smile and voices doubts about the authenticity of Marian visions.

In all video reports of the vision event at Our Lady of the Rock, certain themes and images prevail. Videographers usually follow the testimonies of selected witnesses with an interview of one unusually fervent pilgrim. One such scene featured a woman complaining about gang-banging Satanists who sacrificed cats in her neighborhood; another featured witness recalled how Maria Paula helped her grandson rise from a wheelchair to walk.[12] Cameras love weeping witnesses overcome by devotion to the Virgin. Filmmakers frequently pan the crowd of working-class worshippers sheltering under colorful umbrellas and tents, thus juxtaposing pilgrims' ordinariness with their faith in supernatural experience. None of the films consider how pilgrims integrate their witnessing into their lives. No reporter has probed Maria Paula's origins or the Marian Movement's sources of funding. No one has investigated the group's relations with Catholic pastors and officials. Diocesan officials will not comment about the vision event in videos. Instead, the filmmakers rely on statues and portraits of the Virgin to suggest the vision community's connections to institutional Catholicism as well as their Marian-centric beliefs.[13]

In a similar way, both amateur and professional photographs of Our Lady of the Rock emphasize the emotional enthusiasm of the witnesses and their strange ritual of photographing of the sun rather than the visionary's character or performance. The pictures all look alike, whether they appear in print, on television, or social networking sites, such as Flickr and YouTube. Certain subjects and angles appeal to photographers of desert religion, whether believers or critics, and offer cues to viewers.[14] For example, almost all the photo collections include close-ups of Maria Paula speaking into her microphone. Her white habit suggests official religious status, while the microphone signals her leadership in a religious community that does not normally permit female preachers. Big skies feature prominently in the photographs. So do sun rays breaking through cloud formations, the giant metal cross looming at one side of the sanctuary, the chalk-white grotto, and the mournful face of the Lady's statue. Shots of the sun enhanced by lens flare and clever pictures of reflections in the grotto's windows hint at the elusive Mother of God and the pilgrims' attempts to see her. Images of weeping or rapt pilgrims suggest local, historical, emotional, and bodily centered ritual rather than institutional, universal, timeless, and interiorized religion.[15] The azure sky and golden desert lend vitality to repetitive images of pilgrims in prayer but also emphasize their isolation. This landscape is distant from urban turmoil, the pictures say. In this place, as Ortiz contends, everyone is united in scrutiny of the heavens.

The pictures are not critical of Maria Paula and the pilgrims, but they have not aided the Marian Movement's professed mission to spread the Virgin's message around the world. It doesn't help that Movement members are wary of photographers and reporters. Between late 2006 and late 2009, the only photographer greeted warmly by the Marian Movement was Matt Gainer. Matt won their confidence by repeatedly visiting the shrine and through his friendly exchanges with witnesses and Movement people. His images are informed by a growing familiarity with the vision event as well as his experience in chronicling grassroots political movements. Matt spent more than a year crouching before Maria Paula to shoot portraits and dashing around the sanctuary during visions before the visionary and her handlers elected to trust him. One day in 2007, Maria Paula blessed him in front of the whole crowd. The visionary suggested more than once that Matt should create a permanent visual record of the shrine and the apparitions on behalf of the Marian Movement. She has mugged for his camera.

Matt has not become the official photographer of the Movement, but he has struggled to picture religion and its makers authentically and empathetically. He learned to avoid rendering stereotypes of religion as he documented changes in the desert event over the years. Month after month, he compiled a thick description of the grotto and its community. Matt's images also reveal his shifting attitudes toward extraordinary religion in the desert. His earliest images of Maria Paula emphasized the seer's most human characteristics. He caught her grimaces of weariness and irritation. He documented the stock gestures of a faith healer as well as the visionary's hands reaching out to caress a child's cheek or accept donations from grateful pilgrims. The sky was enormous in photographs taken in 2006 and 2007, when Maria Paula loomed large in wide-angled shots from ground level. The visionary appeared to overwhelm her distracted and perplexed witnesses, who drifted in isolated groups of two or three looking in different directions. Among the several thousand images, the most sympathetic are close-ups of pilgrim faces suddenly still in ecstasy, concentration, or despair.

Lately, though, Matt has imposed more distance between his camera and its subjects. Now pilgrims stand farther away and their expressions are harder to read, as if an invisible barrier shields pilgrim consciousness and the deeper meaning of the monthly liturgies from any camera. The photographer seems to have realized that no visual technology can ever capture genuine religious experience—or, rather, that photographers can never completely escape the tropes of depicted religion. Like other witnesses, he can only retell the original story. Perhaps as a result, in the summer of 2011 Matt lost the visionary's approval. When he attended a vigil held on the night before the annual hem touching, members of the Movement warned him not to take any more pictures of Maria Paula. She was wearing civilian clothes that evening, rather than her usual white nun's habit, and had swathed her face in a dark shawl against desert winds. Matt watched her rake the sanctuary to prepare the grotto for the next day's liturgies. Maria Paula refused to speak to him. She had cautioned him before to be selective with his camera. No one has explained the reasons for the photographer's fall from grace, but I think he saw too much.

Sooner or later, Maria Paula turns against all reporters of her visions. In summer of 2009, the visionary told Jake Bloch that he would become the visual historian of the Mariano Army. She agreed to discuss the apparitions at Our Lady of the Rock in a video interview that the Movement would use to spread the Virgin's messages to the world. Jake agreed to Maria Paula's terms: the visionary would tell her story on camera in her own way, without prompting. Public showings of the work would be subject to her permission. In late 2010, Jake conducted an interview in Spanish of about eleven minutes. His cameraman, George, was present, along with Sister Thelma and a small audience of the visionary's helpers and pilgrims. With Maria Paula's approval, Jake also interviewed Sister Thelma and a member of the Marian Movement named Juan. Jake duly submitted a copy of his work to Maria Paula but has not yet gained her approval of his film.

Jake suspects that Maria Paula's distrust of public media may be causing the delay. A few months earlier, he had been filming on site when the visionary publicly denounced all videographers and news photographers. In previous sermons she had several times accused the news media and other unbelievers of trying to disprove the apparitions in the Mojave. On that particular day, she reviled filmmakers as "snakes" who misrepresented her and the Movement. It was an especially stinging insult, given the symbolism of the serpent in her accounts of the Lady's first appearance. One angry pilgrim immediately began to berate Jake and George, despite their protests that the visionary had invited them to film. In fact, the visionary had already promised Jake and George conditional salvation. The Virgin had revealed to Maria Paula that she would "rise to heaven" in

Mary's company, and, the visionary told Jake, "if God decides, it would be the greatest happiness for me . . . that many go with me, including the two of you."[16]

Maria Paula's unhappiness with professional observers results partly from her ambivalence about the technologies of deception. She longs to commemorate and monumentalize the vision event and her part in it. She speaks often and with conviction about her mission to spread the Virgin's words to sinners beyond the desert. Her goal, she says, is to "fix families." She feels "a desperation" to make "all the people of the world unite and see." God gave her "that grace to see: oh yes, I like this; oh no I do not like this, I am going to fix it." Unfortunately, though, the sinners of the world have donned blinders and refuse to hear the Virgin's pleas. "Mother," Maria Paula complained to the Lady on July 24 of 2010, "I have done what you ask, I have accomplished your request, Holy One, [but] I have not received a response from your children here on Earth. Holy Lord, make them respond to you."[17] It seems that Matt and Jake, along with all other reporters of words and images, have apparently not responded to Our Lady's requests either.

Maria Paula has often inveighed against the causes of spiritual blindness among the human population. She has denounced consumerism, drugs, alcohol, gang violence, the lure of sex, and Satan. Yet her deepest pain, she has declared, has come from the curse of modernism and its instruments of communication, including television, film, photography, and the Internet. She views these technologies, which expand human eyesight and facilitate the exchange of information, as dangerous when wielded by critics of apparitions. Bad pictures and false reports have prevented recruitment to Mary's cause. "There are many Mariano movements," she pointed out on the 2010 anniversary, which official Catholicism has consistently ignored. The cause, according to Maria Paula, is modernism. "If modernism has made them ignore the prayer of the Holy Rosary, each one of us must report our accountability to the Eternal Father," she announced that day. "I hope that the accountabilities are very good and clear for our salvation and the salvation of all of our brothers in the entire world."[18]

In Maria Paula's eyes, modernism is the culture of skepticism and its media, which has prevented the clergy from welcoming her as an authentic Christian visionary. Modern technologies have been unable to reveal what she sees. New modes of communication have kept Catholics from understanding and responding to the Virgin. Television, she has cautioned, is a weapon of government.[19] Computers, she has warned her audiences, are like drugs (*las drogas*) that divert believers from more virtuous pursuits.[20] Professional photographers and videographers have only made things worse by misrepresenting Our Lady of the Rock. Maria Paula continues to pray for all unbelievers, but she doubts that they can detach themselves from the visual wonders of secularized culture. "My obligation is to ask on my knees to Father God, Son God, Holy Spirit God that the faith grows in the entire world. That there be a lot of Mariano groups, not modernized." She prays for "all who are wrong . . . to repent and to be sweet with Father God, with Son God, and Holy Spirit God. Repent and you will enter through the door of heaven. May God bless all of them and also you," she declared in 2010, without specifying who, exactly, is *them* and who, by contrast, is *you*.[21]

No wonder, then, that the Marian Movement refuses to advertise the vision event except through the medium of human lips. Words on the handmade signs that mark Lincoln Boulevard remain misspelled, and directions to the grotto are still hard to come by. Given the superficiality of news reports and videos about the vision event, it is easy to see why Maria Paula might be discouraged by even modest publicity, why she has refused interviews, and why she is suspicious of photographers. Her resistance may seem ironic to outsiders, given that photography is the ritual technology of choice among her pilgrims, but both Maria Paula and her witnesses believe that cameras work correctly only when wielded by genuine believers who have practiced looking the right way through their lenses.

Nonetheless, without more pilgrims, and without reliable public records of Maria Paula's sermons and the vision events or news of the miracles that occur by the grace of Our Lady of the Rock, the shrine will probably not become a famous pilgrimage site. In 2007 a comment posted to the *Catholic Daily's* website included a link to the first *Los Angeles Times* article about the vision event in the Mojave. Readers of the article had never heard of Maria Paula and her apparitions, so they began wrangling over the authenticity of the visionary and her crowd. "I DON'T UNDERSTAND," lamented one perplexed commenter from Florida. "Is this supossed [sic] to be real or is it a movie or what. . . . It sounds like a copy cat of Medjugorje as the so-called visionaries seem to just be repeating the Medjugorje messages. . . . Does anyone know anything about this?"[22] A blogger called Mike responded, "I would tend to take it with a grain of salt, depending on who the L.A. visionaries are. It's a pretty well known fact that the Virgin Mary only appears to the poor. If these are L.A. or Beverly Hills people with tons of money, then it's likely a hoax."

These long-distance viewers doubted the quality of evidence before them. Commenting on an amateur video of the vision event, a blogger from Chino Hills added, "I can't be 100% sure but that looks like some independent filmmaker's attempt at making a 'mockumentary.' The 'visionaries' all have photogenic good looks and perfect makeup." A blogger called Observer agreed that "[The Virgin] has never, as far as I know, appeared to a wealthy or a middle class individual, which is why I tend to think that these L.A. apperitions [sic] are not authentic. That's not to say that there aren't poor people in L.A. but it sounds to me like these kids have pots full of money in addition to their photogenic good looks."

None of the discussants had visited the Mojave except one who announced that "the location where these visions took place is in the same general area (Mohave Desert) where I returned to the Lord. It's not far from Los Angeles. I don't think it's a coincidence that the Virgin Mary was seen there before the Lord came to me." Yet another participant, from Chicago, offered to investigate personally: "Next time I am in the area (I was there last week) I will go along to one of the apparitions if possible."

Without proof of the eyes or the opportunity to negotiate firsthand the meaning of Maria Paula's monthly visions, these witnesses from elsewhere had to rely on comparisons with more famous vision events and the typical attributes of reliable visionaries and witnesses. What little they knew about Californian visionaries came from an entertainment industry that often portrayed Los Angeles as a city of self-centered, decadent consumers interested in little besides movies, traffic, and drug gangs. Long-distance witnesses were apparently suspicious of the same news media that annoy Maria Paula, yet they relied on the conventions of that media to evaluate Maria Paula's apparitions. To the *Catholic Daily's* discussants, the Medjugorje visionaries looked more authentic than Maria Paula's pilgrims—even though the former have been widely criticized for their extravagant lifestyles and bourgeois aspirations, which followed their international fame. Unfortunately, no one from the Marian Movement joined the conversation to testify on behalf of Maria Paula and devout Angelenos.

Maria Paula Acuña has not directly addressed her failure to swell the ranks of the Virgin's army over the last twenty years. She sees it as a problem of insufficient faith rather inept advertising. She has repeatedly and pugnaciously challenged doubters. "What does everyone think?" she demanded one month in her sermon. "Do you think it is a lie that the Virgin descends to earth? Tell me, do you doubt it?" She warned skeptics with a probably unintended paraphrase of Pascal's famous dilemma: "If you continue not believing that the Mother of God comes to this place you will see the consequences at the time of death. We don't need proof that it's true or isn't true that the Mother is with us because we're going to feel her, she sends us to the other side, and Maria Paula doesn't want any of you to go to the wrong side."[23]

In Maria Paula's view, the burden of evangelization does not lie on visionaries such as herself but on self-identified Christians who turn off the screens through which they see but darkly. For their own sakes, pilgrims must journey to the desert and witness with their own eyes the Virgin's miraculous intervention in human affairs through the medium of Maria Paula. "Here you need no more than look to see if it is true or not true," she declared to witnesses, "what we are doing in the desert."[24]

Your Holy Mother and Jesus Are Real

The visual technologies that have opened our eyes to deep space and the bottom of oceans have not made it easier to see apparitions or clarified the task of discernment. More evidence about apparitions and visions circulates more rapidly now than in previous eras, but the accumulated data are neither more nor less trustworthy to Internet audiences than immediate sense perceptions at a vision site. In fact, the sheer quantity of messages from the Gospa of Medjugorje, all duly recorded and available online, has caused Vatican authorities to reinvestigate visionaries there. If more believers than ever before can now download the official catechism of Catholicism, more of them can also devour news of bleeding statues, stigmata, and Virgins in tree stumps. Only some of these data gain meaning, however, in the negotiations of visually savvy, long-distance witnesses. They face the age-old task of reviewing visual evidence to discern the truth of an exclusive theophany, made more difficult by editorial impositions specific to the new media of communicating visions.

Remote audiences pose a threat to religious visionaries and local witnesses, in the same way that the most skilled witnesses challenge established seers. Enhanced skills of discernment also enable viewers to criticize or discredit false seers. Yet if reports of a vision do not escape the immediate community and reach the larger discriminating public, then the revelations will be lost. History will lack precious details about the Virgin's continuing interventions in human affairs. A lesson in discernment will not be taught, and a model for determining visionary authenticity will disappear without anyone's noticing. Eventually the visionary herself or himself will disappear, witnesses will forget what they saw, and the grotto will crumble into the desert.

The mutual dependence of visionary and both groups of witnesses has become more fraught recently, but not only because of the dismaying quantity of evidence available. Visions are increasingly harder to parse and negotiate for a couple of reasons. First, the distance between local seers and remote witnesses has grown as large as the world itself. Translating the personal vision of one seer into the visual and spoken babel of diverse discerners is far more complicated than it used to be. This does not mean, as some have argued, that the negotiation of visionary authenticity has become private or routinized, since new communications technologies have brought with them fresh ways of articulating and evaluating visionary experience.[25] But each time a visionary experience moves from one medium of communication to another, it loses some of the immediate details that may help prove its authenticity. The terms for its evaluation are necessarily more general than in local discernment. In public discussion, standards of visionary authenticity are shifting to accommodate this broader purview.

One good example is the case of the visionary from Batavia, Ohio, whose sightings of the Virgin have been published electronically by a group called the Ministries of Light. She was one of several people who first saw Mary hovering over a Kentucky field in 1991. The Virgin urged her to reveal the vision to a priest, but the seer had initially balked. "Let me tell you," she explains ruefully on the website, "if you are ever faced with the dilemma of approaching a priest and telling him that the Blessed Virgin sent you to him, then you will understand the inner conflict I experienced."[26] After more urging from Mary and her son, the visionary eventually solicited the help of local priests and began organizing "public manifestations" of the Virgin at the church of one of the priests in Kentucky. The little group gained followers and allied with other Marian organizations, including the local Gospa prayer group dedicated to apparitions at Medjugorje. They established the Our Lady of Light Foundation and Ministries and began raising money, eventually purchasing several properties and constructing the Our Lady of the Holy Spirit Center at an abandoned seminary complex. The visionary, who still remains anonymous, has published five volumes of messages from the Virgin and Jesus, a selection of which appears on the ministries' friendly website. On the same site readers may study the full history of the Batavia visionary, buy her books, and consult a Q&A page where she answers basic questions about visions and apparitions such as these: How do you see Our Lady? How do you know these visions are of God and not the devil? How do you know which messages are personal (for you only) and which are for all?[27] Her answers, along with all the other useful evidence on the website, comprise a primer for aspiring visionaries.

Unlike Maria Paula Acuña, the anonymous Batavian does not claim leadership of her movement or assert control over her own legend. She has not taken orders or donned a nun's habit. She received her visions in private and, at Mary's command, kept some messages to herself until ordered to reveal them at the appropriate moment to priests at the ministries. In 2004, however, the visionary received her last message from the Lady of the Light, which directly pertained to the process of communicating revelations in modern times: "Your written work for me is now completed. I thank you for the sacrifice of your time and for saying 'yes' to my call. I now request that you retreat from the public view as much as possible. In private works I ask that you continue to lead others to Jesus with my hand to guide you."[28]

The ministries' website continues to advertise the visionary's alliance with clergy and guarantees her authenticity, based on the premise that no fewer than five priests have discerned and approved the website's published contents. One sign of negotiations between the seer and her witnesses is the visionary's admission of occasional doctrinal errors committed unintentionally over the thirteen years of relaying the Virgin's dicta.[29] The apparitions of Our Lady of Light have not gained official diocesan approval, but no religious authority has officially condemned the Ministries of Light or challenged its financial activities, as was the case with the Marian Movement and Maria Paula Acuña. The visionary's collaborative openness to questions and reprimand has won her approval from local and long-distance witnesses as well as ordained confessors and donors. Unlike Maria Paula, the Batavia visionary did not set clergy against loyal witnesses when confronting the Catholic leadership's wariness about Marian visions. She learned how to influence the process of discernment as early as November of 1991, when she related the following message from Mary, later published online: "To the Priests: I wish all priests to realize that your Holy Mother and Jesus are real. We are not some mystical ghosts or spirit forms in some far-off place. We are here among you, and we are real! Portray this to the people in your charge."[30]

"We are here among you, and we are real!" This is the gist of every visionary's message to immediate witnesses, who then pass the news to family and friends, who relay it to other, more remote audiences. This is the same biblical claim made by apostolic visionaries, potentially available to all Jesus followers. The Batavian did not claim exclusive enlightenment but instead revealed her understanding of modern discernment and the Virgin's role in the process. The ministries' website reinforces this apparitional reality by emphasizing the Virgin's words rather than the visionary's authority, especially the

Virgin's correction of the seer's errors. The humble assertion of orthodoxy is a powerful argument. In a similar way, a website devoted to the infamous apparitions at Bayside, New York, features a cheerful photo of Pope Benedict XVI in his many-tiered papal miter, along with the image of a monstrance displaying the Communion host, clearly calculated to suggest Vatican approval of the visionary, Veronica Leuken. It takes some hunting around the site to learn that Leuken's visions were actually denounced by the bishop of Brooklyn in 1986, nine years before she died in 1995.[31] Only a link tucked into one corner of the Bayside site's main page reveals the continuing battle between Leuken's followers and local church officials—the link leads to an article entitled "Very Few Clergy Will Make It to Heaven: They Have Too Much to Answer For."[32]

Discernment at a distance is like standing at the back of the crowd on a windy day, unable to see or hear much of what is going on in the sanctuary, depending on snatched glances and relayed whispers for clues. As strangers linked only by Marian devotion and the Internet, viewers interact with apparition websites in order to evaluate visionaries whom they may never meet in person. They refine their understanding of the Virgin Mary's appearances, her purposes, and proofs of her interventions, conscious that others around the Catholic world are doing the same and hoping that they make the right judgment. Just as visionaries teach and inspire new visionaries, websites about Marian apparitions inspire additional long-distance discernment. The Internet draws users into an expansive conversation about Christian revelatory heritage. "After all," wrote the webmaster of the Ministries of Light, "since loving Our Lord and Our Lady is a duty for us all, we believers all are responsible for helping one another along the way. And what better way to do that than bringing information to you, the visitor?"[33] The Internet has directly fueled the visionary perception of thousands, maybe millions, of viewers, whose discernment at a distance informs discernment at actual vision sites. The discerners of Christian vision are taking their refined methods for interpreting Marian apparitions back to Bayside, Batavia, the Mojave, and all the other places where apparitions occur. Those who fail to learn the new *sacra lingua* will not be able to participate in the continuing negotiation of visionary authenticity.

Conclusion

The *Longue Durée* of Christian Religious Vision

Religious visionaries are as numerous and various as the stars in the sky and the sands on the shore. Recent studies of Marian apparitions have emphasized the ways that each particular group of witnesses develops its own collective imaginary, or justification for a vision event, which is responsive to local events, shared histories and politics and, especially, the group's relations with local religious authorities.[1] From this perspective, witnesses to Marian visions and apparitions seem to be seeking alternatives to the Catholic Church and its ordained leaders. Faith leaders, as well as social scientists and journalists who write about historical and contemporary Christianities, used to believe that extrainstitutional religious experience reflected religious or political dissent or signaled deeply rooted spiritual dissatisfaction. In other words, since the Catholic leadership systematically refuses to approve Marian apparitions, visionaries and their witnesses must always be at odds with official religion, even when their visionary practices and messages promote Catholic orthodoxy.

Yet the tension between ordained clergy and ordinary believers is ancient. Although visions occur in historically specific and local idioms, visionaries and prophets have always caused trouble for larger society, as Hebrew and Christian scriptures attest. Visionaries must always be recognizable members of their faith tradition but different enough from other seers to gain a following. They must resemble historical prophets and invoke earlier revelations yet never so closely that they seem merely imitative rather than inspired. What a quandary the rabbi, prophet, and Savior Jesus created for his followers when, according to Gospel writers, he walked the earth among living men and women. He looked like an ordinary human and yet, as witnesses to his resurrection learned, he was God. His return to life brought an end to perceptible reality. Ever since then, Christian believers have been forced to do what no human can: choose to disregard their most important sense, eyesight, and try to focus on the unseen. If they are successful, they face the impossible task of conveying their inexpressible vision to other people. Others must determine the truth of what they themselves cannot see or know. This is what Christians call a mystery.

As the crowds at Our Lady of the Rock—and at Knock, Batavia, Conyers, Bayside, Medjugorje, Cuapa, and all the known vision sites, old and ancient—have repeatedly demonstrated, even the faithful have good reasons for doubting visions, apparitions, and revelations. Jesus followers have been arguing among themselves about the possibility of personal revelation and its most reliable forms ever since stories about Christ's resurrection first circulated. Saint Paul, who wrote the earliest lines of the New Testament, was also the first Christian author to express ambivalence about visionaries and prophets. His report on the Jesus follower "caught up" to heaven remains a paradigm for Christian visionary experience, while his suspicion of visions echoes through the works of other Gospel writers, theologians, ecclesiastical bureaucrats, and priestly leaders of all subsequent centuries.

Saint Augustine of Hippo considered the problem of vision and its proofs more than three centuries after Paul, just before the year 400 CE. The bishop wrote a treatise on the topic of Christian faith in an invisible, heavenly reality created by God and made available to humankind through Jesus' self-sacrifice. Augustine entitled his treatise *De fide rerum quæ non videntur* or *Faith in Things Unseen*. This was the same Augustine—bishop, memoirist, and eventual Doctor of the Church—who systematically categorized the three major ways of religious looking, creating the template for revelation still promoted by Catholic leaders today. The lowest form of looking, Augustine argued, is human eyesight; memory and imagination of religious phenomena are higher forms of vision, but direct experience of the divine, undetectable by the human senses, is the most rare and exalted. The bishop of Hippo acknowledged, though, that respectable people of the fourth century typically laughed at believers in Christian visions for their reliance on a hidden God.

Yet, Augustine demanded of vision's critics, who does not believe in some things despite not being able to see them? What about friendship or parental affection? One cannot see these things, yet one experiences them and believes in their existence. "What is as naked, as clear, as certain to the inner eyes of our minds," he demanded, as love? No one can actually see love, only its visible clues. The material world offers proof for this particular form of the invisible. Hence, Augustine concluded, we need only examine visible clues from Nature to prove the resurrection of Christ and the salvation that awaits all true believers. "For if the things that you see have been foretold long before, and have obviously come to pass; if a truth is obvious because of events that preceded it and resulted from it—O unbelieving stragglers!—then you may believe in things that you cannot see, and blush at what you do see."[2] For Augustine, it followed that even those who have not experienced authentic religious visions may logically choose to believe in them.

This is exactly what visionaries and their witnesses around the Catholic world believe and practice to this day. At Our Lady of the Rock, pilgrims gather together and learn how to look. They have negotiated a *modus credendi* in response to a self-identified visionary's assertions of Marian apparitions. They have met Maria Paula Acuña's claims by recalling the sights of their own personal histories. They have negotiated a common visionary heritage, enriched by individual memories, shared adventures in popular visual culture, the available scientific data, the latest news, cutting-edge communications technologies, and every other tool they can lay their hands on, in order to scrutinize the heavens and the desert for signs of divinity. They expect rewards for their efforts, just as they hope for a better life, a healthier body, and a just society, along with a thousand other things that they can visualize but do not yet enjoy. They do not wait passively for heaven's graces, though. They work hard to see better, see more, and see more accurately by journeying together into the deserts of religion.

They practice discernment in order to get better at it. Believers in religious visions will not accept just any old apparition proposed by an unexpected seer. As they have learned to look for signs of heaven, they have also absorbed the lessons of other witnesses to visions and apparitions. Witnesses seek definitions of visionary authenticity from the faith's long history of revelation. They refer to iconographies of orthodox apparitions and case studies of popularly approved visionaries. They examine each vision event in light of previous visions and the visions to come. They consider the effects of each apparition, determining whether other pilgrims' reports of better health or improved lives result from a particular visionary's encounter with the Virgin and the Blessed Mother's consequent pleas to her heavenly Son or whether good fortune has arrived for other reasons. They scrutinize personal collections for evidence of divine presence and intent. At Our Lady of the Rock, pilgrims rely primarily on photographs of the skies; at other vision events, witnesses examine bleeding or weeping icons, written locutions, or stigmata. Still others discern the authenticity of apparitions and revelations with research in the archives of cyberspace.

Despite an occasional tussle between Maria Paula Acuña and her witnesses, their disagreements about how and where to look for heavenly signs are usually easily resolved. The vision community in the Mojave has created a reliable set of intelligible signs of divinity. In the desert, everyone quickly begins to speak in the same visual language, and they are always ready to renegotiate the terms of revelation in order to maintain a rudimentary consensus. Witnesses who decide to see for themselves—such as Juan, Carolina, and Adelia—must also choose whether to speak of new kinds of seeing, keep quiet, or leave the group. There is no doubt that the great majority of Christian visionaries at vision sites across history have done the latter. Countless seers will never face the ridicule of outsiders or rejection by other believers. Nor will those silent seers enter the canon of Christian visionary history, as Maria Paula still hopes to do. No one will lose or profit by what unrecognized prophets think they may have seen.

Religious vision exists only in the difficult negotiation carried on by those who can see with those who cannot. No one has ever claimed that Christian revelation should be left to God. Besides intercessors, such as the Blessed Mother, the saints, angels, and other spirits and signs, genuine Christian epiphany also involves volatile, impermanent, flawed humans. To put it in Augustinian terms, revelation results from a combination of grace and free will: the divine grace that opens human eyes to Christian ways of looking and a believer's decision to accept the perceived illogic of Jesus' resurrection. This revelation was handed down from Christ to apostles and Gospelists, thence to converts and catechumens in one century after another. Each generation of Christian visionaries and witnesses adds additional bits of evidence to that history for the discernment of future generations. The argument between Christian visionaries and their institutional leaders has kept their shared faith tradition vital, in all its global historical variety, for two millennia and counting. The complex relationship of preachers, theologians, visionaries, witnesses, and skeptics enables each cohort of Christians to reinvent its religion all over again—if not forever, then at least until the Savior returns or the Virgin appears once more.

The proliferation of Marian apparitions over the last almost-two centuries reveals another mystery of religion: humans make it every day, whether they realize it or not. They make it with whatever tools and technologies they command, based on whatever liturgies and iconographies they like. Despite the fact that American religion typically hides under the roofs of churches, temples, mosques, and shrines, our daily environments remain littered with the detritus of historic faith traditions. Like it or not, religion is built into the shape and traffic of supposedly secularized cities, governments, and societies. Beliefs and rituals mark our landscapes. Wherever we go, we accumulate bits of religions and carry them like lint in our pockets. Cues to religious ways of looking turn up in greeting cards for sale in the drugstore and the foods we put on our holiday tables, jokes told in television comedies, and the speeches of politicians. Our calendar, our constitution, and our public architecture recall liturgies of the believing past. Universities, scholarly research, and critical analysis—even the very idea of interpreting a speech or text or image for more than one meaning—come from originally religious ways of examining sacred scriptures and objects. The sciences that we sometimes wield to discredit religious visions, apparitions, and prophecies are descended from much older methods for analyzing the relation of human consciousness to nature and divinity. Faith and religious custom drive our lives, regardless of whether that faith and custom belong to us or to others.

The popularity of Catholic visionaries and Marian apparitions in the last sixty years is thus nothing especially new. The ubiquitous presence of the Virgin in news media and cyberspace signals no religious revival or worldwide re-enchantment. Nor are visions and apparitions necessarily specific to particular groups disgruntled by modernism, secularism, or any other seismic shift in human perspectives. Marian apparitions are simply religion taking place and capturing attention as usual. Christians have maintained their faith in personal revelation not despite, but in company with, competing theories about the discernment of material and cosmic realities. All of us, Christians or not, constantly assess alternative ways of looking at these shared realities. For help in the daily business of looking, we all rely on some mix of personal perception, effects of local visual environments, historical conditions, and negotiations with fellow viewers.

As Maria Paula and her witnesses know, believers cannot reveal all that their wandering eyes capture. Humans cannot adequately report theophanies for the simple reason that they are humans and whatever they recognize as theophany comes, by definition, from beyond the bounds of humanity. If they can easily explain the experience, they have not seen anything godlike. For more centuries than Christianity has been around, philosophers have wrangled over the limits of human senses to grasp and convey realities, but no philosophers, scientists, physicians, or faith leaders—from any faith or cultural tradition—have invented a universal mode of expressing divinity. Nor has anyone dreamed up a foolproof method for seeing what anyone else sees. This is the religious visionary's dilemma: revelation cannot be, yet must be, shared so that others may empathize, mimic, and commemorate it, and sometimes dismiss it.

As biologists will tell you, it is almost impossible to deny the evidence of the eyes when supported by other sense perceptions. A congregation of witnesses is like a single mind unwilling to deny its visionary's eyes. Witnesses at Our Lady of the Rock might disagree about what the visionary sees or complain of some collective ocular trouble, but given the basic revelatory premise—and promise—of historical Christianity, most of them figure that Maria Paula probably sees the Blessed Virgin Mary in the Mojave Desert. They inherited this view from parents, grandparents, and more distant ancestors, who got it from older, earlier Christians. They practice looking as best they can in whatever country, congregation, or desert they may inhabit. Sometimes they look like Catholics, sometimes more like Angelenos, Mexicans, foreigners, scientists, or citizens of modernity. To some, they probably look like heretics or lunatics. But they try always and everywhere to look like Christians.

Notes

Preface

1 Carla Hall and Paula Bryant Pratt, "Waiting for Mary," *Los Angeles Times*, February 16, 1997, http://articles.latimes.com/1997–02–16/news/mn-29383_1_virgin-mary.

2 Gastón Espinosa and Mario T. García, ed., *Mexican American Religions: Spirituality, Activism, and Culture* (Durham: Duke University Press, 2008), 41–42.

3 Courtney Bender, *The New Metaphysicals: Spirituality and the American Religious Imagination* (Chicago: University of Chicago Press, 2010), esp. 1–7, 56–74.

4 Paul Vanderwood, "Religion: Official, Popular, and Otherwise," *Mexican Studies/Estudios Mexicanos* 16 (2000): 414.

5 As just two examples: Clarissa Pinkola Estés, "I Am Your Mother," *U.S. Catholic* 67 (2002): 16–19; Beverly Donofrio, *Looking for Mary (or, The Blessed Mother and Me)* (New York: Viking Compass, 2000).

6 Jennifer Scheper Hughes, *The Biography of a Mexican Crucifix: Lived Religion and Local Faith from the Conquest to the Present* (Oxford: Oxford University Press, 2010), ix.

1. Déjà Vu

1 L. Roure, "Visions and Apparitions," in *The Catholic Encyclopedia* (New York: Robert Appleton, 1910), New Advent, http://www.newadvent.org/cathen/15477a.htm.

2 As the anthropologist Paolo Apolito points out, it is difficult to "write in a way that is at once conditional and yet lively, methodologically cautious while literarily engaging." *The Internet and the Madonna: Religious Visionary Experience on the Web* (Chicago: University of Chicago Press, 1995), 20. Like Apolito, I have chosen to use direct, indicative forms, such as "she sees" or "she saw," rather than qualified constructions, such as "she claims to have seen." I treat Maria Paula Acuña, as her witnesses do, as a religious visionary.

3 Barbie Zelizer, "The Voice of the Visual in Memory," in *Framing Public Memory*, ed. Kendall R. Phillips (Tuscaloosa: University of Alabama Press, 2004), 157–86; David Morgan, *Visual Piety: A History and Theory of Popular Religious Images* (Berkeley: University of California Press, 1998), esp. 140–43.

4 Colleen McDannell, *Material Christianity: Religion and Popular Culture in America* (New Haven: Yale University Press, 1995), esp. 1–66; Stewart M. Hoover, "Visual Religion in Media Culture," in *The Visual Culture of American Religions*, ed. David Morgan and Sally M. Promey (Berkeley: University of California Press, 2001), 146–59; Marita Sturken and Lisa Cartwright, *Practices of Looking: An Introduction to Visual Culture* (Oxford: Oxford University Press, 2001), 21–42 passim.

5 For example: Our Loving Mother's Foundation of Hollywood, Inc., "Miraculous Photos," http://www.lovingmother.org/MiraculousPhotoPages/PhotosPage1.htm; Latinaxpert, "Miracles of Apparitions in Conyers," http://www.youtube.com/watch?v=sbdJMBPkloE; Visions of Jesus Christ.com, "Photos of Door to Heaven . . . Photos Kindly Shared from Visionaries [*sic*] Private Collection," http://www.visionsofjesuschrist.com/weeping135.htm.

6 Pew Forum on Religion and Public Life, "A Portrait of American Catholics on the Eve of Pope Benedict's Visit to the U.S.," http://pewforum.org/Christian/Catholic/A-Portrait-of-American-Catholics-on-the-Eve-of-Pope-Benedicts-Visit-to-the-US-%282%29.aspx; Pew Forum on Religion & Public Life/U.S. Religious Landscape Survey, "Summary of Key Findings," http://religions.pewforum.org/pdf/report2religious-landscape-study-key-findings.pdf.

7 Among many related scholarly assessments of Guadalupan literacy: Jeanette Rodriguez, *Our Lady of Guadalupe: Faith and Empowerment among Mexican-American Women* (Austin: University of Texas Press, 1994), esp. xxvii–xxx; Timothy Matovina, *Guadalupe and Her Faithful: Latino Catholics in San Antonio, from Colonial Origins to the Present* (Baltimore: Johns Hopkins University Press, 2005); Luis D. León, *La Llorona's Children: Religion, Life, and Death in the U.S.-Mexican Borderlands* (Berkeley: University of California Press, 2004). All three emphasize the role of collective memory, or history, in Latino/a religions.

8 Easily available online, too, via simple Google search or links from Wikipedia (in multiple languages), e.g., http://es.wikipedia.org/wiki/Apariciones_marianas; also links listed on popular Catholic websites such as EWTN (Catholic television network website), http://www.ewtn.com/spanish/Maria/advocaciones_marianas.htm.

9 Robert A. Orsi, "The Many Names of the Mother of God," in *Between Heaven and Earth: The Religious Worlds People Make and the Scholars Who Study Them* (Princeton: Princeton University Press, 2005), 48–72.

10 Catechism of the Catholic Church, http://www.vatican.va/archive/ccc_css/archive/catechism/p122a3p2.htm#II ; Council of Ephesus, *Epistle of Celestine*, cap. 4, in *Patrologiae Cursus Completus: Series Latina*, ed. J-P. Migne (Paris, 1844), vol. 50, col. 505; http://www.tertullian.org/fathers2/NPNF2-14/Npnf2-14-77.htm#P4464_849311; Jaroslav Pelikan, *The Christian Tradition: A History of the Development of Doctrine*, vol. 1, *The Emergence of the Catholic Tradition (100–600)* (Chicago: University of Chicago Press, 1971), 261.

11 Pius IX, Apostolic Constitution *Ineffabilis Deus* (1854), *Pii IX Pontificis Maximi Acta. Pars prima*, (Rome 1854), 597, http://www.intratext.com/IXT/ITA0483/_INDEX.HTM.

12 Catechism, cap. 507; Pope Paul VI, Dogmatic Constitution of the Church, *Lumen gentium* (November 21, 1964), http://www.vatican.va/archive/hist_councils/ii_vatican_council/documents/vat-ii_const_19641121_lumen-gentium_en.html, 64; cf. cap. 63.

13 Pope Benedict XV, Apostolic Letter *Inter soldalica*, *Acta Apostolicae Sedis* 10 (1918): 181, http://www.vatican.va/archive/aas/documents/AAS%2010%20%5B1918%5D%20-%20ocr.pdf; *Vox Populi Mariae Mediatrici*, http://www.fifthmariandogma.com; "Address of John Paul II to the Plenary Session of the Congregation for the Clergy," November 23, 2001, http://www.vatican.va/roman_curia/congregations/cclergy/documents/rc_con_cclergy_doc_20020804_istruzione-presbitero_en.html.

14 *Lumen gentium*, esp. cap. 62; Lawrence Cunningham, "The Virgin Mary," in *From Trent to Vatican II: Historical and Theological Investigations*, ed. Raymond Bulman and Frederick Parrella (Oxford: Oxford University Press, 2006), 179–92.

15 Father Gerard Mura, "The Third Secret of Fatima: Has It Been Completely Revealed?," *Catholic*, March 2002, http://www.devilsfinalbattle.com/content2.htm; Antonio Socci, "Who Between—You and Me—Is Deliberately Lying?" *Libero*, May 12, 2007 (Milan, Italy); see English translation at http://www.fatima.org/news/newsviews/052907socci.asp.

16 Joseph Cardinal Ratzinger, Prefect of the Congregation for the Doctrine of the Faith, *The Message of Fatima*, "Theological Commentary," http://www.vatican.va/roman_curia/congregations/cfaith/documents/

rc_con_cfaith_doc_20000626_message-fatima_en.html.

17 W. Fanning, "Confraternity (Sodality)," in *The Catholic Encyclopedia* (New York: Robert Appleton, 1908), New Advent, http://www.newadvent.org/cathen/04223a.htm; David Blackbourn, "The Catholic Church in Europe since the French Revolution," *Comparative Studies in Society and History* 33, no. 4 (October 1991): 778–90; William D. Dinges, "'An Army of Youth': The Sodality Movement and the Practice of Apostolic Mission," *U.S. Catholic Historian* 19, no. 3 (Summer 2001): 35–49; Sisters of Mary, Mother of the Church, "Sodality," http://www.sistersofmary-motherofthechurch.org.

18 Paul Allatson and Laura Gutiérrez, *Key Terms in Latino/a Cultural and Literary Studies* (Oxford: Blackwell, 2006), 154–55; Rodriguez, *Our Lady of Guadalupe*; Evelyn P. Stevens, "Marianismo: The Other Face of Machismo in Latin America," in *Female and Male in Latin America*, ed. Ann Pescatelo (Pittsburgh: University of Pittsburgh Press, 1973), 89–102.

19 Donald Calloway, *The Virgin Mary and Theology of the Body* (Stockbridge, MA: Marian Press, 2005); Clarissa Pinkola Estés, *Untie the Strong Woman: Blessed Mother's Immaculate Love for the Wild Soul* (Boulder, CO: Sounds True, Inc., 2007).

20 Catholic.net, "Worldwide Cardinal-Bishop Petition for the Proclamation of a Marian Dogma,"http://www.catholic.net/index.php?option=dedestaca&id=224; http://www.fifthmariandogma.com.

21 "Pope Benedict: 'We Learn to Live from Mary': The Holy Father's General Audience on the Feast of the Queenship of Mary, Aug. 22," EWTN News/CNA, August 22, 2012, http://www.ncregister.com/daily-news/pope-benedict-we-learn-to-live-from-mary.

22 Catechism, cap. 487.

23 Deirdre Joy Good, "The Miriamic Secret," in *Mariam, the Magdalen, and the Mother*, ed. Deirdre Joy Good (Bloomington: Indiana University Press, 2005), 3–24.

24 John 19:25, 20:1–18; Luke 8:2; Mark 16:9; Luke 10:38–42; John 12:1–8.

25 Luke 1:26–38.

26 John 2:1.

27 John 19:25.

28 Karen L. King, trans., *The Gospel of Mary of Magdala: Jesus and the First Woman Apostle* (Santa Rosa, CA: Polebridge Press, 2003).

29 Luke 7; John 11–12.

30 Giacomo Ricci and Giuseppe Santarelli, *Virginis Mariae Loretae Historia* (Loreto, Italy: Congregazione universale della Santa Casa, 1987).

31 Bart D. Ehrman, *Lost Scriptures: Books That Did Not Make It into the New Testament* (New York: Oxford University Press, 2003), 63–72.

32 Rev. 12:1.

33 *Beatus of Liébana* (ca.940), Pierpont Morgan Library, MS M. 644, fol. 152v, http://corsair.themorgan.org/cgi-bin/Pwebrecon.cgi?vi=1&ti=1,1&Search_Arg=644%2C%20fol.%2015 2v&Search_Code=GKEY^&CNT=50&PID=5SFWcOxofRrxK4qab8F_UCGM3kyM&SEQ=20140508233718&SID=1.

34 Hilda C. Graef, *Mary: A History of Doctrine and Devotion* (New York: Sheed and Ward, 1963), 31–36.

35 Averil Cameron, "The Virgin in Late Antiquity," in *The Church and Mary: Papers Read at the 2001 Summer Meeting and the 2002 Winter Meeting of the Ecclesiastical History Society*, ed. R. N. Swanson (Woodbridge, UK: Boydell Press, 2004), 1–21; D. F. Wright, "From God-Bearer to Mother of God," in ibid., 22–30.

36 Miri Rubin, *Mother of God: A History of the Virgin Mary* (New Haven: Yale University Press, 2009), 100–118; André Jean Marie Hamon, *Notre-Dame de France ou Histoire du culte de la Sainte Vierge en France: Depuis l'origine du christianisme jusqu'à nos jours*, vol. 4, *Comprenant l'histoire du culte de la Sainte Vierge*

dans les provinces ecclésiastiques de Bordeaux, Tours et Rennes (Paris: Plon, 1864), 247–50.

37 Graef, *Mary*, 103–6.

38 Stephen J. Shoemaker, *Ancient Traditions of the Virgin Mary's Dormition and Assumption* (Oxford: Oxford University Press, 2002); Pope Pius XII, *Munificentissimus Deus* (1950), http://www.vatican.va/holy_father/pius_xii/apost_constitutions/documents/hf_p-xii_apc_19501101_munificentissimus-deus_en.html; Rubin, *Mother of God*, 55–57, 97.

39 Thomas Aquinas, "Commentary on the Angelic Salutation," and "Commentaries on Sacred Scripture," in *Thomas Aquinas: Selected Works*, ed. Ralph McInerney (New York, NY: Penguin Books, 1998), sec. 33; Aquinas, *De commendatione sacrae Scripturae* in *Opuscula theologica*, ed. Raimondo A. Verardo, Raimondo M. Spiazzi, and Mannes M. Calcaterra (Turin: Marietti, 1954), vol. 1, 441-443.

40 See Hans Belting's masterful analysis of icons and their powers, *Likeness and Presence: A History of the Image before the Era of Art* (Chicago: University of Chicago Press, 1994), especially the introduction, 1–16.

41 Ibid., 495–96.

42 Rubin, *Mother of God*, 126–27, 135–36 passim.

43 Margaret R. Miles, "Santa Maria Maggiore's Fifth-Century Mosaics: Triumphal Christianity and the Jews," *Harvard Theological Review* 86 (1993): 157–59; Mariano Armellini, *Le Chiese di Roma dal secolo IV al XIX*, 2nd ed. (Rome: Vatican, 1891), 229–30; William Dunn Macray, *Chronicon abbatiae de Evesham: Ad annum 1418* (London: Roll Series, 1863), 9; William Dugdale et al., *Monasticon anglicanum: A History of the Abbies and Other Monasteries, Hospitals, Frieries, and Cathedral and Collegiate Churches, with Their Dependencies, in England and Wales: Also of All Such Scotch, Irish, and French Monasteries, as Were in Any Manner Connected with Religious Houses in England* (London: Longman, Hurst, Rees, Orme & Brown, 1817–30), 2:16; Michael Lapidge, *Byrhtferth of Ramsey: The Lives of St Oswald and St Ecgwine* (Oxford: Clarendon Press, 2009), 246–51; *The Victoria History of the Counties of England: Worcestershire* (Folkstone, UK: Dawsons of Pall Mall for the University of London, Institute of Historical Research, 1971), 112–13.

44 William A. Christian, *Visionaries: The Spanish Republic and the Reign of Christ* (Berkeley: University of California Press, 1996), 4–5; Christian, *Local Religion in Sixteenth-Century Spain* (Princeton, NJ: Princeton University Press, 1981), 7–105.

45 Yves Chiron, *Enquête sur les apparitions de la Vierge* (Paris: Perrin, 1995), 18–48; Peter Heintz, *A Guide to Apparitions of Our Blessed Virgin Mary* (Sacramento, CA: Gabriel Press, 1995), li–liv; Angelo de Santi, "Litany of Loreto," in *The Catholic Encyclopedia*, vol. 9 (New York: Robert Appleton Company, 1910), New Advent, http://www.newadvent.org/cathen/09287a.htm.

46 Among other works, see Virgilio Elizondo, *La Morenita: Evangelizer of the Americas* (San Antonio: Mexican American Cultural Center, 1994); Stafford Poole, *Our Lady of Guadalupe: The Origins and Sources of a Mexican National Symbol, 1531–1797* (Tucson: University of Arizona Press, 1995); Louise Burkhardt, *Before Guadalupe: The Virgin Mary in Early Colonial Nahuatl Literature* (Albany: SUNY Press, 2001); Miguel León-Portillo, *Tonantzin Guadalupe: Pensamiento náhuatl y mensaje crisitiano en el "Nicuan mompohua"* (Mexico City: El Colegio Nacional, 2000); Davíd Carrasco, *Religions of Mesoamerica: Cosmovision and Ceremonial Centers* (San Francisco: Harpers, 1990); Ana Castillo, ed., *Goddess of the Americas: Writings on the Virgin of Guadalupe* (New York: Riverhead, 1996).

47 Linda B. Hall, *Mary, Mother and Warrior: The Virgin in Spain and the Americas* (Austin: University of Texas Press, 2004).

48 See http://www.saintemarieamongthehurons.on.ca/sm/en/Home/index.htm.

49 See http://www.shrineofourladyofgoodhelp.com.

50 Florent E. Fanke, *Six Thousand Titles for Our Lady*, originally printed for private distribution (Webster Groves, Missouri), now online as "Titles of the Blessed Virgin Mary," http://saints.sqpn.com/titles-of-the-blessed-virgin-mary; Rogelio Zelada and Agustín Román, *Las Imágenes de Jesús y María en Hispanoamérica* (Washington, DC: Instituto Nacional Hispano de Liturgia, n.d.).

51 *Lumen gentium*, cap. 8.4.66.

52 *Lumen gentium*, cap. 2.12.

53 Carol Glatz, "Misreading of Vatican II Led to 'Collapse' in Marian Devotion, Studies," Catholic News Service, September 7, 2012, http://www.catholicnews.com/data/stories/cns/1203755.htm.

54 See http://www.nationalgallery.org.uk/paintings/leonardo-da-vinci-the-virgin-of-the-rocks; http://www.louvre.fr/oeuvre-notices/la-vierge-aux-rochers.

55 Lisa Bitel field notes, December 13, 2009; *Acta Apostolicae Sedis* 37 (1945), 264–67, http://www.vatican.va/holy_father/pius_xii/speeches/1945/documents/hf_p-xii_spe_19451012_Guadalupe-mexico_sp.html#_edn. See also John XXIII, *Acta Apostolicae Sedis* 62 (1970), 681–683.

56 Lisa Bitel field notes, May 13, 2010.

57 Ana E. Ruiz, "Milagros de nuestra senora del desierto de mojave," 18 September 2010, http://youtu.be/PqChokLv1hY.

58 Adelia, interview by Lisa Bitel and Matt Gainer, August 18, 2010; Lisa Bitel field notes, May 13, 2007.

59 On apparitions at Phoenix and Scottsdale—which differ from each other as well as from devotions at California City in significant ways—see Kristy Nabhan-Warren, *The Virgin of El Barrio: Marian Apparitions, Catholic Evangelizing, and Mexican American Activism* (New York: NYU Press, 2005).

60 Heintz, *Guide to Apparitions*, xliii–xlviii; see also René Laurentin and Patrick Sbalchiero, *Dictionnaire des "apparitions" de la Vierge Marie: Inventaire des origines à nos jours: Méthodologie, bilan interdisciplinaire, prospective* (Paris: Fayard, 2007).

61 Charles Le Brun, "Blessed Jean Eudes," *The Catholic Encyclopedia* (New York: Robert Appleton, 1909), New Advent, http://www.newadvent.org/cathen/05596a.htm.

62 Marian Movement of Southern California, *Our Lady of the Rocks* (brochure, n.d.).

63 Gary Nougues, "Our Lady of Perpetual Apparitions," *Prism* 1 (Fall 1997), http://archive.today/cMsJJ.

64 Carla Hall and Paula Bryant Pratt, "Waiting for Mary," *Los Angeles Times*, February 16, 1997, http://articles.latimes.com/1997–02–16/news/mn-29383_1_virgin-mary.

65 Matt Gainer field notes, June 13, 2006.

66 Michel Pastoureau, *Blue: The History of a Color* (Princeton, NJ: Princeton University Press, 2001), 50–55.

67 William A. Christian, *Apparitions in Late Medieval and Renaissance Spain* (Princeton, NJ: Princeton University Press, 1981), 201–03.

68 *Nican Mopohua*, ed. Antonio Valeriano (México: Centro de Estudios Guadalupanos, 1989), secs. 8–20.

69 Hall, *Mary, Mother and Warrior*, 108–37, esp. 135–37, and related notes.

70 Rodrigo Martínez Baracs, *La secuencia tlaxcalteca: Orígenes del culto a Nuestra Señora de Ocotlán* (Mexico City: INAH, 2000); Davíd Carrasco, "Cuando Dios y Usted Quiere: Latina/o Studies between Religious Powers and Social Thought," in *A Companion to Latina/o Studies*, ed. Juan Flores and Renato Rosaldo (Malden, MA: Blackwell, 2007), 61–67.

71 Heintz, *Guide to Apparitions*, 405.

72 Sandra Zimdars-Swartz, *Encountering Mary: From La Salette to Medjugorje* (Princeton, NJ: Princeton University Press, 1991), 80–81, 125.

73 Ruth Harris, *Lourdes: Body and Spirit in the Secular Age* (New York: Viking, 1999), 78–82.

74 Heintz, *Guide to Apparitions*, 2, 23.

75 Ibid., 2, 102, 132, 152, 161, 200, 217, 309, 353, 284–85, 576, 601.

76 Ibid., 276–77.

77 Apolito, *Internet and the Madonna*, 52–53, 121–30.

78 Christian, *Apparitions*, esp. pp. 188–203.

79 Eugene Hynes, *Knock: The Virgin's Apparition in Nineteenth-Century Ireland* (Cork, Ire.: Cork University Press, 2008), 211–14.

80 "The Horitz Passion Play," *New York Times*, November 23, 1897; Pamela Grace, *The Religious Film: Christianity and the Hagiopic* (Malden, MA: Wiley-Blackwell, 2009), 17–19; Moisés Viñas, *Índice general del cine mexicano* (México City: CONACULTA, 2005).

81 *The Song of Bernadette*, directed by Henry King (Twentieth Century Fox, 1943)

82 William A. Christian Jr., "The Eyes of the Beholders: Systematic Variation in Visions of the Christ of Limpias in Northern Spain, 1919–1936," in *The "Vision Thing": Studying Divine Intervention*, ed. William A. Christian Jr. and Gábor Klaniczay, Workshop Series 18 (Budapest: Collegium Budapest, 2009), 65–81, esp. 68–69.

83 Sherry Velasco, "The Transverberation Scene in Four Films Featuring the Life of Saint Teresa of Avila," *Critical Commons Web*, September 24, 2009, http://criticalcommons.org/Members/svelasco/lectures/the-transverberation-scene-in-four-films-featuring-the-life-of-saint-teresa-of-avila-by-sherry-velasco.

84 See, for example, the animation at *Insigne y Nacional Basilica de Santa Maria de Guadalupe* (2011), http://www.virgendegualupe.org.mx/apariciones/multimedia/apariciones1.htm.

85 Blog posted by ildi, November 2, 2009, in response to Ed Brayton, "I'm Breathless with Anticipation," *ScienceBlogs*, November 1, 2009, http://scienceblogs.com/dispatches/2009/11/im_breathless_with_anticipatio.php.

86 Jerry Saltz, "Chris Ofili Africanizes an Icon," *Village Voice*, October 5, 1999.

87 Karen Mary Davalos, *Yolanda M. López* (Los Angeles: UCLA Chicano Studies Research Center Press, 2008); Alicia Gaspar de Alba and Alma López, *Our Lady of Controversy: Alma Lopez's "Irreverent Apparition"* (Austin: University of Texas Press, 2011); Renee Cox, http://www.reneecox.org.

88 Alex Dobuzinskis, "Nude Virgin Mary Cover Prompts Playboy Apology," Reuters, December 15, 2008, http://www.reuters.com/article/2008/12/15/us-playboy-idUSTRE4BE54F20081215.

89 Davalos, *Yolanda M. López*.

90 Orsi, "Many Names," 64.

91 Apolito, *Internet and the Madonna*, 22–36.

2. The Desert Is Wide

1 KTLA News, "Virgin Mary Sightings Draw Believers to SoCal Desert," KTLA News, May 13, 2008, http://ktla.com/news/ktla-virgin-mary-kern,0,4856534.story#axzz31FIpcTxg; Peter Hartlaub, "Visions of the Virgin; Sightings of Mary Lure Faithful," *LA Daily News*, December 21, 1997; Carla Hall and Paula Bryant Pratt, "Waiting for Mary," *Los Angeles Times*, February 16, 1997, http://articles.latimes.com/1997–02–16/news/mn-29383_1_virgin-mary.

2 Juan Rubio, interview by Lisa Bitel and Matt Gainer, December 19, 2008; Lisa Bitel field notes, March 13, 2009.

3 Gideon Avni, "From Standing Stones to Open Mosques in the Negev Desert: The Archaeology of Religious Transformation on the Fringes," *Near Eastern Archaeology* 70, no. 3 (2007): 124–38.

4 Victor Turner, "The Center Out There: Pilgrim's Goal," *History of Religions* 12, no. 3 (1973): 191–230, esp. 196, http://www.jstor.org.libproxy.usc.edu/stable/1062024.

5 Gala Valtichinova, "Re-inventing the Past, Re-enchanting the Future: Visionaries and National Grandeur in Interwar Bulgaria," in *The "Vision Thing": Studying Divine Intervention*, ed. William A. Christian and Gábor Klaniczay, Workshop Series 18 (Budapest: Collegium Budapest, 2009), 157–94.

6 California City official website, http://www.californiacity.com.

7 Robert F. Heizer, ed., *California*, vol. 8 of *Handbook of North American Indians* (Washington, DC: Smithsonian Institution, 1978), 26–32, 564–69, 656–57 passim.

8 Francisco Tomás Hermenegildo Garcés, *On the Trail of a Spanish Pioneer: The Diary and Itinerary of Francisco Garcés (Missionary Priest) in His Travels through Sonora, Arizona, and California, 1775–1776; Translated from an Official Contemporaneous Copy of the Original Spanish manuscript, and Ed. with Copious Critical Notes by* Elliott Goues (New York: F. P. Harper, 1900), 228–29.

9 Chris Brewer, *Historic Kern County* (Bakersfield, CA: Kern County Museum, 2001).

10 "The Legend of the Mojave Desert's Lost Ships," http://www.angelfire.com/journal/difleys/legend.htm; "Secrets of the Mojave," http://www.bibliotecapleyades.net/esp_sociopol_mojave.htm. Unfortunately, the Mojave's utter flatness made it too dull for Cecil B. DeMille's retelling of the Exodus story, which was filmed farther north in Pismo Dunes.

11 *Pioneers in Progress*, twentieth anniversary brochure ([California City], 1985); *Los Angeles Times*, sec. J, Real Estate, May 20, 1962; *Life* magazine 1962 cover, "Opening Up the Desert for Living"; Mike Anton, "A Desert City That Didn't Fan Out," *Los Angeles Times*, August 14, 2010, http://articles.latimes.com/2010/aug/14/local/la-me-cal-city-20100814; Al Gagnon, "Chronological History of the Antelope Valley, Fremont Valley, Indian Wells Valley and Surrounding Areas in Kern County, California," http://www.califcity.com/history-1958.html.

12 City-data.com, "California City, CA (California) Houses and Residents," http://www.city-data.com/housing/houses-California-City-California.html.

13 U.S. Census Bureau Quick Facts, 2010 Census, for California City, http://quickfacts.census.gov/qfd/states/06/0609780.html.

14 California City official website, http://www.californiacity.com/churches.html.

15 California office of the U.S. Bureau of Land Management, *California Desert Area Conservation Area: Plan Alternatives and Environmental Impact Statement* (draft, 1980).

16 Matt Gainer field notes, fall 2011.

17 Exod. 33: 11, 19. See also Seth Landers, "Old Light on Moses' Shining Face," *Vetus Testamentum* 52 (2002): 400–406.

18 David Jasper, *The Sacred Desert: Religion, Literature, Art, and Culture* (Malden, MA: Blackwell, 2004); Jeff Cavins, "Temptations of Jesus Christ," the Crossroads Initiative, http://www.crossroadsinitiative.com/library_article/460/Temptations_of_Jesus_Christ_Jeff_Cavins.html; Michael Guinan, "In the Desert with Jesus," http://www.americancatholic.org/Newsletters/CU/ac0205.asp.

19 Gastón Espinosa, "History and Theory in the Study of Mexican American Religions," in *Mexican American Religions: Spirituality, Activism, and Culture*, ed. Gastón Espinosa and Mario T. García (Durham, NC: Duke University Press, 2008), 25–27.

20 Helen Waddell, *The Desert Fathers* (1936; repr., Ann Arbor: University of Michigan, 1957), 38.

21 Useful works in the extensive literature: Liz Herbert McAvoy and Mari Hughes-Edwards, eds., *Anchorites, Wombs, and Tombs: Intersections of Gender and Enclosure in the Middle Ages* (Cardiff: University of Wales, 2005); Sabina Flanagan, *Hildegard of Bingen, 1098–1179: A Visionary Life* (London: Routledge, 1989); Alison Weber, *Teresa of Avila and the Rhetoric of Femininity* (Princeton, NJ: Princeton University Press, 1990); Caroline Walker Bynum, *Holy Feast and Holy Fast: The Religious*

Significance of Food to Medieval Women (Berkeley: University of California Press, 1987).

22 Thomas Merton, *The Wisdom of the Desert; Sayings from the Desert Fathers of the Fourth Century* (New York: New Directions, 1961); Merton, *The Seven Storey Mountain* (New York: Harcourt, Brace, 1948).

23 Edward Lewine, "My Life as a Hermit," *New York Times*, September 9, 2007; Gayda Hollnagel, "Alone with God: Hermit Nun Lives Life of Prayer and Solitude," *La Crosse Tribune*, July 17, 2005, http://www.cultural-catholic.com/hermitnun.htm; R. W. Sims, "Salvation Mountain," 2004, http://www.salvationmountain.us.

24 Lisa Bitel field notes, March 13, 2009.

25 Archdiocese of Los Angeles, "Biography: Most Reverend José H. Gomez Archbishop of Los Angeles," http://www.la-archdiocese.org/archbishop/Pages/bio.aspx.

26 Pew Forum on Religion and Public Life, "A Portrait of American Catholics on the Eve of Pope Benedict's Visit to the U.S.," http://pewforum.org/Christian/Catholic/A-Portrait-of-American-Catholics-on-the-Eve-of-Pope-Benedicts-Visit-to-the-US-%282%29.aspx; Pew Forum on Religion & Public Life/U.S. Religious Landscape Survey, Summary of Key Findings, religions.pewforum.org/report2religious-landscape-study-key-findings.pdf. On clergy, see George J. Sanchez, *Becoming Mexican American: Ethnicity, Culture and Identity in Chicano Los Angeles, 1900–1945* (Oxford: Oxford University Press, 2003), 151–70; Adrian A. Bantjes, "Mexican Revolutionary Anticlericalism: Concepts and Typologies," *The Americas* 65 (2009): 467–80.

27 Gustavo Gutiérrez, *Teología del liberación: Perspectivas* (Lima: Centro de Estudios y Publicaciones, 1971); Moises Sandoval, *Fronteras: A History of the Latin American Church in the USA Since 1513* (San Antonio: Mexican American Cultural Center, 1983); Virgilio Elizondo, *Mestizaje: The Dialectic of Cultural Birth and the Gospel, A Study in the Intercultural Dimension of Evangelization* (San Antonio: Mexican American Cultural Center, 1978); also Elizondo, *La Morenita, Evangelizer*

of the Americas: A Study in Evangelization and the Dialectic of Violence (San Antonio: Mexican American Cultural Center, 1976), among other works.

28 Alyshia Gálvez, *Guadalupe in New York: Devotion and the Struggle for Citizenship Rights among Mexican Immigrants* (New York: NYU Press, 2010); Luis D. León, *La Llorona's Children: Religion, Life, and Death in the U.S.-Mexican Borderlands* (Berkeley: University of California Press, 2004), esp. 93–126; Davíd Carrasco and Roberto Lint Sagarena, "The Religious Vision of Gloria Anzaldúa: *Borderlands/La Frontera* as a Shamanic Space," in Espinosa and García, *Mexican American Religions*, 223–41.

29 Jeanette Rodriguez, *Our Lady of Guadalupe: Faith and Empowerment among Mexican American Women* (Austin: University of Texas Press, 1994); Kristy Nabhan-Warren, *The Virgin of El Barrio: Marian Apparitions, Catholic Evangelizing, and Mexican American Activism* (New York: NYU Press, 2005).

30 Gálvez, *Guadalupe*, esp. 75–79.

31 Linda B. Hall, "The Virgin as National Symbol," in *Mary, Mother and Warrior: The Virgin in Spain and the Americas* (Austin: University of Texas Press, 2004), 169–206; Socorro Castañeda-Liles, "Our Lady of Guadalupe and the Politics of Cultural Interpretation," in Espinosa and García, *Mexican American Religions*, 156–79.

32 Pablo Vila, *Border Indentifications: Narratives of Religion, Gender, and Class on the U.S.-Mexico Border* (Austin: University of Texas Press, 2005), esp. 4–10; N. Ross Crumrine and Alan Morinis, eds., *Pilgrimage in Latin America* (Westport, CT: Greenwood, 1991), esp. Morinis and Crumrine, "*La Pergrinación*: The Latin American Pilgrimage," 1–17.

33 Cf. Acts 7:33.

34 Lisa Bitel field notes, November 13, 2007; March 13, 2009; Juan Rubio, interview by Lisa Bitel and Matt Gainer, December 19, 2008.

35 Lawrence Taylor, "Centre and Edge," *Mobilities* 2 (2007): 383–93.

36 Augustine, *De civitate Dei* 15:1, 19:17, http://www.thelatinlibrary.com/august.html.

3. The Model Visionary

1 Matt. 7:15.

2 Benedict XIV, *Heroic Virtue: A portion of the Treatise of Benedict XIV on the Beatification and Canonization of the Servants of God*, vol. 3 (London: Thomas Richardson and Son,1850), esp. chaps. 5–14.

3 Galia Valtichinova, "Re-inventing the Past, Re-enchanting the Future: Visionaries and National Grandeur in Interwar Bulgaria," in *The "Vision Thing": Studying Divine Intervention*, ed. William A. Christian Jr. and Gábor Klaniczay, Workshop Series 18 (Budapest: Collegium Budapest, 2009), 185–89; Monique Scheer, "Taking Shelter under Mary's Mantle: Marian Apparitions in the Early Cold War Years, 1947–1953," in Christian and Klaniczay, "*Vision Thing*," 203–4.

4 Élisabeth Claverie, "Peace, War, Accusations, Criticism, and the Virgin (Medjugorje and the Anthropology of Marian Apparitions)," in Christian and Klaniczay, "*Vision Thing*," 219–38.

5 Julio César Ortiz, "Fe Entre la Arena," pt. 2, Univision, 2009, http://archivo.univision.com/content/content.jhtml?cid=1869070#2.

6 Thelma interview by Jake Bloch, February 13, 2011.

7 Telephone interview with local pastor by Lisa Bitel, fall 2010.

8 Marie Romero Cash, *Living Shrines: Home Altars of New Mexico* (Albuquerque: Museum of New Mexico Press, 1998); Laura Elisa Pérez, *Chicana Art: The Politics of Spiritual and Aesthetic Altarities* (Durham, NC: Duke University Press, 2007), 6–7, 91–145; Valtchinova, "Reinventing the Past," 157–94.

9 Frank Graziano, "What Speech Conceals and Silence Reveals: Possession Trance, Votive Texts, and the Silence of God in Mexican Devotions" (paper presented in seminar series "Haunting Religions," University of Southern California, April 16, 2013); Richard Bauman, *A World of Others' Words: Cross-cultural Perspectives on Intertextuality* (Malden, MA: Blackwell), esp. 2–3.

10 Acuña sermon, May 13, 2007.

11 David Morgan, *The Embodied Eye: Religious Visual Culture and the Social Life of Feeling* (Berkeley: University of California Press, 2012), 70–83.

12 Aaron Milavec, trans., *The Didache: Text, Translation, Analysis, and Commentary* (Collegeville, MN: Liturgical Press, 2004), cap. 11. For false prophets, see also Isa. 8:2; Deut. 13,18; Matt. 24:23–24; Mark 13:6, 21–22; 2 Cor. 1:14; 4:1–5; Gal. 1:8–9; Col 2:8; 2 Thess. 2:3; 1 Tim. 1:3–4, 4:1–2; 1 Peter 5:8–9, 2; 2 Peter 2:1–3; 1 John 2:18–23; Rev. 2:2; Jude 4:10–11,16–17; Acts 8:10–25.

13 Bernard McGinn, *The Foundations of Mysticism* (New York: Crossroad, 1991), app.: "Theoretical Foundations: The Modern Study of Mysticism," 265–343.

14 Thomas Aquinas, *Summa Theologica*, trans. Fathers of the English Dominican Province (Benziger Bros., 1947), 1.Q.12.3, http://www.ccel.org/ccel/aquinas/summa.i.html.

15 Saint Augustine, *Confessions*, trans. Edward B. Pusey bk. 9, cap. 10, 23–25, http://www.ccel.org/ccel/augustine/confess.toc.html.

16 Saint Augustine, *De Genesi ad Litteram libri duodecim*, in J.-P. Migne, *Patrologiae Cursus Completus: Series Latina* (Paris, 1844), vol. 34, bk. 1, cap. 12:7; see also Moreira, *Dreams, Visions, and Spiritual Authority*, 29–34; Bernard McGinn, *The Foundations of Mysticism* (New York: Crossroad, 1991), 228–62.

17 Ruth Harris, *Lourdes: Body and Spirit in the Secular Age* (New York: Viking, 1999), 363–64; Eugene G. D'Aquili and Andrew B. Newberg, *The Mystical Mind: Probing the Biology of Religious Experience* (Minneapolis: Fortress Press, 1999); Jerome Kroll and Bernard S. Bachrach, *The Mystic Mind: The Psychology of Medieval Mystics and Ascetics* (New York: Routledge, 2005.)

18 Ann Taves, *Fits, Trances, & Visions: Experiencing Religion and Explaining Experience*

from Wesley to James (Princeton, NJ: Princeton University Press, 1999), 7–8.

19 William James, *The Varieties of Religious Experience: A Study in Human Nature: Being the Gifford Lectures on Natural Religion Delivered at Edinburgh in 1901–1902* (New York: Signet Classic, 2003), 53.

20 "The Marian Movement of Southern California," letter from Archbishop Roger Mahony of Los Angeles to priests of the archdiocese, September 20, 1995, Archives of the Archdiocese of Los Angeles; "'Marian Movement' Not Supported by Church, Says Cardinal," *Tidings*, October 13, 1995.

21 Juan Rubio, interview by Lisa Bitel and Matt Gainer, December 18, 2008.

22 John Cooney, "Shrine Staff Forced to Clean Up Mess Left by Knock Pilgrims," *Irish Independent*, November 3, 2009; Henry O'Donnell, "Thousands Await Knock's New Vision," *Observer*, November 1, 2009; "Unholy Row Is Brewing over Visionary Claims at Shrine," *Belfast Telegraph*, November 2, 2009.

23 William A. Christian, "Afterword: Islands in the Sea," *Visual Resources* 25 (2009): 159.

24 Barbara Newman, "What Did It Mean to Say 'I Saw'? The Clash between Theory and Practice in Medieval Visionary Culture," *Speculum* 80 (2005): 1–43.

25 Harris, *Lourdes*, 83–109; Sandra Zimdars-Swartz, *Encountering Mary: From La Salette to Medjugorje* (Princeton, NJ: Princeton University Press, 1991), 245–70.

26 Gregory of Tours, *Liber in Gloria Martyrum*, trans. Raymond Van Dam as *Glory of the Martyrs* (Liverpool: Liverpool University Press, 1988), 12; Bede, *Ecclesiastical History of the English People*, ed. and trans. Bertram Colgrave and R. A. B. Mynors (Oxford: Clarendon Press, 1969), 1.17, 19, 34 passim.

27 David Albertson, *Nicholas of Cusa's Mathematical Theology* (Oxford: Oxford University Press, 2014); Dallas Denery, *Seeing and Being Seen in the Late Medieval World: Optics,* *Theology and Religious Life* (Cambridge: Cambridge University Press, 2005).

28 Kenneth Mills, *Idolatry and Its Enemies: Colonial Andean Religion and Extirpation, 1640–1750* (Princeton, NJ: Princeton University Press, 1997).

29 Hilda C. Graef, *Mary: A History of Doctrine and Devotion* (New York: Sheed and Ward, 1963), 432–33.

30 Catechism of the Catholic Church, http://www.vatican.va/archive/ccc_css/archive/catechism/p122a3p2.htm#II, 67.

31 Catholic Church and Pietro Gasparri, *Codex Iuris Canonici Pii X Pontificus Maximi* (Freiburg: Herder, 1919), canon 1399: 5; "Q: What about apparitions yesterday and today?," University of Dayton, http://campus.udayton.edu/mary/questions/yq/yq66.html.

32 Gianni Cardinale, "Intervista con Monsignor Angelo Amato di Gianni Cardinale," *Avvenire*, July 9, 2008, http://pda.medjugorje.ws/it/articles/timing-criteria-judging-apparitions.

33 Congregation for the Doctrine of the Faith, *Normae de modo procedendi in diudicandis praesumptis apparitionibus ac revelationisbus* (1978), http://www.doctrinafidei.va/documents/rc_con_cfaith_doc_19780225_norme-apparizioni_en.html; Joachim Bouflet and Philippe Boutry, *Un signe dans le ciel : Les apparitions de la Vierge* (Paris: Grasset, 1997), 396–99; an English translation of the French is available as "Norms of the Sacred Congregation of the Doctrine of the Faith on the Manner of Proceeding in Judging Alleged Apparitions and Revelations," trans. attrib. to Richard Chonak, Kevin Symonds et al. (2010), http://www.scribd.com/doc/73756470/Normae-Congregationis-2010-translation. See also "Pope Urges Crackdown on Reported Visions of Mary," *Times Online*, September 12, 2008, http://www.thetimes.co.uk/tto/faith/article2099617.ece.

34 Avila (deacon), interview by Lisa Bitel May 2, 2008.

35 2 Cor. 12:3–5.

36 Cardinale, "Intervista."

37 The Mary Page, Marian FAQ 16, University of Dayton, http://campus.udayton. edu/mary/questions/faq/faq16.html.

38 *Normae Congregationis*, I.B.e.

39 Jerome, "To Rusticus," trans. W. H. Fremantle in *Nicene and Post-Nicene Fathers*, vol. 6, 249, http://www.ccel.org/ccel/schaff/ npnf206.v.CXXII.html. Thanks to Andrew Fogleman for this reference.

40 Andrew Fogleman, "Believe Not Every Spirit" (PhD diss., University of Southern California, 2009).

41 David Blackbourn, *Marpingen: Apparitions of the Virgin Mary in a Nineteenth-Century German Village* (New York: Vintage, 1995), 114–16.

42 Peter Heintz, *A Guide to Apparitions of Our Blessed Virgin Mary* (Sacramento, CA: Gabriel Press, 1995), 261; see also videos made during apparition events at Garbandal: St. Joseph Publications, "Garabandal Apparitions," http://www.youtube.com/user/ GarabandalVideos; Elisabeth Claverie, *Les guerres de la vierge: Une anthropologie des apparitions* (Paris: Gallimard, 2003), 201–4; René Laurentin and H. Joyeux, *Études médicales et scientifiques sur les apparitions de Medjugorje* (Paris: OEIL, 1985); Paolo Apolito, *The Internet and the Madonna: Religious Visionary Experience on the Web* (Chicago: University of Chicago Press, 1995), 130–43.

43 American Psychiatric Association, *Diagnostic and Statistical Manual of Mental Disorders: DSM-IV-TR* (Washington, DC: American Psychiatric Association, 2000), 297.1: "Delusional Disorder."

44 *Normae Congregationis*, app.

45 Ibid.

46 Johan Rotem, "Frequently Asked Questions": "How does the bishop of a diocese go about verifying an apparition, and what does it mean if ecclesial approval is granted?," University of Dayton, http://campus.udayton. edu/mary/questions/faq/faq16.html; Frederick Jelly, O.P., "Discerning the Miraculous: Norms for Judging Apparitions and Private Revelations" (1993); Fr. Michael Smith Foster, JCD, "Canonical Considerations regarding Alleged Apparitions" (1995), both abridged, combined, and rearranged by Fr. Johann G. Roten, S.M., as "Norms and Process for Judging Revelations," University of Dayton, http:// campus.udayton.edu/mary/resources/newsltr. html.

47 Daniel Wojcik, *The End of the World As We Know It: Faith, Fatalism, and Apocalypse in America* (New York: New York University Press, 1997), 69–70.

48 Roses from Heaven: Apparitions of the Virgin Mary to Veronica Lueken, http:// www.rosesfromheaven.com.

49 Daniel Wojcik, ""Polaroids from Heaven': Photography, Folk Religion, and the Miraculous Image Tradition at a Marian Apparition," *Journal of American Folklore: Journal of the American Folklore Society* 109 (1996): 129–48.

50 Bishop Francis Mugavero of Brooklyn, "Declaration concerning the Bayside Movement," letter of November 4, 1986, EWTN, http://www.ewtn.com/Library/NEWAGE/ MUGABAY.TXT; see also Mugavero's source for discernment practices later published as James J. LeBar, *Cults, Sects, and the New Age* (Huntington, IN: Our Sunday Visitor, 1989.)

51 Harris, *Lourdes*, 80–81.

52 Claverie, *Les guerres*, 134–85.

53 This is the argument of Zimdars-Swartz, *Encountering Mary*.

54 "Ratzinger Rejects Rumors on Secret of Fatima," *Catholic World News*, October 15, 1997, http://www.catholicculture.org/news/ features/index.cfm?recnum=6056&repos=4&s ubrepos=1&searchid=872621.

55 "Church Status of the Bayside Apparitions," Roses from Heaven: Apparitions of the Virgin Mary to Veronica Leuken, http://www. rosesfromheaven.com/church_status.htm.

56 Augustin Poulain, "Private Revelations," *The Catholic Encyclopedia*, vol. 13 (New York: Robert Appleton, 1912), New Advent, http://

www.newadvent.org/cathen/13005a.htm;
David Frankfurter, *Evil Incarnate: Rumors of Demonic Conspiracy and Satanic Abuse in History* (Princeton: Princeton University Press, 2006),13–30 passim.

57 Congregation for the Doctrine of the Faith, "Christian Faith and Demonology," *L'Osservatore Romano*, English ed., July 10, 1975, 6–10, http://www.vatican.va/roman_curia/congregations/cfaith/documents/rc_con_cfaith_doc_19750626_fede-cristiana-demonologia_en.html.

58 Geralidine McKendrick and Angus McKay, "Visionaries and Affective Spirituality during the First Half of the Sixteenth Century, in *Cultural Encounters: The Impact of the Inquisition in Spain and the New World*, ed. Mary Elizabeth Perry and Anne J. Cruz (Berkeley: University of California Press, 1991), 93–104; J. Imirizaldu, *Monjas y beatas embaucadoras* (Madrid: Editora Nacional, 1977), 33–62.

59 Claverie, *Les Guerres*, 146–47; Michael Davies, "Megjugorje after Twenty-One Years—The Definitive History" (2004), http://www.olrl.org/prophecy/mdavies_medj21yrs.pdf, p. 14

60 Synod of Bishops, Special Assembly for America, "Encounter with the Living Jesus Christ: The Way to Conversion, Communion, and Solidarity in America," in *Instrumentum Laboris* (Rome: Vatican, 1997).

61 William J. Levada, "Congregation for the Doctrine of the Faith (2010–03–17) Investigative Commission on Medjugorje," *Osservatore Romano* 2139 (weekly ed. in English), April 7, 2010.

62 Pope John Paul II, *Memory and Identity: Conversations at the Dawn of a Millennium* (Waterville, ME: Thorndike, 2005), 184.

63 Simon Caldwell, "Pope Declares 'Holy War' against People Falsely Claiming to See the Virgin Mary," Mail Online.com, January 9,2011, http://www.dailymail.co.uk/news/article-1113943/Pope-declares-holy-war-people-falsely-claim-seen-Virgin-Mary.html; "Pope Orders Bishops to Investigate Claims of Seeing Jesus, Virgin Mary's Visions," Britain News.net, January 9, 2011, http://www.britainnews.net/story/453128; "Vatican confirms Pope Benedict XVI has set up an international commission on Medjugorje," *Rome Reports*, March 17, 2011, http://www.romereports.com/palio/vatican-confirms-pope-benedict-xvi-has-set-up-an-international-commission-on-medjugorje-english-1779.html; Benedict XVI, "Post-Synodal Apostolic Exhortation: Verbum Domini," September 30, 2010, http://www.vatican.va/holy_father/benedict_xvi/apost_exhortations/documents/hf_ben-xvi_exh_20100930_verbum-domini_en.html; John L. Allen, Jr., "Benedict Brings 'Marian Cool' to Fevered Fatima Devotion," *National Catholic Reporter*, May 12, 2011, http://ncronline.org/blogs/ncr-today/benedict-brings-marian-cool-fevered-fatima-devotion; Carol Glatz, "Is Seeing Believing?" How the Church Faces Claims of Marian Apparitions," Catholic News Service, January 21, 2011, http://www.catholicnews.com/data/stories/cns/1100252.htm.

64 *Annuario pontificio per l'anno* [. . . .] (Città del Vaticano: Libreria editrice vaticana, 1716–), 2003; Lezione de Religione, "Maria, la Madre di Dio—le apparizioni,"http://www.lezionidireligione.it/joomla/index.php/en/materiale-multimediale/item/338-maria-la-madre-di-dio/338-maria-la-madre-di-dio.html?start=12.

65 Joseph Cardinal Ratzinger, "Theological Commentary," in Congregation for the Doctrine of the Faith, "Message of Fatima," http://www.vatican.va/roman_curia/congregations/cfaith/documents/rc_con_cfaith_doc_20000626_message-fatima_en.html.

66 Jamie Manson, "Pope Francis, Women and 'Chauvinism with Skirts,'" *National Catholic Reporter*, April 25, 2013, http://ncronline.org/blogs/grace-margins/pope-francis-women-and-chauvinism-skirts.

67 Nancy47, "Prophesey [sic] and speaking in tounges [sic]," Catholic Answers Forums, Non-Catholic Religions, February 28, 2008), http://forums.catholic.com/showthread.php?p=3371708#post3371708.

68 Mahony pastoral letter, September 20, 1995; "'Marian Movement' Not Supported."

69 Peter Hartlaub, "Visions of the Virgin: Sightings of Mary Lure Faithful," *LA Daily News*, December 27, 1997.

70 Lisa Bitel field notes, August 13, 2006; April 13, 2006; April 13, 2008; Ortiz, "Fe Entre la Arena."

71 Lisa Bitel field notes, July 24, 2010.

72 Luis Laso de la Vega, *Huey tlamahuiçoltica omonexiti in ilhuicac tlatocacihuapilli Santa Maria totlaçonantzin Guadalupe in nican huey altepenahuac Mexico itocayocan Tepeyacac* (Mexico City: Imprenta de Iuan Ruiz, 1649); Lisa Sousa, Stafford Poole, and James Lockhart, eds. and trans., *The Story of Guadalupe: Luis Laso de la Vega's Huei tlamahuiçoltica of 1649* (Stanford, CA: Stanford University Press, 1998.) For the vexed problem of original sources testifying to Juan Diego's visions, see also Stafford Poole, *Our Lady of Guadalupe: The Origins and Sources of a Mexican National Symbol, 1531–1797* (Tucson: University of Arizona, 1995), esp. 110–26.

73 Stafford Poole, *The Guadalupan Controversies in Mexico* (Stanford, CA: Stanford University Press, 2006); "Our Lady of Guadalupe, Historical Sources," EWTN, http://www.ewtn.com/library/mary/ladyguad.htm; John Paul II, "Canonization of Juan Diego Cuauhtlatoatzin, Homily of the Holy Father John Paul II" (Mexico City, July 31, 2002), http://www.vatican.va/holy_father/john_paul_ii/homilies/2002/documents/hf_jp-ii_hom_20020731_canonization-mexico_en.html.

74 For modern acknowledgment of the motif, see Father Angelo Mary Geiger, "Hail Mary, Hammer of Dragons!" December 8, 2010, http://maryvictrix.wordpress.com/tag/immaculate-conception.

75 Lisa Bitel field notes, August 13, 2006.

76 Lisa Bitel field notes, May 13, 2007; August 13, 2006.

77 Lisa Bitel field notes, April 13, 2008.

78 Luis D. León, *La Llorona's Children: Religion, Life, and Death in the U.S.-Mexican Borderlands* (Berkeley: University of California Press, 2004); Maritza Montiel Tafur, Terry K. Crowe, and Eliseo Torres, "A Review of *Curanderismo* and Healing Practices among Mexicans and Mexican Americans," *Occupational Therapy International* 16 (2009): 82–88.

79 Luis D. León, "Borderlands Bodies and Souls: Mexican Religious Healing Practices in East Los Angeles," in Gastón Espinosa and Mario T. García, eds., *Mexican American Religions: Spirituality, Activism, and Culture* (Durham: Duke University Press, 2008), 296–322.

80 Suzanne Kaufman, *Consuming Visions: Mass Culture and the Lourdes Shrine* (Ithaca, NY: Cornell University Press, 2005), 98–105.

81 Thelma, interview by Jake Bloch February 13, 2011.

82 Ibid.

83 Robert A. Orsi, "Mildred, Is It Fun to Be a Cripple? The Culture of Suffering in Mid-twentieth Century American Catholicism," in *Between Heaven and Earth: The Religious Worlds People Make and the Scholars Who Study Them* (Princeton, NJ: Princeton University Press, 2005), 19–47.

84 As one famous example, see "Saint Gemma Galgani," ETWN, http://www.ewtn.com/library/mary/galgani.htm.

85 Oliver Sacks, *Migraine*, rev. ed. (New York: Vintage, 1999), 299–301.

86 Rudolph M. Bell, *Holy Anorexia* (Chicago: University of Chicago Press, 1985); Biro Barton, "Saint Teresa of Avila: Did She Have Epilepsy?" *Catholic Historical Review* 68 (1982): 581–98.

87 Margery Kempe, *The Book of Margery Kempe*, trans. Liz Herbert McAvoy (Woodbridge, UK: Boydell & Brewer, 2003), 79–80; Giunta Bevegnati, *Life and Revelations of Saint Margaret of Cortona: Dedicated to Her Brothers and Sisters of the Third Order of Saint Francis*, trans. F. M'Donogh Mahony (London: Burns and Oates, 1883), sec. 2.6. See also Steven Justice, "Did the Middle Ages Believe in Their Miracles?," *Representations* 103 (2008): 1–29.

88 John Paul II, *Beatificazione di Laura Vicuña*, September 3, 1988, http://www.vatican.va/holy_father/john_paul_ii/homilies/1988/documents/hf_jp-ii_hom_19880903_colle-don-bosco_it.html.

89 Kathleen Z. Young, "The Imperishable Virginity of Saint Maria Goretti," *Gender and Society* 3 (1989): 474–82; Pius XII, *In Solemni Canonizatione Beatae Mariae Goretti, Virginis et Martyris*, June 24, 1950, http://www.vatican.va/holy_father/pius_xii/homilies/documents/hf_p-xii_hom_19500624_maria-goretti_lt.html.

90 Acuña sermon, July 24, 2010, translated by Sandra Ruiz.

91 Yves Chiron, *Enquête sur les apparitions de la Vierge* ([Paris]: Perrin, 1995); David Blackbourn, *Marpingen: Apparitions of the Virgin Mary in a Nineteenth-Century German Village* (New York: Vintage, 1993), 22–27.

92 "Spirit Daily" discussion list, *Catholic Daily*, August 18, 2006–December 20, 2006, http://www.catholicdaily.com/forum/viewtopic.php?f=17&t=4290.

93 Congregation for the Doctrine of the Faith, "The Message of Fatima," http://www.vatican.va/roman_curia/congregations/cfaith/documents/rc_con_cfaith_doc_20000626_message-fatima_en.html.

94 Pavao Zanic, "A Statement of the Chancellor of the Diocese of Mostar concerning the Alleged Apparition of the Blessed Virgin Mary in Medjugorje," June 22, 1997, in "Answers About Medjugorje," http://members.tripod.com/~chonak/documents/medj_index.html.

95 Cindy Wooden, "Cardinal Says Commission to Review Alleged Apparitions at Medjugorje," Catholic News Service, July 25, 2006.

96 "Virgin Mary Sightings Draw Believers to SoCal Desert," KTLA News, May 13, 2008.

97 Lisa Bitel field notes, July 24, 2009.

98 Ibid.

99 Lisa Bitel field notes, March 13, 2009.

100 World Apostolate of Fatima, Blue Army Shrine, http://www.wafusa.org/about_blue_army/history.html; Legion of Mary, http://www.legionofmary.org and http://www.legionofmary.ie.

101 Acuña, interview by Jake Bloch, February 13, 2011.

102 Form 990 for 2002, 2003, and 2005–10 available via the Urban Institute, National Center for Charitable Statistics, http://nccsdataweb.urban.org.

103 KTLA News, "Virgin Mary Sightings": "She says she cannot speak about her past without the permission of a 'spiritual father,' whom she refuses to name."

104 For examples of contemporary visionaries and their messages, see http://www.cuapa.com/las_apariciones.html; http://www.conyers.org/w_intro.aspx; and http://www.maryheartcrusaders.org/the_story.html.

105 Interview by Jake Bloch, February 13, 2011.

106 Lisa Bitel field notes, April 13, 2008.

107 Interview by Jake Bloch, February 13, 2011.

108 Acuña sermon, July 24, 2010.

109 Acuña sermon, July 13, 2007, translated by Barbara Soliz.

110 Jake Bloch field notes, December 13, 2010.

111 Stefano Gobbi *To the Priests, Our Lady's Beloved Sons* (St. Francis, ME: Marian Movement of Priests, 1998).

112 Juan Rubio, interview with Lisa Bitel and Matt Gainer, December 19, 2008.

113 John T. Steinbock, bishop of Fresno, pastoral message (Fresno KNXT Catholic television, aired May 2004.

114 Dragicevic tours annually: "Ivan Dragicevic's Speaking Schedule," Medjugorje Web, http://www.medjugorje.org/ivanse.htm.

115 Claverie, "Peace, War, Accusations," esp. 222–25.

116 Juan interview by Jake Bloch, February 13, 2011.

4. Looking Like Pilgrims

1 "Virgin Mary Sightings Draw Believers to SoCal Desert," May 13, 2008, http://www.youtube.com/watch?v=QK5Fb4ZR8YE.

2 Lisa Bitel field notes, July 24, 2008.

3 Jake Bloch field notes, July 24, 2010.

4 P. Debuchy, "Discernment of Spirits," *Catholic Encyclopedia* (New York: Robert Appleton, 1909), http://www.newadvent.org/cathen/05028b.htm.

5 Jerome P. Baggett, *Sense of the Faithful: How American Catholics Live Their Faith* (New York: Oxford University Press, 2009), 89–98, 109–13.

6 Jake Bloch field notes, July 24, 2010.

7 Richard Kieckhefer, *Theology in Stone: Church Architecture from Byzantium to Berkeley* (New York: Oxford University Press, 2004), 41–43, 86–87; see 1 Kings 6.

8 R. A. Stalley, *Early Medieval Architecture* (Oxford: Oxford University Press, 1999), 65–81; Annie Shaver-Crandell, Paula Lieber Gerson, and Alison Stones, *The Pilgrim's Guide to Santiago De Compostela: A Gazetteer* (London: Harvey Miller Publishers, 1995), esp. introduction, 13–57.

9 Lisa Bitel, *Landscape with Two Saints: How Genovefa of Paris and Brigit of Kildare Built Christianity in Barbarian Europe* (Oxford: Oxford University Press, 2009), xi, 210.

10 Lisa Bitel field notes, May 13, 2006; July 24, 2008.

11 Frank Graziano, *Cultures of Devotion: Folk Saints of Spanish America* (New York: Oxford University Press, 2007), 61–65.

12 Birgit Meyer, "Religious Sensations: Media, Aesthetics, and the Study of Contemporary Religion," in *Religion, Media and Culture: A Reader*, ed. Gordon Lynch and Jolyton Mitchell with Anna Strhan (London: Routledge, 2012), 158–70.

13 Julio César Ortiz, "Fe Entre la Arena," pts. 1 and 2, Univision, 2009, http://archivo.univision.com/content/content.jhtml?cid=1869070#1 and http://archivo.univision.com/content/content.jhtml?cid=1869070#2

14 Jake Bloch field notes, July 24, 2010; Galia Valtichinova, "Re-inventing the Past, Re-enchanting the Future Visionaries and National Grandeur in Interwar Bulgaria," in *The "Vision Thing": Studying Divine Intervention*, ed. William A. Christian and Gábor Klaniczay, Workshop Series 18 (Budapest: Collegium Budapest, 2009), 160–63.

15 Peter Heintz, *A Guide to Apparitions of Our Blessed Virgin Mary* (Sacramento, CA: Gabriel Press, 1995), 408, 427, 467.

16 Acuña sermon, July 24, 2010.

17 Adelia, interview by Lisa Bitel and Matt Gainer, August 18, 2010.

18 U.S. Conference of Catholic Bishops, "Backgrounder: Asian and Pacific Islander Catholics in the United States," http://www.uspapalvisit.org/backgrounders/asian-pacific.htm.

19 Adelia, interview by Lisa Bitel and Matt Gainer, August 18, 2010.

20 Juan Hurtado, *An Attitudinal Study of Social Distance between the Mexican American and the Church* (San Antonio: Mexican American Cultural Center, 1975); Pew Foundation, "Changing Faiths: Latinos and the Transformation of American Religion" (Pew Forum on Religion and Public Life, 2007), http://www.pewhispanic.org/files/reports/75.pdf.

21 Lisa Bitel field notes, July 24, 2010.

22 Juan Rubio, interview by Lisa Bitel and Matt Gainer, December 19, 2008.

23 Gastón Espinosa, "Reflections on Social Science Research on Latino Religions," in *Rethinking Latino(a) Religion and Identity*, ed. Miguel A. De La Torre and Gastón Espinosa (Cleveland: Pilgrim Press, 2006), 40–41; "Separated Brothers: Latinos Are Changing the Nature of American Religion," *Economist*, July 16, 2009, http://www.economist.com/node/14034841?story_id=14034841.

24 Pew Forum on Religion and Public Life, U.S. Religious Landscape Survey (2007), http://religions.pewforum.org/pdf/report2religious-landscape-study-key-findings.pdf.

25 William A. Christian, *Person and God in a Spanish Valley* (New York: Seminar Press, 1972), 182ff.; Victor W. Turner and Edith L. B. Turner, *Image and Pilgrimage in Christian Culture: Anthropological Perspectives* (New York: Columbia University Press, 1978), 206–9.

26 Carolina, interview by Jake Bloch, fall 2010.

27 Lisa Bitel field notes, April 13, 2008.

28 Lisa Bitel field notes, March 13, 2009.

29 Michael Kearney, "Religion, Ideology, and Revolution in Latin America," *Latin American Perspectives* 13 (1986): 3–12; Carol Ann Drogus, "The Rise and Decline of Liberation Theology: Churches, Faith, and Political Change in Latin America," *Comparative Politics* 27 (1995): 465–77.

30 Priest at Our Lady of Lourdes, telephone interview by Lisa Bitel, fall 2010.

31 Luis D. León, *La Llorona's Children: Religion, Life, and Death in the U.S.-Mexican Borderlands* (Berkeley, Calif: University of California Press, 2004), 42–45.

32 "Visions of Mary," pt. 2, Paranormal TV, episode PTV0159 (2010), http://youtu.be/mkzjyaQbfy4.

33 Joseph Treviño, "Crucified Again: Eastside Priest Accused of Sex Sins," *LAWeekly*, May 5, 2002, http://www.laweekly.com/2002-05-23/news/crucified-again; n.b. comments by victims. See also Jesse Katz, "Jesus' Homeboy: Slaying Aftermath: Father Juan Santillan Walks a Fine Line as Peacemaker and Spiri-tual Leader in Tense Ramona Gardens. He Is Respected by Gang Members, Politicians and the Police," *Los Angeles Times*, July 10, 1991.

34 Lisa Bitel field notes, May 13, 2007.

35 Lisa Bitel field notes, March 13, 2009; April 13, 2008; July 24, 2008.

36 Cf. Luis D. León, "Borderland Bodies and Souls: Mexican Religious Healing Practices in East L.A.," in *Mexican American Religions: Spirituality, Activism, and Culture*, ed. Gastón Espinosa and Mario T. García (Durham: Duke University Press, 2008), 297.

37 Lisa Bitel field notes, March 13, 2009.

38 Ibid.; "Our Lady of the Rock: A Holy Place?," KTNV, December 1, 2008, http://health.ktnv.com/story/9416581/our-lady-of-the-rock-a-holy-place.

39 Alice-Mary Talbot, "Pilgrimage to Healing Shrines: The Evidence of Miracle Accounts," *Dumbarton Oaks Papers* 56 (2002): 153–73; Valtchinova, "Re-interventing the Past," 186–87; Györfy Eszter, "'That Is Why Miracles Happen Here': The Role of Miracles Narratives in the Legitimation Process of a New Shrine," in *"Vision Thing,"* 252–53; "Ancient or Modern Miracles? Yes," *The Pilgrim's Path*, http://thepilgrimspath.net/2011/11/29/ancientmoder; Our Lady of Good Help Pilgrimage, "Wisconsin Public TV Covers 3-Year-Old Boy's Healing," http://goodhelppilgrimage.com/2011/04/wisconsin-public-tv-covers-3-year-old-boys-healing.

40 Jacalyn Duffin, *Medical Miracles: Doctors, Saints, and Healing in the Modern World* (Oxford: Oxford University Press, 2009.).

41 A. Wallis field notes, April 13, 2008.

42 Ortiz, "Fe Entre la Arena."

43 Jake Bloch field notes, February 13, 2011.

44 J.M. Martinez et al., "La Virgen de Mojave," pt. 1, "Muy cerca del Cielo," and pt. 2, "La FE en el Desierto," Onevision Productions, 2006, http://youtu.be/lp-5ERQWp-8.

45 "Sea real o no, la gente se va convencida de haber sentido la presencia de la Virgen y haber obtenido un regalo de Dios que los cure

de todos sus males." J. M. Martinez et al., "La Virgen de Mojave," pt. 3, "Encuentro con María," Onevision Productions, 2006, http://youtu.be/SXuFwNVG9E4.

46 Lisa Bitel field notes, July 24, 2008.

47 Alex McInnis, "Mary over Mojave," 2007, http://youtu.be/8t-K3XtyZM4.

48 Lisa Bitel field notes, May 13, 2007.

49 Juan Rubio, interview with Lisa Bitel and Matt Gainer, December 19, 2008.

50 "Our Lady of the Rock: A Religious Destination in the CA Desert Has Visitors from All over the World Coming in Search of Faith and Healing," KTNV-LAS VEGAS, November 25, 2008, http://www.youtube.com/watch?v=QK5Fb4ZR8YE.

51 Ross McDermott and Andrew Owen, "Our Lady of the Rock," National Geographic Travel, http://travel.national-geographic.com/travel/american-festivals/our-lady-rock-photos/#festival-our-lady-rock-1_17005_600x450.jpg; Ross McDermott and Andrew Owen, "Our Lady of the Rock," http://vimeo.com/6896428.

52 California City Real Estate homepage, http://www.califcity.com; link to /virginmary.html.

53 Paolo Apolito *The Internet and the Madonna: Religious Visionary Experience on the Web* (Chicago: University of Chicago Press, 1995), 107–26.

54 Daniel Wojcik, "'Polaroids from Heaven': Photography, Folk Religion, and the Miraculous Image Tradition at a Marian Apparition Site," *Journal of American Folklore* 109 (1996): 129–48; Dale Heatherington, "The Mystery of the Golden Door," http://www.wa4dsy.net/skeptic/goldendoor.html; latinaexpert, "Miracle Pictures of Apparitions in Conyers, Georgia 1991–1998.wmv," http://www.youtube.com.

55 Apolito, *Internet and the Madonna*, 15, 20–60, esp. 40–41.

56 Catholic Tools, "Marian Apparitions of the 20th Century Video," http://www.catholictools.com/marian-apparitions-20th-century.

57 "Miraculous Statues and Photographs," Angelfire, http://www.angelfire.com/ky/dodone/MiraculousStatues.html.

58 Apolito, *Internet and the Madonna*, 76–77.

59 William A. Christian Jr., "The Eyes of the Beholders Systematic Variation in Visions of the Christ of Limpias in Northern Spain, 1919-1936," in *"Vision Thing,"* 76–79.

60 Brian Britt, "Snapshots of Tradition: Apparitions of the Virgin Mary," *Nova Religio: The Journal of Alternative and Emergent Religions* 2 (1998): 108–25.

61 Yves Chiron, *Enquête sur les apparitions de la Vierge* ([Paris]: Perrin, 1995), 352–59.

62 Hans Belting, *Likeness and Presence: A History of the Image before the Era of Art* (Chicago: University of Chicago Press, 1994), 47–77.

63 Carol Glatz, "Shroud of Turin to Be Displayed to Public in 2010," Catholic News Service, June 2, 2008; Jeanette Favrot Peterson, "Creating the Virgin of Guadalupe: The Cloth, the Artist, and Sources in Sixteenth-Century New Spain," *Americas* 61, no. 4 (2005): 571–610.

64 John Harvey, *Photography and Spirit* (London: Reaktion, 2007), esp.70–80; Michael Leja, *Looking Askance: Skepticism and American Art from Eakins to Duchamp* (Berkeley : University of California Press, 2004), esp. "Mummler's Fraudulent Photographs," 21–58.

65 Harvey, *Photography and Spirit*, 28–46.

66 Cf. Apolito, *Internet and the Madonna*, 117–21.

67 Sandra Zimdars-Swartz, *Encountering Mary: From La Salette to Medjugorje* (Princeton, NJ: Princeton University Press, 1991), 136–37.

68 Lisa Bitel field notes, July 24, 2010.

69 Lisa Bitel field notes, August 13, 2006.

70 McDermott and Owen, "Our Lady of the Rock," National Geographic Travel.

71 Paolo Apolito, *Apparitions of the Madonna at Oliveto Citra: Local Visions and Cosmic Drama* (University Park: Penn State University Press, 1998), 102–6, 216–20, on the negotiation of what witnesses see with eyes and cameras. For the iconography of Bayside visions, see Roses from Heaven, "Photo Symbolism," http://www.rosesfromheaven.com/photoStory2.html.

72 Wojcik, "'Polaroids from Heaven,'" 135; Jessy C. Pagliaroli, "Kodak Catholicism: Miraculous Photography and Its Significance at a Post-Conciliar Marian Apparition Site in Canada," *Historical Studies* 70 (2004): 89–91.

73 Jake Bloch field notes, December 13, 2010.

74 Lisa Bitel field notes, April 13, 2008.

75 David Yamane, "Narrative and Religious Experience," *Sociology of Religion* 61 (2000): 171–89.

76 Carolina, interview by Jake Bloch, fall 2010.

77 Yamane, "Narrative and Religious Experience"; Birgit Meyer and Dick Houtman, "Introduction: Material Religion, How Things Matter," in *Things: Religion and the Question of Materiality*, ed. Birgit Meyer and Dick Houtman (New York: Fordham University Press, 2012), 1–26.

78 Lynn Davidson, "Truth, Subjectivity, and Ethnographic Research," in *Personal Knowledge: Reshaping the Ethnography of Religion*, ed. James V. Spickard, J. Shawn Landres, and Meredith B. McGuire (New York: NYU Press, 2002), 17–26.

79 Valtchinova, "Re-inventing the Past," 189.

80 See Courtney Bender, *The New Metaphysicals Spirituality and the American Religious Imagination* (Chicago: University of Chicago Press, 2010), 66–70.

81 Carolina, interview Jake Bloch, fall 2010.

82 Adelia, interview with Lisa Bitel and Matt Gainer, August 18, 2010.

83 Bender, *New Metaphysicals*, 56–73.

84 Jake Bloch field notes, March 13, 2011.

85 Ortiz, "Fe Entre la Arena."

86 Jake Bloch field notes, March 13, 2011.

87 Ibid..

88 Interview with Jake Bloch, February 13, 2011.

5. From Witness to Visionary

1 Danièle Hervieu-Léger and Simon Lee, *Religion as a Chain of Memory* (New Brunswick, NJ: Rutgers University Press, 2000); Peter Jan Margry,"Paradoxes of Marian Apparitional Contestation: Networks, Ideology, Gender, and the Lady of All Nations," in *Moved by Mary*, ed. Anna-Karina Hermkens, Wilhelmina Helena Maria Jansen, and Catrien Notermans (Farnham, UK: Ashgate, 2009), esp. 192–93.

2 Lisa Bitel field notes, April 13, 2008.

3 Juan Rubio, interview by Lisa Bitel and Matt Gainer, December 19, 2008.

4 Emiliano Chamorro, 'La Virgen del cerro Cacaulí,' *La Prensa*, July 18, 2004, http://archivo.laprensa.com.ni; Leoncio Vanegas, "Foto impresiona a feligreses de las Segovias," *El Nuevo Diario—Managua*, March 23, 2007; Vanegas, "Miles veneraron a la Virgen de Cacaulí," *El Nuevo Diario—Managua*, December 10, 2007.

5 Cuapa, www.cuapa.com.

6 Tatiana Morales, "Virgin Mary Crying Blood?" CBSNews, February 11, 2009, www.cbsnews.com.

7 Sacred Congregation for Divine Worship, "Letter 'En reponse a la demande,' to presidents of those conferences of bishops petitioning the indult for communion in the hand, May 29, 1969," *Acta Apostolicae Sedis* 61 (1969): 546–47; Robert J. Daly, "Robert Bellarimine and Post-Tridentine Eucharistic Theology," in *From Trent to Vatican II*, ed. Raymond F. Bullman and

Frederick J. Parrella (Oxford: Oxford University Press, 2006), 79–88.

8 Bulman and Parrella, *From Trent to Vatican II*, 65, 68–69, 81–98.

9 Californiacity395, "Our Lady of the Rock," pt. 4, 2010, http://youtu.be/pdKT6m-HII3A; *LA VIRGEN DE MOJAVE—Parte II*, 2006, http://www.youtu.be/ m6ajQyWxKtg.

10 Interview with Jake Bloch, fall 2010.

11 Jake Bloch field notes, November 13, 2010.

12 Jake Bloch field notes, February 13, 2011.

6. Discernment at a Distance

1 Kim tieu thu, "Our Lady of the Rock," http://www.flickr.com/photos/tieu_thu/ sets/72157626329907994/with/5551899016.

2 "Milagros y mensajes de la Virgen," Univision, "Opiniones," December 11, 2006, http://foro.univision.com/t5/El-Show-de-Cristina/Milagros-y-mensajes-de-la-Virgen/m-p/130498599.

3 Grethel Miranda Villejos, "Festejarán 31 aniversario de apariciones en Cuapa," *La Prensa*, May 7, 2011, http://www.laprensa.com. ni/2011/05/07/nacionales/59807; El grupo Ave Maria Cuapa, "¡Bienvenidoa a Cuapa! Lugar de Las Apariciones de La Virgen María," http://www.cuapa.com/31_aniversario_de_las_ apariciones.htm.

4 For example, Conyers.org, "A Holy Place of Peace, Healing & Conversion," http://www.conyers.org; Shrine of Our Lady of Good Help, "Marian Apparitions," http://www.shrineofourladyofgoodhelp.com/ htmPages/g_hst_p3.html; The Prophecies of Our Lady of Emmitsburg, www.prourlady ofemmitsburg.org.

5 Jesse Washington, "For Minorities, New 'Digital Divide' Seen," *USA Today* January 20, 2011, http://www.usatoday.com/ tech/news/2011–01–10-minorities-online_N. htm; Gretchen Livingston, "The Latino

Digital Divide: The Native Born versus the Foreign Born," Pew Hispanic Center, Pew Research Center, http://www.pewhispanic. org/2010/07/28/the-latino-digital-divide-the-native-born-versus-the-foreign-born.

6 Kerrytown Apparitions, http://www. kerrytown-apparitions.com; Michael Commins, "Knock 'Apparition' to Attract 50,000," *Mayo News*, October 5, 2009, http://www. mayonews.ie/index.php?option=com_conte nt&task=view&id=7836&Itemid=38; Radio Telefís Éireann, "Apparitions at Knock," You-Tube, July 25, 2010, http://www.youtube.com/ watch?v = Or6L0Y1JZ-w; "Joe Coleman Sends Bunch of Delusional Twats to Miracle Statue—without a Camera," *Fatmammycat's Blog*, http:// fatmammycat.wordpress.com/2009/10/03/ joe-coleman-sends-bunch-of-delusional-twats-to-miracle-statue-without-a-camera.

7 "God's Close-up," *This American Life* 3.1, originally aired April 5, 2007), http://www. thisamericanlife.org/tv-archives/season-one/ gods-close.

8 Frank Suffert, Peter Fonda, and Lillemor Mallau, *Desert Dreamers* (Venice, CA: Tivoli Entertainment, 2006.)

9 "Conductores," Univision 34.com, Los Angeles, http://losangeles.univision.com/ contactanos/conductores/article/2008-03-12/ bio-julio-cesar-ortiz

10 Julio César Ortiz, "Fé entre la Arena," Univision, 2008), pt.1, http://www.univision. com/content/video.jhtml?cid=1630506; pt. 2, http://www.univision.com/content/video. jhtml?cid=1632296.

11 Paranormal TV, "Visions of Mary—Part 1," 2010, http://youtu.be/C5jIUgglpfk; "Part 2," 2010, http://www.youtu.be/mkzjyaQbfy4.

12 Vorkalex, "Mary over Mojave," 2007, http://youtu.be/8t-K3XtyZM4.

13 J. M. Martínez et al., "La Virgen de Mojave," pt. 1, "Muy cercla del Cielo," 2006, http://www.youtu.be/lp-5ERQWp-8.

14 Photograph collections available online include Hector Villablanca, "Our Lady of the Rock," http://www.flickr.com/photos/

fotovillablanca/5722508743/ and http://
www.flickr.com/photos/fotovillablanca/
sets/72157626607017203/; Kim Tieu
Thu, "Our Lady of the Rock," http://
www.flickr.com/photos/tieu_thu/
sets/72157626329907994/; American
Festivals Project, http://americanfestivals
project.net/photos/album/72157622504235568/
Our-Lady-of-the-Rock.html; Dave Malkoff,
http://www.flickr.com/search/?q=lady%20
of%20the%20rock&w=74193050%40N00.

15 Catherine Lutz and Jane Lou Col-
lins, *Reading National Geographic* (Chicago:
University of Chicago Press, 1993); Elaine
Graham, "Religious Literacy and Public
Service Broadcasting: Introducing a Research
Agenda," in *Religion, Media and Culture: A
Reader*, ed. Gordon Lynch, Jolyon P. Mitchell,
and Anna Strhan (Abingdon, Oxon: Rout-
ledge, 2012), 228–35.

16 Jake Bloch field notes, December
13, 2010.

17 Lisa Bitel field notes, July 24, 2010.

18 Acuña sermon, July 24, 2010.

19 Lisa Bitel field notes, August 13, 2006.

20 Jake Bloch field notes, December
13, 2010.

21 Acuña sermon, July 24, 2010.

22 *Catholic Daily*, "Spirit Daily" discussion
board, http://www.catholicdaily.com/forum/
viewtopic.php?f=17&t=4290.

23 Acuña sermon, July 13, 2007.

24 Ibid.

25 Paolo Apolito, *The Internet and the
Madonna: Religious Visionary Experience on the
Web* (Chicago: University of Chicago Press,
1995), 101–30.

26 Our Lady of Light Ministries, "Our
Lady of Light: Visits and Messages to a Batavia, Ohio Visionary," http://www.ourladyo
flight.org/messages.htm.

27 Ibid., http://www.ourladyoflight.org/
qa.htm.

28 Ibid., http://www.ourladyoflight.org/
messages.htm.

29 Ibid.,message from July 13, 1998,
http://www.ourladyoflight.org/messages.
htm#Hidden_Messages.

30 Ibid., "Hidden Messages," http://www.
ourladyoflight.org/messages.htm#Hidden_
Messages.

31 Our Lady of the Roses, http://www.
tldm.org/no-invest/investigation1.htm.

32 Roses from Heaven, http://www.
rosesfromheaven.com/few_clergy_saved.html.

33 Our Lady of Light Ministries, http://
www.ourladyoflight.org/activities.htm.

Conclusion

1 William A. Christian Jr. and Gábor Klan-
iczay. ed., *The "Vision Thing": Studying Divine
Intervention*, Workshop Series 18 (Budapest:
Collegium Budapest, 2009), esp. 7–19.

2 Augustine, *De fide rerum quae non
videntur*, in *Aurelii Augustini opera. Pars 13,
2, Pars 13, 2* (Turnholti: Brepols, 1969), bk.
I, cap. 4: "Si vero haec quae videtis, et longe
ante praedicta sunt, et tanta manifestatione
complentur; si se ipsa veritas et praecedentibus
vobis et consequentibus declarat effectibus,
o reliquiae infidelitatis, ut credatis quae non
videtis, iis erubescite quae videtis!"

Index

Gomez, José H. (archbishop of Los Angeles), 36, 86
Goretti, Maria, 60
Gospels, 15–16, 43–44, 90; noncanonical, 138. *See also* New Testament
grace, 45, 90, 96, 136, 145, 153–54
Green Bay, Wisconsin, 19
Gregory of Tours, 47
Guadalupe (Mexico), Our Lady of (Nuestra Señora de) or The Virgin of (La Virgen de), 3, 11, 19; cult of, 21, 36–37; feast of (December 12), 9; iconography of, 23, 26–27, 85, 104; Marian apparitions (at Tepeyac), 19, 21, 23, 26, 56–57, 104, 141

hem touching event, 69, 71–72, 74, 89, 108, 134
heretics, 47, 155
hermanas. See *monjas*
hermits, 29, 34–35
Hildegard of Bingen, 35, 60
Hispanics, 81–82
Hodgetria, 99. *See also* archeiropoieta
holy cards, 98
Holy Spirit, 133
Holy Virgin Mary, The (Ofili), 26
Horitz Passion play, 25
humility, 49, 56, 61
Huxley, Aldous (*Devils of Loudon*), 53

illegal immigrants, 118–19, 122–25, 140–41
imagination, 2, 40, 46, 152
Immaculate Conception, 13, 23, 52, 57, 127
Incarnation of God, witnesses of, 43–44
India, 37, 69
interiority, xi, 46, 108, 123, 142
Internet: and discernment of visionary authenticity, 137–39, 141, 144, 146–49; Marian apparition websites, 26, 96–98, 137–39, 146–49
Israelites, 34, 38

James, Saint (apostle), 43, 75
James, William, 46
Jerome, Saint, 50, 53
Jesuits, 19
Jesus Christ, 2, 13–17; and the desert, 29, 34; Mary's influence on, 42; miraculous healing by, 90; portraits of, 99; resurrection of, 151–52, 154; and visionaries, 41–45, 131–32
Je vous salu, Marie (Goddard), 25

Jews, 34
John, Gospel of, 16, 43
John Paul II (pope), 13–14, 54–55, 60
John the Baptist, 29, 34
Juan Diego, Saint, 19, 22–23, 37, 41, 56–57; tilma of, 23, 57, 99

Kempe, Margery, 60
Kennedy, Robert F., 52
Knock (Ireland), Marian apparitions, 25

La Reina de Reinas (film), 25
La Salette (France), Marian apparitions, 21, 67
La Señora de la Roca. *See* Our Lady of the Rock
Laso de la Vega, Luis, 56
Last Temptation of Christ (Altman), 25
Latin America, 19; healers, 58; liberation theology, 34. *See also* Mexico
Latino/a Catholics, 36–37, 81–82, 85–87
Legion of Mary, 14, 63
Leonardo da Vinci, 21
liberation theologians, 14, 34
Litany of Loreto, 18–19
Lopez, Alma (*Our Lady*), 27
López, Yolanda, 26–27
Lopez Canyon, 2–3, 22, 38, 78, 110
Los Angeles, 1, 29–31, 36–37, 61, 81, 119, 122–26, 145–46; clergy of, 47, 55, 81, 128
Los Angeles Times, 137, 145
Lourdes (France), Marian apparitions, 21, 41, 52, 57, 67, 75, 98, 116
Lueken, Veronica, 51–53, 149
Luke (evangelist), 99
Luke, Gospel of, 15–16
Lumen gentium (Paul VI), 20

Magdalena de la Cruz, 53
Magisterium, 20, 48
Mahony, Cardinal Roger (archbishop of Los Angeles), 55
Mandylion, 99. *See also* archeiropoieta
Marian apparitions, ix, 11, 21–27, 54–55, 64–68, 128, 154; and the Internet, 26, 96–98, 137–39, 145–49. *See also* Bayside; Cacaulí; Conyers; Cuapa; Emmitsburg; Fátima; Garabandal; Guadalupe; La Salette; Lourdes; Marpingen; Medjugorje; Phoenix; Scottsdale
Marian Apparitions of the 20th Century (film), 97

marianismo, 14. *See also* Marian organizations

Marian Movement of Southern California, 41; activities at vision events, 5, 8–11, 62–63, 69, 77, 81; cenacles, 63, 133–34; on desert site, 37; evangelization, 146; finances, 55, 63, 111, 141; official T-shirts, 6, 63, 85; overview of, 63; publicity, 139–46; sale of photographs, 10–11, 66, 112; work on Our Lady of the Rock site, 1, 29–30, 33

Marian organizations, 13, 14, 63, 147. *See also* Marian Movement of Southern California

Marian shrines, 18–22, 75–80; pilgrimages to, 97–98

Maria Paula. *See* Acuña, Maria Paula

mariophany, xii, 4, 116, 135; use of term, 2. *See also* Marian apparitions

Mark, Gospel of, 15, 43

Marpingen (Germany), Marian apparitions, 50, 98

Martínez, Bernardo, 127

Martínez, Edward, 87

Mary: Assumption of, 16, 17, 27; biblical history, 15–16; Catholic popular opinion on, 20; Christian doctrine of, 13–20; clothing worn by, 22–23; as co-redemptrix with Jesus, 13, 14–15; cult of, 14, 17–18, 23; death of (Dormition), 16, 17, 27; iconography, 3–4, 17, 21–27; light from, 23–24; as mediatrix, 13, 15, 17; and medieval Christians, 17–19, 23; as Mother of God, 13, 16–17; names of, 18–19; one-and-many Virgins doctrine, 13, 21; petitions to, 42, 79, 90–93; portraits of, 99; representation in film and visual media, 25–27; as sinless, 13, 17; titles for, 18–20. *See also* Marian apparitions; Marian shrines; Our Lady of the Rock

Mary Magdalene, 44

Matthew, Gospel of, 15, 43–44

Medieval. *See* Middle Ages

medievalists, ix, xii, 60

Medjugorje (Bosnia-Herzegovina), Marian apparitions: credibility of visionaries, 61–62, 145–46; and demonic deception, 53; description of, 23–24; Gospa of, 22, 116; Gospa prayer groups, 147; images of, 11, 97, 105; material evidence, 101; medallions, 21; medical examination of seers, 50; reinvestigation of, 54, 146; visionaries, 66–67; websites, 139

memory, 3, 46, 116, 152

Mendelsohn, Nathan, 31, 33

Merton, Thomas, 35

Mexican American Catholics, 36–37, 81, 85

mexicanidad, 37

Mexico, 9, 11, 19, 23, 25, 56–57, 58, 117–18, 122, 141

Middle Ages: Christianity during, 17–19, 23; pilgrims, 75, 83; theologians, 45, 47, 131. *See also* medievalists

migration, 38. *See also* illegal immigrants

milagros, 122, 124. *See also* miracles

Ministries of Light, 147–49

miracles, 67, 119, 121, 122, 124. See also *milagros*

miraculous healing, 70, 73, 86–87, 89–93, 119, 128

missionaries, 19

modernism, 144

Mojave, California, 1, 30, 76, 137

Mojave Desert, 41; history and uses of, 30–33; media coverage, 139–40; as refuge, 33, 35. *See also* Our Lady of the Rock

monjas, 6, 41, 57, 59, 62, 85–86, 112, 128–30, 134–36

monjitas. See monjas

monks, 29, 34–35

morals, 20, 43, 45, 49

Moses, 34–35, 37, 43

Munificentissimus Deus (Pius XII), 13

mysteries, 152, 154

Neoplatonic philosophy, 46

New Testament, 15–16, 34, 43–44, 138. *See also* Gospels

Nuestra Señora de Guadalupe. *See* Guadalupe

observers, 4, 9, 47, 65, 79, 108, 110, 121, 130–31; academic and professional, 70, 88, 90, 107, 144. *See also* witnesses

Ofili, Chris (*The Holy Virgin Mary*), 26

Old Testament, 34, 43, 118

orthodoxy, 20, 42–48, 51, 61, 66, 79, 86, 141, 149, 151, 153

Ortiz, Julio César, 140–41

Our Lady (Lopez), 27

Our Lady of Help Church, 86

Our Lady of Light Foundation and Ministries, 147–48

Our Lady of Lourdes Roman Catholic Church, 31, 85, 88, 129

Our Lady of the Holy Spirit Center, 147

salvation, 2, 15–17, 20, 83, 143–44, 152

Sandinistas, 122, 127

Santa Muerte, 104

Santería, 58

Santiago de Compostella, 75

Santillan, Juan, 86–87, 141

Santos, Lúcia dos, 61, 98, 104

Satan, 53, 57. *See also* demons and devils

Scottsdale (Arizona), Marian apparitions, 66, 138

Second Peter, 45

Second Vatican Council, xi, 13–15, 54, 82

secrecy and secrets, 13–14, 52, 61–62, 64–66, 126, 136

seeing and sight: Christian ways of looking, xi, 43–48, 151–55; eyesight, 152, 155; fallibility of, 44; hierarchy of, 43, 46, 152

seers. *See* prophets; visionaries

sensus fidelium, 20, 48

shrines: architectural elements, 75–76; Marian, 18–22, 75–80; pilgrimages to, 97–98. *See also* pilgrims

shroud of Turin, 99

simulacra, 17, 99, 112

skeptics, 106, 110, 131, 139, 144, 146

snakes, iconography of, 11, 57, 143

Solomon's Temple, 75

Somoto, Nicaragua, 122–24, 127–28

Song of Bernadette (film), 26

Soubirous, Bernadette. *See* Bernadette Soubirous, Saint

Spielberg, Steven (*Close Encounters of the Third Kind*), 24

spirit photos, 99

spiritual blindness, 43, 144

spiritual retreats, 29, 31–32

Steinbock, Bishop John, 66

St. Robert Bellarmine Church, Bayside, New Jersey, 51–52

Suffert, Frank (*Desert Dreamers*), 140

Talone-Sullivan, Giana, 138

technologies: communications, 144, 147; electronic, 96–106; visual, 144, 146–47. *See also* Internet; photography

Tercero, Francisco. *See* Panchito

Teresa de Ávila, Saint, 35, 52

Thelma, Sister, xi, 10, 41, 59–60, 62–63, 64, 67, 91, 133, 140, 143

theophany, 43–44, 47, 50, 155; use of term, 2. *See also* epiphany; mariophany

theotokos (God bearer), 13

Thérèse of Lisieux, Saint, 60

This American Life (television show), 139–40

Thomas (apostle), 44, 126

Thomas Aquinas, 17–18, 46

tilma of Juan Diego, 23, 57, 99

Torah, 34, 43. *See also* Old Testament

trances, x, 50, 98, 107

transcendence, 46, 107

unbelievers, 65, 72, 106, 110, 139, 143–44, 152

Univision network, 140

unseen, 151–52; photography as enhancement for, 96–97

U.S. Army and Air Force bases, 30–31

U.S. Bureau of Land Management, 32

Vatican II. *See* Second Vatican Council

Vera Icon (Veronica), 99. *See also* archeiropoieta

Vicuña, Laura, 60

Virgin Mary. *See* Mary

visionaries: and Catholicism, 53, 148, 151; domestic and social lives, 52; educational backgrounds, 52; media coverage of, 52–53; medical examinations of, 49–51; mental health of, 49–51, 60; orthodoxy, 42–48; physical health of, 49–51, 60; reproduction of, 116, 130; secrecy of, 61–62; sociocultural context and community, 51–52, 151–52; witnesses as, 115–36; women as, 60. *See also* Acuña, Maria Paula; prophets

visionary authenticity, 25, 30, 50, 60–61, 116, 128, 130, 138–39, 147–49; doubts about, 24, 25, 44, 152; evaluation of, 40, 44–55, 137–49, 153; photographs as proof of, 98–101, 106; physical symptoms, 60. *See also* discernment

visionary experiences, descriptions of, 24, 70–74, 88–93, 106–14, 116–21, 123–28, 130–36, 153. *See also* Acuña, Maria Paula, visions of

visions and apparitions: cultural trends and fads, 47–48; evidence of, 146, 147; images of, 96–106; as inexpressible things, x, 61–68; lifting of Catholic ban on publishing, 54; medieval, ix, 17, 41, 45, 47, 53, 60; modern, xii–xiii; political contexts, 52; provenance of apparitional objects, 99; use of terms, 2. *See also* Marian apparitions; mariophany; revelation

"Visions of Mary" (Paranormal TV), 141
visual experiences, hierarchy of, 43, 46, 152. *See also* seeing and sight

Wenzieger, Anna, 25
wilderness: biblical, 34; passage through, 38; as site of visions and apparitions, 29–30, 33; uses of, 30–33. *See also* deserts
witches, 24, 47
witnesses, 51–55; discernment by, 47, 61; eyewitnesses, 44, 138, 147, 155; global culture of, 137–49; live witnessing, 138; of the living Incarnation, 43–44

witnesses at Our Lady of the Rock, x–xi, 1–11, 69–80; characteristics of, 80–88; skills for successful witnessing, 108–10; testimonies, 88–93, 141; as visionaries, 115–36; visions and personal religious experiences, 24, 70–74, 88–93, 106–14, 153. *See also* photography; pilgrims
Wizard of Oz, The (film), 24, 108
Wojcek, Dan, 98

Yo Mamadonna and Child (Cox), 27
Yo Mama's Last Supper (Cox), 27